Matthew Arnold

The popular education of France

With notices of that of Holland and Switzerland

Matthew Arnold

The popular education of France
With notices of that of Holland and Switzerland

ISBN/EAN: 9783337197933

Printed in Europe, USA, Canada, Australia, Japan

Cover: Foto ©Paul-Georg Meister /pixelio.de

More available books at **www.hansebooks.com**

THE

POPULAR EDUCATION OF FRANCE

WITH NOTICES OF THAT OF

HOLLAND AND SWITZERLAND

BY

MATTHEW ARNOLD, M.A.

FOREIGN ASSISTANT-COMMISSIONER TO THE COMMISSIONERS APPOINTED TO INQUIRE INTO THE STATE OF POPULAR EDUCATION IN ENGLAND;
PROFESSOR OF POETRY IN THE UNIVERSITY OF OXFORD;
ONE OF HER MAJESTY'S INSPECTORS OF SCHOOLS.

LONDON
LONGMAN, GREEN, LONGMAN, AND ROBERTS
1861

I know that, since the Revolution, along with many dangerous, many useful powers of Government have been weakened.

BURKE (1770).

CONTENTS.

CHAPTER VII.

CHAPTER VIII.

CHAPTER IX.

CHAPTER X.

CHAPTER XI.

CHAPTER XII.

CHAPTER XIII.

CHAPTER XIV.

POPULAR EDUCATION OF SWITZERLAND.

CHAPTER XV.

POPULAR EDUCATION OF HOLLAND.

CHAPTER XVI.

CHAPTER XVII.

CHAPTER XVIII.

INTRODUCTION.

In the following account of popular education in certain countries of the Continent, the State and its action are occasionally spoken of in a way which, if quite unexplained, is likely, I know, to offend some of my readers, and to surprise others. With many Englishmen, perhaps with the majority, it is a maxim that the State, the executive power, ought to be entrusted with no more means of action than those which it is impossible to withhold from it; that it neither would nor could make a safe use of any more extended liberty; would not, because it has in itself a natural instinct of despotism, which, if not jealously checked, would become outrageous; could not, because it is, in truth, not at all more enlightened, or fit to assume a lead, than the mass of this enlightened community. According to the long-cherished convictions of a great many, it is for the public interest that Government should be confined, as far as possible, to the bare and indispensable functions of a police officer and a revenue collector. It is to be always the mere delegated hand of the nation, never its originating head.

No sensible man will lightly go counter to an opinion firmly held by a great body of his countrymen. He will take for granted, that for any opinion which has taken deep root among a people so powerful, so successful, and so well worthy of respect as the people of this country, there certainty either are, or have been, good and sound reasons. He will venture to impugn such an opinion with real hesitation, and only when he thinks he perceives that the reasons which once supported it exist no longer, or at any rate seem about to disappear very soon. For undoubtedly there arrive periods when, the circumstances and conditions of Government having changed, the guiding maxims of Government ought to change also. *J'ai dit souvent,* says Mirabeau*, admonishing the Court of France in 1790, *qu'on devait changer de manière de gouverner, lorsque le gouvernement n'est plus le même.* And these decisive changes in the political situation of a people happen gradually as well as violently. "In the silent lapse of events," says Burke†, writing in England twenty years before the French Revolution, "as material alterations have been insensibly brought about in the policy and character of governments and nations, as those which have been marked by the tumult of public revolutions."

The wish for a more deliberate and systematically reasoned action on the part of the State in dealing with

* *Correspondance entre le Comte de Mirabeau et le Comte de la Marck*, publiée par M. de Bacourt, Paris, 1851, vol. ii. p. 143.

† Burke's Works, (edit. of 1852), vol. iii. p. 115.

education in this country, is more than once expressed or implied in the following pages. In this introduction I propose to submit to those who have been accustomed to regard all State-action with jealousy, some reasons for thinking that the circumstances which once made that jealousy prudent and natural have undergone an essential change. I desire to lead them to consider with me, whether, in the present altered conjuncture, that State-action, which was once dangerous, may not become, not only without danger in itself, but the means of helping us against dangers from another quarter. To combine and present the considerations upon which these two propositions are based, is a task of some difficulty and delicacy. My aim is to invite impartial reflexion upon the subject, not to make a hostile attack against old opinions, still less to set on foot and fully equip a new theory. In offering, therefore, the thoughts which have suggested themselves to me, I shall studiously avoid all particular applications of them likely to give offence, and shall use no more illustration and development than may be indispensable to enable the reader to seize and appreciate them.

The dissolution of the old political parties which have governed this country since the Revolution has long been remarked. It was repeatedly declared to be happening long before it actually took place, while the vital energy of these parties still subsisted in full vigour, and was threatened only by some temporary obstruction. It has been eagerly deprecated long after it had actually begun to take place, when it was in full progress, and inevitable. These parties, differing in so much else, were yet alike in this, that they were both, in a certain broad sense, *aristocratical* parties. They were combinations of persons considerable, either by great family and estate, or by Court favour, or, lastly, by eminent abilities and popularity; this last body, however, attaining participation in public affairs only through a conjunction with one or other of the former. These connections, though they contained men of very various degrees of birth and property, were still wholly leavened with the feelings and habits of the upper class of the nation. They had the bond of a common culture; and, however their political opinions and acts might differ, what they said and did had the air and style imparted by this culture, and by a common and elevated social condition.

Aristocratical bodies have no taste for a very imposing Executive, or for a very active and penetrating domestic administration. They have a sense of equality among themselves, and of constituting in themselves what is greatest and most dignified in the realm, which makes their pride revolt against the overshadowing greatness and dignity of a commanding Executive. They have a temper of independence, and a habit of uncontrolled action, which makes them impatient of encountering, in the management of the interior concerns of the country, the machinery and regulations of a superior and peremptory power. The different parties amongst them, as they successively get possession of the Government, respect this jealous disposition in their opponents, because they share it themselves. It is a disposition proper to them as great personages, not as

Ministers; and as they are great personages for their whole life, while they may be Ministers but for a very short time, the instinct of their social condition avails more with them than the instinct of their official function. To administer as little as possible, to make its weight felt in foreign affairs rather than in domestic, to see in ministerial station rather a means of grandeur and dignity than a means of searching and useful administrative activity, is the natural tendency of an aristocratic Executive. It is a tendency which is creditable to the good sense of aristocracies, honourable to their moderation, and at the same time fortunate for their country, of whose internal development they are not precisely fitted to have the full direction.

One strong and beneficial influence, however, the administration of a vigorous and high-minded aristocracy is calculated to exert upon a robust and sound people. I had occasion lately, in speaking of Homer, to say very often, and with much emphasis, that he is *in the grand style.* It is the chief virtue of a healthy and uncorrupted aristocracy, that it is, in general, in this grand style. That elevation of character, that noble way of thinking and behaving, which is an eminent gift of nature to some individuals, is also often generated in whole classes of men, (at least, when these come of a strong and good race), by the possession of power, by the importance and responsibility of high station, by habitually dealing with great things, by being placed above the necessity of constantly struggling for little things. And it is the source of great virtues. It may go along with a not very quick or open intelligence, but it cannot well go along with a conduct vulgar and ignoble. A governing class imbued with it, may not be capable of intelligently leading the masses of its people to the highest pitch of welfare possible for them; but it sets them an invaluable example of qualities without which no really high welfare can exist. This has been done for their nation by the best aristocracies. The Roman aristocracy did it: the English aristocracy has done it. They each fostered in the mass of the peoples they governed, peoples of sturdy moral constitution and apt to learn such lessons, a greatness of spirit, the natural growth of the condition of magnates and rulers, but not the natural growth of the condition of the common people. They made, the one of the Roman, the other of the English people, in spite of all the shortcomings of each, great peoples, peoples *in the grand style.* And this they did, while wielding the people according to their own notions, and in the direction which seemed good to them; not as servants and instruments of the people, but as its commanders and heads; solicitous for the good of their country, indeed, but taking for granted that of that good they themselves were the supreme judges, and were to fix the conditions.

The time has arrived, however, when it is becoming impossible for the aristocracy of England to conduct and wield the English nation any longer. It still, indeed, administers public affairs; and it is a great error to suppose, as many persons in England suppose, that it administers but does not govern. He who administers, governs *, because he infixes his own mark and stamps his own character on all public affairs as they pass through his hands; and therefore, so long as the English aristocracy administers the State, it still governs it. But signs not to be mistaken show that its headship and leadership of the nation by virtue of the substantial acquiescence of the body of the nation in its predominance and right to lead is nearly over. That acquiescence was the tenure by which it held its power: and it is fast giving way. The superiority of the upper class over all others is no longer so great; the willingness of the others to recognise that superiority, is no longer so ready.

This change has been brought about by natural and inevitable causes, and neither the great nor the multitude are to be blamed for it. The growing [illegible] and [illegible] of the latter, the encroaching spirit of democracy, are, indeed, matters of loud complaint with some persons. But these persons are complaining of human nature itself when they thus complain of a manifestation of its native and [illegible] impulse. Life itself consists, say the philosophers, in the effort to [illegible]; [illegible] to develope one's own existence fully and freely, to have ample

* [illegible]

the more they crave.

This movement of democracy, of nature, merits properly neith Its partisans are apt to give it cre deserve, while its enemies are apt Its friends celebrate it as the a but political freedom may very v aristocratic founders; and, certai dom of England owes more to barons than to democracy. Soc —that is rather the field of the cracy. And here what I must ca enemies comes in. For its seekin cracy is often, in this country abo

hearts of many of those who cry for equality. No doubt there are ignoble natures which prefer equality to liberty. But what we have to ask is, when the life of democracy is admitted as something natural and inevitable, whether this or that product of democracy is a necessary growth from its parent stock, or merely an excrescence upon it. If it be the latter, certainly it may be due to the meanest and most culpable passions. But if it be the former, then this product, however base and blameworthy the passions which it may sometimes be made to serve, can in itself be no more reprehensible than the vital impulse of democracy is in itself reprehensible; and this impulse is, as has been shown, identical with the ceaseless vital effort of human nature itself. Now, can it be denied, that a certain approach to equality, at any rate a certain reduction of signal inequalities, is a natural, instinctive demand of that impulse which drives society as a whole—no longer individuals and limited classes only, but the mass of a community—to develope itself with the utmost possible fulness and freedom? Can it be denied, that to live in a society of equals tends in general to make a man's spirits expand, and his faculties work easily and actively; while, to live in a society of superiors, although it may occasionally be a very good discipline, yet in general tends to tame the spirits and to make the play of the faculties less secure and active? Can it be denied, that to be heavily overshadowed, to be profoundly insignificant, has, on the whole, a depressing and benumbing effect on the character? I know that some individuals react against the strongest impediments, and owe success and greatness to the efforts which they are thus forced to make. But the question is not about individuals. The question is about the common bulk of mankind, persons without extraordinary gifts or exceptional energy, and who will ever require, in order to make the best of themselves, encouragement and directly favouring circumstances. Can any one deny, that for these the spectacle, when they would rise, of a condition of splendour, grandeur, and culture, which they cannot possibly reach, has the effect of making them flag in spirit, and of disposing them to sink despondingly back into their own condition? Can any one deny, that the knowledge how poor and insignificant the best condition of importance and culture attainable by them must be esteemed by a class incomparably richer-endowed, tends to cheapen this modest possible amelioration in the account of those classes also for whom it would be relatively a real progress, and to disenchant their imaginations with it? It seems to me impossible to deny this. And therefore a philosophic observer*, with no love for democracy, but rather with a terror of it, has been constrained to remark, that "the common people is more uncivilised in aristocratic countries than in any others;" because

* M. de Tocqueville. See his *Démocratie en Amérique* (edit. of 1835); vol. i. p. 11. "Le peuple est plus grossier dans les pays aristocratiques que partout ailleurs. Dans ces lieux, où se rencontrent des hommes si forts et si riches, les faibles et les pauvres se sentent comme accablés de leur bassesse; ne découvrant aucun point par lequel ils puissent regagner l'égalité, ils désespèrent entièrement d'eux-mêmes, et se laissent tomber au-dessous de la dignité humaine."

there, "the lowly and the poor feel themselves, as it were, overwhelmed with the weight of their own inferiority." He has been constrained to remark *, that "there is such a thing as a manly and legitimate passion for equality, prompting men to desire to be, *all* of them, in the enjoyment of power and consideration." And, in France, that very equality, which is so impetuously decried, while it has by no means improved (it is said) the upper classes of French society, has undoubtedly given to the lower classes, to the body of the common people, a self-respect, an enlargement of spirit, a consciousness of counting for something in their country's action, which has raised them in the scale of humanity. The common people, in France, seems to me the soundest part of the French nation. They seem to me more free from the two opposite degradations of multitudes, brutality and servility; to have a more developed human life, more of what distinguishes elsewhere the cultured classes from the vulgar, than the common people in any other country with which I am acquainted.

I do not say that grandeur and prosperity may not be attained by a nation divided into the most widely distinct classes, and presenting the most signal inequalities of rank and fortune. I do not say that great national virtues may not be developed in it. I do not even say that a popular order, accepting this demarcation of classes as an eternal providential arrangement, not questioning the natural right of a superior order to lead it, content within its own sphere, admiring the grandeur

* *Démocratie en Amérique*; vol. i. p. 60.

and highmindedness of its ruling class, and catching on its own spirit some reflex of what it thus admires, may not be a happier body, as to the eye of the imagination it is certainly a more beautiful body, than a popular order, pushing, excited, and presumptuous; a popular order, jealous of recognising fixed superiorities, petulantly claiming to be as good as its betters, and tastelessly attiring itself with the fashions and designations which have become unalterably associated with a wealthy and refined class, and which, tricking out those who have neither wealth nor refinement, are ridiculous. But a popular order of that old-fashioned stamp exists now only for the imagination. It is not the force with which modern society has to reckon. Such a body may be a sturdy, honest, and sound-hearted lower class; but it is not a democratic people. It is not that power, which at the present day in all nations is to be found existing; in some, has obtained the mastery; in others, is yet in a state of expectation and preparation.

The power of France in Europe is at this day mainly owing to the completeness with which she has organised democratic institutions. The action of the French State is excessive; but it is too little understood in England that the French people has adopted this action for its own purposes, has in great measure attained those purposes by it, and owes to having done so the chief part of its influence in Europe. The growing power in Europe is democracy; and France has organised democracy with a certain indisputable grandeur and success. The ideas of 1789 were working everywhere in the eighteenth century; but it was because in

France the State adopted them that the French Revolution became an historic epoch for the world, and France the lode-star of Continental democracy. Her airs of superiority and her overweening pretensions come from her sense of the power which she derives from this cause. Every one knows how Frenchmen proclaim France to be at the head of civilisation, the French army to be the soldier of God, Paris to be the brain of Europe, and so on. All this is, no doubt, in a vein of sufficient fatuity and bad taste; but it means, at bottom, that France believes she has so organised herself as to facilitate for all members of her society full and free expansion; that she believes herself to have remodelled her institutions with an eye to reason rather than custom, and to right rather than fact; it means, that she believes the other peoples of Europe to be preparing themselves, more or less rapidly, for a like achievement, and that she is conscious of her power and influence upon them as an initiatress and example. In this belief there is a part of truth and a part of delusion: I think it is more profitable for a Frenchman to consider the part of delusion contained in it; for an Englishman, the part of truth.

It is because aristocracies almost inevitably fail to appreciate justly, or even to take into their mind, this instinct pushing the masses towards expansion and fuller life, that they lose their hold over them. It is the old story of the incapacity of aristocracies for ideas; the secret of their want of success in modern epochs. The people treats them with flagrant injustice, when it denies all obligation to them. They can, and often do, impart a high spirit, a fine ideal of grandeur, to the people: thus they lay the foundations of a great nation: but they leave the people still the multitude, the crowd; they have small belief in the power of the ideas which are its life. Themselves a power reposing on all which is most solid, material, and visible, they are slow to attach any great importance to influences impalpable, spiritual, and viewless. Although, therefore, a disinterested looker-on might often be disposed, seeing what has actually been achieved by aristocracies, to retain them or to replace them in their preponderance, rather than commit a nation to the hazards of a new and untried future; yet the masses instinctively feel that they can never consent to this without renouncing the inmost impulse of their being, and that they should make such a renunciation cannot seriously be expected of them. Except on conditions which make its expansion, in the sense understood by itself, fully possible, democracy will never frankly ally itself with aristocracy; and on these conditions perhaps no aristocracy will ever frankly ally itself with it. Even the English aristocracy, so politic, so capable of compromises, has shown no signs of being able so to transform itself as to render such an alliance possible. The reception given by the Peers to the bill for establishing life peerages was, in this respect, of ill omen. The separation between aristocracy and democracy will probably, therefore, go on still widening.

And it must in fairness be added, that as in one most important part of general human culture, openness to ideas and ardour for them, aristocracy is less advanced than democracy, to replace or keep the latter under the tutelage of the former would in some respects actually be unfavourable to the progress of the world. At epochs when new ideas are powerfully fermenting in a society, and profoundly changing its spirit, aristocracies, as they are in general not long suffered to guide it without question, so are they by nature not well fitted to guide it intelligently.

In England democracy has been slow in developing itself, having met with much to withstand it, not only in the worth of the aristocracy, but also in the fine qualities of the common people. The aristocracy has been more in sympathy with the common people than perhaps any other aristocracy. It has rarely given them great umbrage: it has neither been frivolous, so as to provoke their contempt, nor impertinent, so as to provoke their irritation. Above all, it has in general meant to act with justice, according to its own notions of justice. Therefore the feeling of admiring deference to such a class was more deep-rooted in the people of this country, more cordial, and more persistent, than in any people of the Continent. But, besides this, the vigour and high spirit of the English common people bred in them a self-reliance which disposed each man to act individually and independently; and so long as this disposition prevails through a nation divided into classes, the predominance of an aristocracy, of the class containing the greatest and strongest individuals of the nation, is secure. Democracy is a force in which the concert of a great number of men makes up for the weakness of each man taken by himself; democracy accepts a certain relative rise in their condition, obtainable by this concert for a great number, as something desirable in itself, because though this is undoubtedly far below grandeur, it is yet a good deal above insignificance. A very strong, self-reliant people neither easily learns to act in concert, nor easily brings itself to regard any middling good, any good short of the best, as an object ardently to be coveted and striven for. It keeps its eye on the grand prizes, and these are to be won only by distancing competitors, by getting before one's comrades, by succeeding all by one's self; and so long as a people works thus individually, it does not work democratically. The English people has all the qualities which dispose a people to work individually; may it never lose them! A people without the salt of these qualities, relying wholly on mutual co-operation, and proposing to itself second-rate ideals, would arrive at the pettiness and stationariness of China. But it is no longer so entirely ruled by them as not to show visible beginnings of democratic action: it becomes more and more sensible to the irresistible seduction of democratic ideas, promising to each individual of the multitude increased self-respect and expansion with the increased importance and authority of the multitude to which he belongs, with the diminished preponderance of the aristocratic class above him.

While the habit and disposition of deference are thus dying out among the lower classes of the English nation, it seems to me indisputable that the advantages which command deference, eminent superiority in high feeling, dignity and culture, tend to diminish among the highest class. I shall not be suspected of any inclination to underrate the aristocracy of this country. I regard it as the worthiest, as it certainly has been the most successful aristocracy, of which history makes record: if it has not been able to develope excellences which do not belong to the nature of an aristocracy, yet it has been able to avoid defects to which the nature of an aristocracy is peculiarly prone. But I cannot read the history of the flowering time of the English aristocracy, the eighteenth century, and then look at this aristocracy in our own century, without feeling that there has been a change. I am not now thinking of private and domestic virtues, of morality, of decorum: perhaps with respect to these there has in this class, as in society at large, been a change for the better; I am thinking of those public and conspicuous virtues by which the multitude is captivated and led—lofty spirit, commanding character, exquisite culture. It is true that the advance of all classes in culture and refinement, may make the culture of one class, which, isolated, appeared remarkable, appear so no longer; but exquisite culture and great dignity are always something rare and striking, and it is the distinction of the English aristocracy, in the eighteenth century, that not only was their culture something rare by comparison with the rawness of the masses, but it was something rare and admirable in itself. It is rather that this rare culture of the highest class has actually somewhat declined *, than that it has come to

* This will appear doubtful to no one well-acquainted with the literature and memoirs of the last century. To give but two illus-

look less by juxtaposition with the augmented culture of other classes. Probably democracy has something to answer for in this falling off of her rival. To feel itself raised on high, venerated, followed, no doubt stimulates a fine nature to keep itself worthy to be followed, venerated, raised on high: hence that lofty maxim, *noblesse oblige*. To feel its culture something precious and singular, makes such a nature zealous to retain and extend it. The elation and energy thus fostered by the sense of its advantages, certainly enhances the worth, strengthens the behaviour, and quickens all the active powers of the class enjoying it. *Possunt quia posse videntur.* The removal of the stimulus a little relaxes their energy. It is not so much that they sink to be somewhat less than themselves, as that they cease to be somewhat more than themselves. But, however this may be, whencesoever the change may proceed, I cannot doubt that, in the aristocratic virtue, in the intrinsic commanding force of the English upper class, there is a diminution. Relics of a great generation are still to be seen amongst them, surviving exemplars of noble manners and consummate culture; but they disappear one after the other, and no one of their order takes their place. At the very moment when democracy becomes less and

trations out of a thousand. Let the reader refer to the anecdote told by Robert Wood in his *Essay on the Genius of Homer* (London, 1775), p. vii., and to Lord Chesterfield's *Letters*, (edit. of 1845), vol. i. pp. 115, 113, vol. ii. p. 54; and then say, whether the culture there indicated as the culture of a *class* has maintained itself at that level.

less disposed to follow and to admire, aristocracy becomes less and less qualified to command and to captivate.

On the one hand, then, the masses of the people in this country are preparing to take a much more active part than formerly in controlling its destinies; on the other hand, the aristocracy, (using this word in the widest sense, to include not only the nobility and landed gentry, but also those reinforcements from the classes bordering upon itself, which this class constantly attracted and assimilated,) while it is threatened with losing its hold on the rudder of government, its power to give to public affairs its own bias and direction, is losing also that influence on the spirit and character of the people which it long exercised.

I know that this will be warmly denied by some persons. Those who have grown up amidst a certain state of things, those whose habits, and interests, and affections, are closely concerned with its continuance, are slow to believe that it is not a part of the order of nature, or that it can ever come to an end. But I think that what I have here laid down will not appear doubtful either to the most competent and friendly foreign observers of this country, or to those Englishmen who, clear of all influences of class or party, have applied themselves steadily to see the tendency of their nation as it really is. Assuming it to be true, a great number of considerations are suggested by it; but it is my purpose here to insist upon one only.

That one consideration is;—on what action may we rely, to replace, for some time at any rate, that action of the aristocracy upon the people of this country, which we have seen exercise an influence in many respects elevating and beneficial, but which is rapidly, and from inevitable causes, ceasing? In other words, and to use a short and significant modern expression which every one understands;—what influence may help us to prevent the English people from becoming, with the growth of democracy, *Americanised?* I confess I am disposed to answer:—*Nothing but the influence of the State.*

I know what a chorus of objectors will be ready. One will say: Rather repair and restore the influence of aristocracy. Another will say: It is not a bad thing, but a good thing, that the English people should be Americanised. But the most formidable and the most widely entertained objection, by far, will be that which founds itself upon the present actual state of things in another country; which says: Look at France! there you have a signal example of the alliance of democracy with a powerful State-action, and see how it works.

This last and principal objection I will notice first: I have had occasion to touch upon the first already, and upon the second I shall touch presently. It seems to me, then, that one may save one's self from much idle terror at names and shadows, if one will be at the pains to remember what different conditions the different character of two nations must necessarily impose on the operation of any principle. That which operates noxiously in the one, may operate wholesomely in the other; because the unsound part of the one's character may be yet further inflamed and enlarged by it, the unsound part of the other's may find in it a corrective and an abatement. This is the great use which two unlike characters may find in observing each other. Neither is likely to have the other's faults, so each may safely adopt as much as suits him of the other's qualities. If I were a Frenchman, I should never be weary of admiring the independent, individual, local habits of action in England; of directing attention to the evils occasioned in France by the excessive action of the State; for I should be very sure, that, say what I might, the part of the State would never be too small in France, nor that of the individual too large. Being an Englishman, I see nothing but good in freely recognising the coherence, rationality, and efficaciousness, which characterise the strong State-action of France; of acknowledging the want of method, reason, and result, which attend the feeble State-action of England; because I am very sure, that, strengthen in England the action of the State as one may, it will always find itself sufficiently controlled. But, when the *Constitutionnel* sneers at the do-little talkativeness of parliamentary government, or when the *Morning Star* inveighs against the despotism of a centralised administration, it seems to me that they lose their labour, because they are hardening themselves against dangers to which they are neither of them liable. Both the one and the other, in plain truth,

> Compound for sins they are inclin'd to,
> By damning those they have no mind to.

So that the exaggeration of the action of the State, in France, furnishes no reason for absolutely refusing to enlarge the action of the State in England; because the genius and temper of the people of this country are such as to render impossible that exaggeration, which the genius and temper of the French rendered easy. There is no danger at all that the native independence and individualism of the English character will ever belie itself, and become weakly prone to lean on others, or blindly confiding in them.

English democracy runs no risk of being overmastered by the State; it is almost certain that it will throw off the tutelage of aristocracy. Its real danger is, that it will have far too much its own way, and be left far too much to itself. "What harm will there be in that?" say some: "are we not a self-governing people?" I answer: "We have never yet been a *self-governing democracy*, or anything like it." The difficulty for democracy is, how to find and keep high ideals. The individuals who compose it are, the bulk of them, persons who need to follow an ideal, not to set one; and one ideal of greatness, high feeling and fine culture, which an aristocracy once supplied to them, they lose by the very fact of ceasing to be a lower order and becoming a democracy. Nations are not truly great solely because the individuals composing them are numerous, free, and active; but they are great when these numbers, this freedom, and this activity are employed in the service of an ideal somewhat higher than that of an ordinary man, taken by himself. Not only the greatness of nations, but their very unity, depends on this. In fact, unless a nation's action is inspired by an ideal commanding the respect of the many as higher than each ordinary man's own, there is nothing to keep that nation together, nothing to resist the dissolvent action of innumerable and conflicting wills and opinions. *Quot homines, tot sententiæ*, and one man's opinion is as good as another's: —there is no basis for a real unity here. In this regard, what is now passing in the United States of America is full of instruction for us. I hear numberless English lamenting the disruption of the American Union; they esteem it a triumph for the enemies of all freedom, a discouragement for the principles of self-government, as they have been long understood and put in practice in this country as well as in America. I, on the contrary, esteem it a great and timely lesson to the over-individualism of the English character. We in England have had, in our great aristocratical and ecclesiastical institutions, a principle of cohesion and unity which the Americans had not; they gave the tone to the nation, and the nation took it from them; self-government here was quite a different thing from self-government there. Our society is probably destined to become much more democratic: who will give the tone to the nation then? That is the question. The greatest men of America, her Washingtons, Hamiltons, Madisons, well understanding that aristocratical institutions are not in all times and places possible; well perceiving that in their Republic there was no place for these; comprehending, therefore, that from these that security for national unity and greatness, an ideal commanding popular reverence, was not to be obtained, but knowing that this ideal was indispensable, would have been rejoiced to found a substitute for it in the dignity and authority of the State. They deplored the weakness and insignificance of the executive power as a calamity. When the inevitable course of events has made our self-government something really like that of America, when it has removed or weakened that security for a noble national spirit, and therefore for unity, which we possessed in *aristocracy*, will the substitute of *the State* be equally wanting to us? If it is, then the dangers of America will really be ours: the multitude in power, with no ideal to elevate or guide it; the spirit of the nation vulgarised; unity imperilled because there is no institution grand enough to unite round.

It would really be wasting time to contend at length, that to give more prominence to the idea of the State is now possible in this country, without endangering liberty. In other countries the habits and dispositions of the people may be such that the State, if once it acts, may be easily suffered to usurp exorbitantly; here they certainly are not. Here the people will always sufficiently keep in mind that any public authority is a trust delegated by themselves, for certain purposes, and with certain limits; and if that authority pretends to an absolute, independent character, they will soon enough (and most rightly) remind it of its error. Here there can be no question of a paternal Government, of an irresponsible executive power, professing to act for the people's good, but without the people's consent, and, if necessary, against the people's wishes; here no one dreams of removing a single constitutional control, of abolishing a single safe-guard for securing a correspondence between the acts of Government and the will of the nation. The question is, whether, retaining all its power of control over a Government which should abuse its trust, the nation may not now find advantage in voluntarily allowing to it purposes somewhat ampler, and limits somewhat wider within which to execute them, than formerly; whether it may not thus acquire in the State an ideal of high reason and right feeling, representing its best self, commanding general respect, and forming a rallying point for the intelligence and for the worthiest instincts of the community, which will herein find a true bond of union.

I am convinced that, if the worst mischiefs of democracy ever happen in England, it will be, not because a new condition of things has come upon us unforeseen, but because, though we all foresaw it, our efforts to deal with it were in the wrong direction. At the present time, almost every one believes in the growth of democracy. Almost every one talks of it, almost every one laments it; but the last thing people can be brought to do, is to make timely preparation for it. Many of those who, if they would, could do most to forward this work of preparation, are made slack and hesitating by the belief that, after all, in England, things may probably never go very far; that it will be possible to keep much more of the past than speculators say. Others, with a more robust faith, think that all democracy wants is vigorous putting-down; and that, with a good will and strong hand, it is perfectly possible to retain the whole Middle Ages. Others, free from the prejudices of class and position which warp the judgment of these, and who would, I believe, be the first and greatest gainers by strengthening the hands of the State, are averse from doing so, by reason of suspicions and fears, once perfectly well-grounded, but in this age and in the present circumstances, well grounded no longer.

I speak of the middle classes. I have already shown how it is the natural disposition of an aristocratical class to view with jealousy the development of a considerable State-power. But this disposition has in England found extraordinary favour and support in regions not aristocratical—from the middle classes; and above all, from the kernel of these classes, the Protestant Dissenters. And for a very good reason. In times when passions ran high, even an aristocratical Executive was easily stimulated into using, for the gratification of its friends and the abasement of its enemies, those administrative engines which, the moment it chose to stretch its hand forth, stood ready for its grasp. Matters of domestic concern, matters of religious profession and religious exercise, offered a peculiar field for an intervention gainful and agreeable to friends, injurious and irritating to enemies. Such an intervention was attempted and practised. The State lent its machinery and authority to the aristocratical and ecclesiastical party, which it regarded as its best support. The party which suffered comprised the flower and strength of that middle class of society, always very flourishing and robust in this country. That powerful class, from this specimen of the administrative activity of the State, conceived a strong antipathy against all intervention of Government in certain spheres. An active, stringent administration in those spheres, meant at that time a High Church and Prelatic administration in them, an administration galling to the Puritan party and to the middle class; and this aggrieved class had naturally no proneness to draw nice philosophical distinctions between State-action in these spheres, as a thing for abstract consideration, and State-action in them as they practically felt it and supposed themselves likely long to feel it, guided by their adversaries. In the minds of the English middle class, therefore, State-action in social and domestic concerns became inextricably associated with the idea of a Conventicle Act, a Five-Mile Act, an Act of Uniformity. Their abhorrence of such a State-action as this, they extended to State-action in general; and, having never known a beneficent and just State-power, they enlarged their hatred of a cruel and partial State-power, the only one they had ever known, into a maxim that no State-power was to be trusted, that the least action, in certain provinces, was rigorously to be denied to the State, whenever this was possible.

Thus that jealousy of an important, sedulous, energetic Executive, natural to grandees unwilling to suffer their personal authority to be circumscribed, their individual grandeur to be eclipsed, by the authority and grandeur of the State, became reinforced in this country by a like sentiment among the middle classes, who had no such authority or grandeur to lose, but who, by a hasty reasoning, had theoretically condemned for ever an agency which they had practically found at times oppressive. *Leave us to ourselves!* magnates and middle classes alike cried to the State. Not only from those who were full and abounded went up this prayer, but also from those whose condition admitted of great amelioration. Not only did the whole repudiate the physician, but also those who were sick.

For it is evident, that the action of a diligent, an impartial, and a national Government, while it can do little to better the condition, already fortunate enough, of the highest and richest class of its people, can really do much, by institution and regulation, to better that of the middle and lower classes. The State can bestow certain broad collective benefits, which are indeed mean and insignificant, if compared with the advantages already possessed by individual grandeur, but which are rich and valuable if compared with the make-shifts of mediocrity and poverty. A good thing meant for the many cannot well be so exquisite as the good things of the few; but it can easily, if it comes from a donor of great resources and wide power, be incomparably better than what the many could, unaided, provide for themselves.

In all the remarks which I am making, I impose on myself the rule carefully to abstain from any attempt to suggest a positive application of them. I do not presume to discuss in what manner the world of facts is to adapt itself to the changed world of ideas which

I have been describing. I offer general considerations, —presented, I hope, without offensiveness, as I am sure they have been formed without prejudice—considerations suggested by watching the course of men and classes in this country, to the silent reflection of thinking minds. This an isolated individual, however humble, may fairly attempt; more he cannot attempt properly; perhaps the time has not yet come for more to be attempted at all. But one breach of my own rule I shall here venture to commit, by dwelling for a moment on a matter of practical institution, designed to meet new social exigencies: on the intervention of the State in public education.

The public secondary schools of France, decreed by the Revolution, and established under the Consulate, are said by many good judges to be inferior to the old colleges. By means of the old colleges and of private tutors, the French aristocracy could procure for its children (so it is said, and very likely with truth) a better training than that which is now given in the lyceums. Yes; but the boon conferred by the State, when it founded the lyceums, was not for the aristocracy, it was for the vast middle class of Frenchmen. This class, certainly, had not already the means of a better training for its children, before the State interfered. This class, certainly, would not have succeeded in procuring by its own efforts a better training for its children, if the State had not interfered. Through the interference of the State, this class enjoys better schools for its children, not than the great and rich enjoy, (that is not the question,) but than the same class enjoys in any country where the State has not interfered to found them. The lyceums may not be so good as Eton or Harrow; but they are a great deal better than a *Classical and Commercial Academy*.

The aristocratic classes in England may, perhaps, be well content to rest satisfied with their Eton and Harrow; the State is not likely to do better for them; nay, the superior confidence, spirit, and style, engendered by a training in the great public schools, constitute for these classes a real privilege, a real engine of command, which they might, if they were selfish, be sorry to lose by the establishment of schools great enough to beget a like spirit in the classes below them. But the middle classes in England have every reason not to rest content with their private schools; the State can do a great deal better for them; by giving to schools for these classes a public character, it can bring the instruction in them under a criticism which the knowledge of these classes is not in itself at present able to supply; by giving to them a national character, it can confer on them a greatness and a noble spirit, which the tone of these classes is not in itself at present adequate to impart. Such schools would soon prove notable competitors with the existing public schools; they would do these a great service by stimulating them, and making them look into their own weak points more closely: economical, because with charges uniform and under severe revision, they would do a great service to that large body of persons, who, at present, seeing that on the whole the best secondary instruction to be found is that of the existing public schools, obtain it for their children from a sense of duty, although they can ill afford it, and although its cost is certainly exorbitant. Thus the middle classes might, by the aid of the State, better their instruction, while still keeping its cost moderate. This in itself would be a gain; but this gain would be nothing in comparison with that of acquiring the sense of belonging to great and honourable seats of learning, and of breathing in their youth the air of the best culture of their nation. This sense would be an educational influence for them of the highest value; it would really augment their self-respect and moral force; it would truly fuse them with the class above, and tend to bring about for them the equality which they desire.

So it is not State-action in itself which the middle and lower classes of a nation ought to deprecate; it is State-action exercised by a hostile class, and for their oppression. From a State-action reasonably, equitably, and nationally exercised, they may derive great benefit; greater, by the very nature and necessity of things, than can be derived from this source by the class above them. For the middle or lower classes to obstruct such a State-action, to repel its benefits, is to play the game of their enemies, and to prolong for themselves a condition of real inferiority.

This, I know, is rather dangerous ground to tread upon. The great middle classes of this country are conscious of no weakness, no inferiority; they do not want any one to provide anything for them; such as they are, they believe that the freedom and prosperity of England are their work, and that the future belongs to them. No one admires them more than I do; but those who admire them most, and who most believe in their capabilities, can render them no better service than by pointing out in what they underrate their deficiencies, and how their deficiencies, if unremedied, may impair their future. They want culture and dignity; they want ideas. Aristocracy has culture and dignity: democracy has readiness for new ideas, and ardour for the ideas it possesses; of these, our middle class has the last only, ardour for the ideas it already possesses. It believes ardently in liberty, it believes ardently in industry; and, by its zealous belief in these two ideas, it has accomplished great things. What it has accomplished by its belief in industry is patent to all the world. The liberties of England are less its exclusive work than it supposes; for these, aristocracy has achieved at least as much; but of one inestimable part of liberty, liberty of thought, it has been (without precisely intending it) the principal champion. The intellectual action of the Church of England upon the nation has been insignificant: its social action has been great and useful. The social action of Protestant Dissent, that genuine product of the English middle class, has been insignificant: its positive intellectual action has been insignificant: its negative intellectual action—in so far as by strenuously maintaining for itself, against persecution, liberty of conscience and the right of free opinion, it at the same time maintained and established this right as a universal principle—has been invaluable. But the actual results of this negative intellectual service rendered by Protestant Dissent—by the middle class—to the whole community, great as they undoubtedly are, must not be taken for something which they are not. It is a very great thing to be able to think as you like; but, after all, an important question remains—*what* you think. It is a fine thing to secure a free stage and no favour: but, after all, the part which you play on that stage will have to be criticised. Now, all the liberty and industry in the world will not ensure two things; a high reason and a fine culture. They may favour them, but they will not of themselves produce them: they may exist without them. But it is by the appearance of these two things, in some shape or other, in the life of a nation, that it becomes something more than an independent, an energetic, a successful nation—that it becomes a *great* nation.

In modern epochs, the part of a high reason, of ideas, acquires constantly increasing importance in the conduct of the world's affairs. A fine culture is the complement of a high reason, and it is in the conjunction of both with character, with energy, that the ideal for men and nations is placed. It is common to hear remarks on the frequent divorce between culture and character, and to infer from this that culture is a mere varnish, and that character only deserves any serious attention. No error can be more fatal: culture without character is, no doubt, something frivolous, vain, and weak, but character without culture is, on the other hand, something raw, blind, and dangerous: the most interesting, the most truly glorious peoples, are those in which the alliance of the two has been effected most successfully, and its result spread most widely. This is why the spectacle of ancient Athens has such profound interest for a rational man: that it is the spectacle of the culture of a *people*. It is not an aristocracy leavening with its own high spirit the multitude which it wields, but leaving it the unformed multitude still; it is not a democracy, acute and energetic, but tasteless, narrow-minded, and ignoble: it is the middle and lower classes in the highest development of their humanity that these classes have yet reached. It was the *many* who relished those arts, who were not satisfied with less than those monuments; in the conversations recorded by Plato, or by the matter-of-fact Xenophon, which for the free yet refined discussion of ideas have set the tone for the whole cultivated world, shopkeepers and tradesmen of Athens mingle as speakers. For any one but a pedant, this is why a handful of Athenians of two thousand years ago are more interesting than the millions of most nations our contemporaries. Surely, if they knew this, those friends of progress, who have confidently pronounced the remains of the ancient world so much lumber, and a classical education an aristocratic impertinence, might be inclined to reconsider their sentence.

The course taken in the next fifty years by the middle classes of this nation, will probably give a decisive turn to its history. If they will not seek the alliance of the State for their own elevation, if they go on exaggerating their spirit of individualism, if they persist in their jealousy of all governmental action, if they cannot learn that the antipathies and the Shibboleths of a past age are now an anachronism for them — that will not prevent them, probably, from getting the rule of their country for a season, but they will certainly *Americanise* it. They will rule it by their energy, but they will deteriorate it by their low ideals and want of culture. In the decline of the aristocratical element, which in some sort supplied an ideal to ennoble the spirit of the nation and to keep it together, there will be no other element present to perform this service. It is in itself a serious calamity for a nation that its tone of feeling and grandeur of spirit should be lowered or dulled: but the calamity appears far more serious still, when we consider that, as we have seen, this high tone of feeling supplies a principle of cohesion by which a nation is kept united; that without this, not only its nobleness is endangered, but its unity. Another consideration is, that the middle classes, remaining as they are now, with their narrow and somewhat harsh and unattractive spirit and culture, will almost certainly fail to mould or assimilate the masses below them, whose sympathies are at the present moment actually wider and more liberal than theirs. They arrive, these masses, eager to enter into possession of the world, to gain a more vivid sense of their own life and activity: in this their irrepressible development, their natural educators and initiators are those immediately above them, the middle classes. If these classes cannot win their sympathy or give them their direction, society is in danger of falling into anarchy.

Therefore, with all the force I can, I wish to urge

upon the middle classes of this country, both that they might be very greatly profited by the action of the State, and also that they are continuing their opposition to such action out of an unfounded fear. But at the same time I say, that the middle class has the right, in admitting the action of Government, to make the condition that this Government shall be one of its own adoption, one that it can trust. To ensure this is now in its own power. If it does not now ensure this, it ought to do so, it has the means of doing so. Two centuries ago it had not; now it has. Having this security, let it now show itself jealous to keep the action of the State equitable and rational, rather than to prevent the action of the State altogether. If the State acts amiss, let it check it; but let it no longer take for granted that the State cannot possibly act usefully.

The State — but what is the State? cry many. Speculations on the idea of a State abound, but these do not satisfy them; of that which is to have practical effect and power they require a plain account. The full force of the term, *the State*, as the full force of any other important term, no one will master without going a little deeply, without resolutely entering the world of ideas; but it is possible to give in very plain language an account of it sufficient for all practical purposes. The State is the representative acting power of the nation; the action of the State is the representative action of the nation. Nominally emanating from the Crown, as the ideal unity in which the nation concentrates itself, this action, by the constitution of our country, really emanates from the Ministers of the Crown. It is common to hear the depreciators of State-action run through a string of Ministers' names, and then say: "Here is really your *State;* would you accept the action of these men as your own representative action? in what respect is their judgment on national affairs likely to be any better than that of the rest of the world?" In the first place I answer:—Even supposing them to be originally no better or wiser than the rest of the world, they have two great advantages from their position: access to almost boundless means of information, and the enlargement of mind which the habit of dealing with great affairs tends to produce. Their position itself, therefore, if they are men of only average honesty and capacity, tends to give them a fitness for acting on behalf of the nation, superior to that of other men of equal honesty and capacity who are not in the same position. This fitness may be yet further increased by treating them as persons on whom, indeed, a very grave responsibility has fallen, and from whom very much will be expected; nothing less than the representing, each in his own department, the collective energy and intelligence of his nation. By treating them as men on whom all this devolves to do, to their honour if they do it well, to their shame if they do it ill, one probably augments their faculty of well-doing; as it is excellently said: "To treat men as if they were better than they are, is the surest way to *make* them better than they are." But to treat them as if they had been shuffled into their places by a lucky accident, were most likely soon to be shuffled out of them again, and meanwhile ought to magnify themselves and their office as little as possible; to treat them as if they and their functions could without much inconvenience be quite dispensed with, and they ought perpetually to be admiring their own inconceivable good fortune in being permitted to discharge them;—this is the way to paralyse all high effort in the executive government, to extinguish all lofty sense of responsibility; to make its members either merely solicitous for the gross advantages, the emolument and self-importance, which they derive from their offices, or else timid, apologetic, and self-mistrustful in filling them; in either case, formal and inefficient.

But in the second place I answer:—If the executive government is really in the hands of men no wiser than the bulk of mankind, of men whose action an intelligent man would be unwilling to accept as representative of his own action, whose fault is that? It is the fault of the nation itself, which, not being in the hands of a despot or an oligarchy, being free to control the choice of those who are to sum up and concentrate its action, controls it in such a manner, that it allows to be chosen agents so little in its confidence, or so mediocre, or so incompetent, that it thinks the best thing to be done with them is to reduce their action as near as possible to a nullity. Hesitating, blundering, unintelligent, inefficacious, the action of the State may be; but, such as it is, it is the collective action of the nation itself, and the nation is responsible for it: it is its own action which it suffers to be thus unsatisfactory. Nothing can free it from this responsibility. The conduct of its affairs is in its own power. To carry on into its executive proceedings the indecision, conflict, and discordance of its deliberative proceedings, may be a natural defect of a free nation, but it is certainly a defect; it is a dangerous error to call it, as some do, a perfection. The want of concert, reason, and organisation in the State, is the want of concert, reason, and organisation in the collective nation.

Inasmuch, therefore, as collective action is more efficacious than isolated individual efforts, a nation having great and complicated matters to deal with must greatly gain by employing the action of the State. Only, the State-power which it employs should be a power which really represents its best self, and whose action its intelligence and justice can heartily avow and adopt; not a power which reflects its inferior self, and of whose action, as of its own second-rate action, it has perpetually to be ashamed. To offer a worthy initiative, and to set a standard of rational and equitable action—this is what the nation should expect of the State; and the more the State fulfils this expectation, the more will it be accepted in practice for what in idea it must always be. People will not then ask the State, what title it has to commend or reward genius and merit, since commendation and reward imply an attitude of superiority: for it will then be felt that the State truly acts for the English nation; and the genius of the English nation is greater than the genius of any individual, greater even than Shakspeare's genius, for it includes the genius of Newton also.

I will not deny that to give a more prominent part

to the State would be a considerable change in this country; that maxims once very sound, and habits once very salutary, may be appealed to against it. The sole question is, whether those maxims and habits are sound and salutary at this moment. A far graver and more difficult change, because a change at variance with maxims far less sound and habits far less salutary, — to reduce the all-effacing prominence of the State, to give a more prominent part to the individual, — is imperiously presenting itself to other countries. Both are the suggestions of one irresistible force, which is gradually making its way everywhere, removing old conditions and imposing new, altering long-fixed habits, undermining venerable institutions, even modifying national character — *the modern spirit.*

Undoubtedly we are drawing on towards great changes; and for all nations the one thing needful is to discern clearly their own condition, in order to know in what particular way they themselves may best meet them. Openness and flexibility of mind are at such a time the first of virtues. *Be ye perfect,* said the Founder of Christianity; *I count not myself to have apprehended,* said its greatest Apostle. Perfection will never be reached; but to recognise a period of transformation when it comes, and to adapt themselves honestly and rationally to its laws, is the nearest approach to perfection of which men and nations are capable. No habits or attachments should prevent their trying to do this; nor indeed, in the long run, can they. Human thought, which made all institutions, inevitably saps them, resting only in that which is absolute and eternal.

POPULAR EDUCATION OF FRANCE

THE

POPULAR EDUCATION OF FRANCE,

ETC.

CHAPTER I.

OBJECTS AND MEANS OF INQUIRY.

HAVING been entrusted by the Royal Commissioners, appointed to inquire into the state of popular education in England, with the charge of reporting to them on the systems of popular education in use in France, Holland, and the French Cantons of Switzerland, I proceeded to Paris on the 15th of March, 1859.

The British Ambassador at Paris, Earl Cowley, to whom my warmest acknowledgments are due for the prompt kindness with which he gave me his assistance on every occasion when I appealed to him for it, introduced me to M. Rouland, the Minister of Public Instruction, who furnished me with all facilities for prosecuting my inquiry. Not only did M. Rouland obligingly place at my disposal the aid, in Paris, of those officers of his department who could best guide me, but he also supplied me with letters to the Prefects and Rectors, by which I was enabled, after leaving Paris, to extend my researches to the provinces, and to visit schools in every part of France.

From every functionary of the French Government with whom I was placed in relation, I experienced uniform courtesy, attention, and assistance. My thanks are due to them all; but I must be allowed to mention by name two gentlemen, whom I had the advantage of consulting constantly, and to whom my obligations are unbounded—M. Magin and M. Rapet.

M. Magin, now Inspector-General of primary instruction, and formerly Rector of the Academy of Nancy, the metropolis of one of the best educated districts in France, has peculiar qualifications, in his wide experience, his thorough mastery of the whole system of French education, his perfect disinterestedness, and his singular clearness of judgment, for guiding an inquirer charged with such an errand as mine. If I have not wholly failed in finding my way through the complicated general question which in France I had to study, it is M. Magin whom I have had, almost always, to thank for my clue.

Recommended by Lord Granville's kindness to the notice of M. Guizot, (whose services in the cause of popular education is one of his many distinctions), I was introduced by M. Guizot to a Primary Inspector, who was, he said, of all men the best qualified to inform me respecting the French schools and the practical working of their system—M. Rapet. This testimony borne by M. Guizot to M. Rapet's excellence I soon found that every other voice—official and unofficial, clerical and lay—cordially confirmed. Indeed, I could not but be astonished to find one, whom all thus united in deservedly praising, placed in the official hierarchy of public instruction so far below his merits. M. Rapet's guidance and information were invaluable to me in prosecuting my visits to schools.

I afterwards visited Holland and the French Cantons of Switzerland. In these countries, also, I received every assistance, both from the British Legation and from the officers of Government. But the time which I was able to pass in Holland and Switzerland was very limited; it was to France that I principally directed my attention. M. Cousin's report on Public Instruction in Holland is in every one's hands; the state of things which it describes is to this day little changed. In Switzerland, the German Cantons, the Cantons most interesting to the student of public education, (Canton Aargau is said to possess the best primary schools in Europe), were beyond the province assigned to me by my instructions. Even had they fallen within it, I should have hesitated, though their schools are undoubtedly superior to the French schools, to shorten my inquiry in France in order to visit them.

The day has gone by, when the actual mechanism of primary schools formed the principal object of inquiries upon public education. Rival school-methods have fought their fight; and at the present day we in England, at any rate, think that we know pretty well in what good school-keeping consists. It was not to arbitrate between the monitorial and simultaneous systems, or to give the palm to the best plan for fitting and furnishing schools, that the Education Commission was appointed. That appetite for school-details must indeed be voracious, which at the present day can make its possessor forget, in the spectacle of highly perfected schools, that the vital question is no longer the perfection of elementary schools, but their creation; their creation, and upon what scale this is accomplished, and under what conditions.

France is a country, in population, in extent, in resources, not ill-matched with our own country. In France, therefore, the problem of popular education is presented in nearly the same terms as to ourselves. How is it solved? What does this great agent of popular education do for this great French people, so like to us in its numbers, so like to us in its power, so like to us in its difficulties? This question, I confess, had invincible attractions for me. Moreover, while the popular education of Holland and Germany has had its historians, that of France has hitherto remained undescribed.*

I begin, therefore, with France; and my notices of primary instruction in Holland and Switzerland will be but supplementary.

* I speak of special works, composed in the English language, or of which English translations exist. But for general works noticing French education along with that of other countries, see Mr. Kay's interesting book, *The Education of the Poor in England and Europe*, London, 1846; and also *National Education in Europe*, by Henry Barnard, Superintendent of Common Schools in Connecticut; Hartford, U. S., 1854.

CHAPTER II.

ORGANISATION OF MODERN FRANCE.

FRANCE contains, according to the last census, a population of 36,039,364 inhabitants. Its 86 departments have, for administrative purposes, a division which it will often be necessary, in reading what follows, to bear in mind. Each *department* is divided into *arrondissements*; each *arrondissement* is subdivided into *cantons* and *communes*. There are 363 arrondissements in France, 2850 cantons, 36,826 communes. The department, the arrondissement, and the commune have each a special civil administration. At the head of the department is the prefect, assisted by a "prefect's council" (*conseil de préfecture*), a judicial body charged with the settlement of legal disputes arising out of the administration of the department; and by an elective council-general, a deliberative body which assigns to the several arrondissements the share to be contributed by each to the State-taxation of the department, and votes the funds employed by the departmental executive. At the head of the arrondissement is the sub-prefect, assisted by another deliberative body, the *conseil d'arrondissement*, which performs for the communes and the arrondissements the same functions which the council-general performs for the arrondissements and the department. Lastly, at the head of the commune is the mayor, assisted by a third deliberative body, the municipal council. The representatives of the executive power in each of the three stages of this hierarchy—the prefects, the sub-prefects, and the mayors—are nominated by the central executive power, the State; the deliberative and tax-voting assemblies are elected by the tax-paying bodies whom they respectively represent.* This organisation was established in 1800, under the government of the First Consul.

The mayors and the municipal councils in France, (with whom popular education is chiefly concerned), form a machinery for local self-government which we do not possess. The commune does not correspond to our parish, (a word still used in France, but as an ecclesiastical term only,) because the commune, even in the largest French town, is but one, while the parishes in most English towns of importance are many. But if we imagine every English borough retaining its unity of municipal organisation, and this organisation extended to every town not a borough, and above all to every country parish; if we imagine, in every small town, in every considerable village of England, an elective local council, answerable for the police, the sanitary condition, the roads, the public buildings, the public schools of their locality, we shall be able to conceive the completeness of the municipal organisation which actually exists in France.

Three forms of religious worship are recognised by the law; the Roman Catholic, the Protestant, and

* It is to be noted, however, that the prefect has the power to dissolve any municipal council of his department, and to replace it by a municipal commission of his own naming. At Paris and in all the great towns this has been done; but it is also often done in the country. About 2000 municipal councils have been thus dissolved since 1851.

the Jewish.* The ministers of these three communions are alike salaried by the State. The Roman Catholic religion is truly, as designated in the Concordat, (the instrument which fixes the modern legal constitution of the French Church), "the religion of the great majority of the French people." It is professed by more than thirteen-fifteenths of the population. There are about five millions† of Protestants, divided between the Lutheran and Calvinist communions. The Calvinists are the more numerous, having 510 salaried ministers, while the Lutherans have but 255. The Jews are in number about 70,000.

* In France always called *Israëlite*, the terms *Jew*, *Jewish*, being considered somewhat opprobrious.

† I quote from the latest information, a work by M. Magin, *Cours de Géographie Moderne*, Paris, 1858, authorised by the French Government for use in the public schools. But on this subject of the numbers of the French Protestants there is the most astonishing diversity of assertion. The lowest estimate which I have seen puts them at one million; the highest at six millions.

CHAPTER III.

POPULAR EDUCATION IN FRANCE BEFORE THE REVOLUTION.

In France, as in other countries, the Christian Church has from the earliest times recognised the duty, and asserted the right, of organising and controlling public education. Besides the monastery schools, besides the ecclesiastical or episcopal schools, the church professed the obligation to provide schools of a humbler order, schools for the poor laity, *les pauvres laïques*. The capitularies of Theodulf, appointed bishop of Orleans by Charlemagne, direct his clergy to open, in the towns and villages of his diocese, schools where the children of the faithful might receive, free of cost, the elements of instruction.* From the fourth century to the sixteenth, canons and decrees enjoined even the village priest to collect at the ecclesiastical dwelling (*pastophorium*) a certain number of readers, and to train them to the study of letters as well as to the ministry of the altar. The Lateran Council of 1179 gave injunctions, renewed by the Lateran Council of 1215, that a prebend in every cathedral should be devoted to the maintenance of a preceptor charged to instruct, without fee, the young. This instruction, like that of the higher schools, was under the superintendence of

* See p. 90 of *Histoire de l'Instruction Publique en Europe, et principalement en France*, par Vallet de Viriville, professeur auxiliaire à l'École des Chartes, &c., Paris, 1849; a work to which, both here and in what follows, I am much indebted.

an ecclesiastical functionary delegated for the purpose by the bishop. He bore the title of *écolâtre*, or master of the schools, and generally filled at the same time the office of *chantre*, or master of the choir.

But, if the Church arrogated to herself the right of governing public education, the State, in France, arrogated it yet more imperiously. This power, which, though maintaining Roman Catholicism, opposed to ecclesiastical encroachment the Propositions of Bossuet in 1682, the Organic Articles of the Concordat in 1802, inherits from the Roman Empire, and has never ceased to put in practice, the loftiest idea of State attributions and State authority. It has maintained this idea against the Pope; it has maintained it against its own subjects. Charlemagne assumed the right of subjecting his bishops to his own examination, in order to assure himself that, amid the distractions of their benefices, they had not let their learning grow rusty. Henry the Fourth, in his Statutes of Reformation for the University of Paris, issued in 1598, takes it upon him to ordain, that no boy who has passed the age of nine years shall be allowed to be educated at home.* Napoleon, after establishing his University, decrees, that after a certain day every educational establishment in France which is not provided with an express authorisation from his Grand-Master, shall cease to exist.† The French State may refuse to concede to the Church the control of public instruction, but it agrees with the Church in holding that public instruction must be in the hands of an authorised body. *Collegia illicita dissolvantur*, said the Roman law; unauthorised asso-

* Art. 1. "Nullus in privatis ædibus pueros, qui nonum annum excesserint, instituat et doceat."

† Decree of 11 September 1808.

ciations are to be dissolved. The greatest of French jurists, the friend of Pascal*, enforces the same maxim: "The first rule for all associations," he says, "is that they be established for some public advantage *and by the order or permission of the Sovereign*; for all assemblages of more than one or two persons without this order or permission would be unlawful." "Every one knows," says another great lawyer†, "that no assembly of persons may take place in the realm unless with the authorisation of the Sovereign." Finally, the same principle is consecrated by the existing law of France, by the Penal Code‡, which declares that "no association of more than twenty persons, whose object shall be to assemble daily or at certain fixed times in order to occupy themselves with religious, literary, political, or other matters, may be formed unless with the consent of the Government, and under such conditions as it shall please the public authorities to impose." Theocracy in France, with M. de Bonald for its organ§, may desire to intrust education to a clerical corporation; modern society in France, with the first Napoleon for its organ, may desire to intrust it to a lay corporation; but both are agreed not to intrust it to itself. Liberty of instruction, such as we conceive it, appears in French legislation once, and once only; it appears there in 1793, under the Reign of Terror.

The high Roman and Imperial theory as to the

* Domat, the author of *Les Lois civiles dans leur Ordre naturel*. He died in 1696.

† Rousseau de Lacombe, author of the *Recueil de Jurisprudence civile*, and of the *Recueil de Jurisprudence canonique*. He died in 1749.

‡ *Code Pénal*, art. 291

§ See his *Théorie du Pouvoir politique et religieux*, published in 1796.

duties and powers of the State has never obtained in England. It would be vain to seek to introduce it; but it is also vain, in a country where this theory is powerless, to waste time in decrying it. I believe, as every Englishman believes, that *over-government* is pernicious and dangerous; that the State cannot safely be trusted to undertake everything, to superintend everywhere. But, having once made this profession of faith, I shall proceed to point out as may be necessary, without perpetually repeating it, some inconveniences of *under-government;* to call attention to certain important particulars, in which, within the domain of a single great question, that of public education, the direct action of the State has produced salutary and enviable results.

From the fifth to the fifteenth century the institutions founded for popular instruction bore little or no fruit, because instruction in Europe was up to that time nearly confined to one class of society, the clergy. From the very earliest times, indeed, a simple shepherd boy, like Saint Patroclus of Berry, might enter a monastery-school and become one of the learned men of his epoch; but it was on condition of embracing the ecclesiastical profession. The urban and rural free schools, of which mention has been made, served chiefly to train boys designed for the service of the choir, like the schools for choristers which still survive; or, like the lesser seminaries, of which they were probably the germ, to give the first teaching to boys designed for the ministry. The collectors of autographs, in their quest of the handwriting of noble and distinguished persons, do not mount beyond the fourteenth century, because up to that time even great personages seldom knew how to write. When such was the school-learning of the rich and noble, it may be imagined what was that of the poor and lowly. It was confined to a little instruction in the catechism and the rudiments of religion, given, where it was given at all, to the children of both sexes alike.

In the fifteenth century there are signs in the laity of France both of a growing demand for school instruction and of a sense that the Church inefficiently performed her duty of supplying it. In 1412, the inhabitants of Saint Martin de Villers, in the diocese of Evreux, founded a school for their own parish. The bishop complained of an encroachment on his privilege. The new school, he said, injured his own school at Touque. The dispute was settled by the consent of the lay founders of the new school to vest in the bishop the appointment of their teacher. On other occasions the dispute was carried into the courts of law; the courts of law upheld the exclusive privilege of the ecclesiastical authority, and the lay school was closed. But while thus maintaining her school rights, the Church failed to amend her discharge of her school duties.* A canon of Notre-Dame, Claude Joly, master of the choir and master of the schools in the metropolitan cathedral, who himself exercised in the seventeenth century the superintendence of the ecclesiastical schools of Paris, and who has left an historical account †

* The great Chancellor of the University of Paris, Jean Gerson, (born 1363, died 1429), was in advance of his order and his age in his zeal for popular education, as in other matters. In his retirement at Lyons, at the end of his life, he himself taught the children of the poor; and his is the remarkable saying, "The Reformation of the Church must be commenced with the young children."

† *Traité historique des Écoles épiscopales et ecclésiastiques*, Paris, 1678.

of them, avows the obligation of the Church and confesses her failure. This confession is made in 1678; not twenty years later* every parish in Scotland had its school.

It is well known how prodigious an impulse the Reformation gave in Protestant countries to the education of the people. The primary instruction of Holland, of Scotland, of Protestant Germany, dates from that event. In France, the ferment of mind, which in England and Germany produced the Reformation, existed; but it took a different course. Yet everywhere the new spirit showed solicitude for popular education, although it could not everywhere found it. In the meetings of the States-General held at Orleans and at Blois in 1560, 1576, and 1588, the Estates called the attention of the sovereign to the want of elementary schools. The nobles proposed to make church benefices contribute yearly a certain sum, to be employed in maintaining schoolmasters and literate persons (*pédagogues et gens lettrés*) in all towns and villages, "for the instruction of the children of the poor in the Christian religion and other needful learning, and in sound morality." The Third Estate insisted on the obligation of the clergy to "instruct or cause to be instructed the children of the poor in all good learning, according to their capacity, even from their earliest years, *not delaying or excusing themselves on pretext of the negligence of parents and sponsors.*" The nobles even demanded that "parents who neglected to send their children to school should be subjected to compulsion and fine." Little was done, however. The ordinance of Orleans, designed to meet the wishes of the Estates of 1560, attempted to revive the ancient prescription of the

* In 1696.

Councils, by directing that in "every cathedral or collegiate church one prebend, or the revenues of the same, should be permanently devoted to maintain a preceptor, and to give free schooling to the children of the place." It added a provision unknown to Councils, that this preceptor should be appointed *by the ecclesiastical and municipal authorities conjointly.* In 1563, Charles IX. attempted by letters patent to put this ordinance into execution at Paris: the ecclesiastical authority, the master of the schools, resisted, complaining that his privilege was infringed; and the king gave way.

The Church owed to the laity some compensation for her obstructiveness, and she paid her debt in a certain measure. Civilisation owes much to the great religious orders which laboured in the work of teaching: to the Dominicans, the Franciscans, the Benedictines, the Oratorians, the Jesuits. These, however, busied themselves with the education of the rich; but humbler efforts were not wanting, devoted to the service of the poor. A member of the severest of religious communities, a Minim of the Order of St. Francis of Paola, the Pere Barré, founded in 1671 an association of teachers for the instruction of poor children of both sexes. The association took the title of "Brothers and Sisters of the Christian and Charitable Schools of the Child Jesus." Towards 1700 the Ursulines and other sisterhoods, by the establishment of their schools for girls, carried onward this effort. In 1789 the religious societies engaged in teaching the poor of France were twenty in number; but the religious society which has prosecuted this work most effectually, which has most merited gratitude by its labours for the education of the poor, and which, at the present day, most claims attention from its numbers and from its influence, is undoubtedly the society of the "Brethren of the Christian Schools."*

It dates from 1679. In that year it was founded by Jean Baptiste de Lasalle, a canon of the cathedral church of Rheims and a man of apostolic piety and zeal, in Rheims, his native town. He resigned his canonry in order to be able to tend his infant institution more assiduously. He drew up for it statutes which are a model of sagacity and moderation, and by which it is still governed. He composed for his schools a handbook of method†, of which later works on the same subject have little improved the precepts, while they entirely lack the unction. He lived long enough to see the fruit of his labours. In 1688 he established at Paris a colony of his *teaching brethren.*‡ In 1705 he fixed the head-quarters of his institute in Rouen, at the house of Saint Yon, from which his community took one of the titles by which it long was familiarly known.§ When he died in 1719, with the title of Superior-General of the Brethren of the Christian Schools, his order was established in eight dioceses. In 1724, when the society received a bull of confirmation and approbation from Pope Benedict XIII., it possessed 23 houses in France. In 1785, the number of children taught by the brethren was reckoned at 30,000. Dispersed at the Revolution, they were re-established under the reign of Napoleon, and in 1825,

* Institut des Frères des Écoles Chrétiennes.

† *Conduite des Écoles Chrétiennes.*

‡ Frères enseignants.

§ The brethren have gone by the names of Frères de Saint Yon, Frères Ignorantins, and Frères des Écoles Chrétiennes. They are now almost universally called by the latter title.

during the Restoration, the number of their houses was 210. In 1848 they had in France 19,114 schools, and taught 1,354,056 children.* Their central house is now at Paris.

The brethren are enjoined by their statutes to devote themselves to the instruction of boys in all things that pertain to an honest and Christian life. They are not forbidden to receive the rich into their schools, but their principal business is to be with the poor, and to their poorer scholars they are to extend a special affection. They are to obey a Superior-General, who, with two assistants, is to be elected by the assembled directors of the principal houses. The Superior-General is chosen for life, the assistants for ten years. The separate houses are to be governed by directors, chosen for three years. No brother is to take holy orders. Their vows, which are for three years only, are the three regular vows of chastity, poverty, and obedience, with another of stability, and of teaching without fee or reward. Even these three-year vows they are not permitted to make until they have been members of the institute two years, one of which is passed in the noviciate, the other in a school. They are always to go in company with others of their order; at first they went in parties of two, now they must be at least three. Together with religious knowledge they are to teach their scholars reading, writing, and arithmetic. They are to have in each of their houses a store of school books and school material,

* I quote from returns supplied by the Superior of the brethren, the Frère Philippe, to M. Vallet de Viriville for his *Histoire de l'Instruction Publique en Europe*, and published in that work. But the above numbers seem to me, I confess, hard to reconcile with those which, taken from official returns, will be given hereafter.

which they are to sell to their scholars at the cost price. They are not to talk or gossip with their scholars, or to hear any news from them. They are to be sparing of punishments. The director of each house is to have the inspection of the schools in connection with it.

Such are the rules to which this remarkable association owes its vitality. The pious founder, to whose thoughts the misery flowing from the debasement and ignorance of the poor and working classes was perpetually present*, and with whom its relief was a passion, took every precaution not to found, instead of an order of schoolmasters, an order of monks. He proscribed bodily mortification: he strictly limited the number of fasts to be observed by his brethren; he tried to dissuade them from perpetual vows. "He was fearful," says his biographer, "to see his disciples bind themselves too hastily." At first he allowed them to engage themselves for but a single year; then he fixed three years as their term of service; finally, and against his will, he consented to admit to perpetual vows some of the most fervent among his followers. The weakness of the disciples was not long in justifying the master's hesitation.

A similar community, established some years later on a much smaller scale, deserves notice, because in connection with its operations we have one of the few

* He established his institute, says Pope Benedict XIII., in his bull of approbation, "piè considerans innumera quæ ex ignorantiâ, omnium origine malorum, proveniunt scandala, præsertim in illis, qui, vel egestate oppressi, vel fabrili operi unde vitam eliciunt operam dantes, quarumvis scientiarum humanarum, *ex defectu æris impendendi*, non solum penitus rudes, sed, quod magis dolendum est, elementa religionis Christianæ persæpè ignorant."

facts, testifying to fruit borne by popular instruction, which are to be met with before the Revolution. In the most populous quarter of Paris, the Faubourg St. Antoine, a society for the education of the poor had been founded under the title of "Brethren of the Christian Schools of the Faubourg St. Antoine," by an ecclesiastic, the Abbé Tabourin. In 1738, this society had established seventeen schools. The functionary at the head of the police of Paris declared that the police of the quarter cost, since the establishment of these schools, 30,000f. less than it cost before.

The labours of these religious societies were, however, principally confined to the towns. To their diffusion through the rural districts was opposed the serious obstacle of their expensiveness—an obstacle pointed out in 1818 by the Education Minister of that day, the excellent and admirable M. Royer Collard.* "The brethren," said M. Royer-Collard, "are undoubtedly highly useful and highly to be respected; they do good service in the towns: *it would not be easy to introduce them into the rural districts, because they cost so much more than the ordinary schoolmasters.*" The rule which forbids the brethren to serve in parties of less than three, excellent in many respects, has the inconvenience of rendering difficult their employment in a poor country village where there are not funds for the

* In a debate on a proposal to exempt the brethren from military service. The whole debate, which is very interesting, is to be found (copied from the *Moniteur*) in M. Ambroise Rendu's *Essai sur l'Instruction publique*, Paris, 1819, vol. ii. p. 581. M. Ambroise Rendu, Inspector-General and afterwards Councillor of the University, distinguished himself by his labours in the cause of public education. His son, M. Eugène Rendu, now employed in the Department of Public Instruction at Paris, has published interesting reports on popular education in Germany and England.

payment of three teachers. To spread instruction through the length and breadth of the country was out of their power; and the State continued to find this service undischarged.

The century which saw the brotherhood founded did not close without seeing an effort of the State to undertake the task which for the brotherhood was impossible. But to this effort the State was prompted by a spirit wholly unlike to that which inspired M. de Lasalle, and it reaped from it no more success than it deserved. After the revocation of the Edict of Nantes, the persecuting government of Louis XIV. bethought itself of the village schoolmaster as a useful agent in its work of forcible conversion. A royal edict of December 13th, 1698, gave orders to take the children of heretics from their families at five years old, in order to bring them up, by compulsion, in Catholic schools. But these Catholic schools did not yet exist. The edict, therefore, went on to provide that "there should be established, so far as it was possible, schoolmasters and schoolmistresses in every parish which was without them, in order to instruct the children of both sexes in the principal mysteries of the Catholic, Apostolic, and Roman religion . . . in order, likewise, to teach reading, *and even writing*, to all who might need them." "To this end, it is our pleasure," the edict continues, "that, in places where there are no other funds, there shall be a power of taxing all the inhabitants to raise stipends for the said schoolmasters and schoolmistresses, up to a sum of 150 livres a year for a master, and of 100 for a mistress."* But the arbitrary and violent provisions of this edict made it inexecutable. The village children of France remained free

* Art. 9.

from forcible initiation into the mysteries of the Catholic, Apostolic, and Roman religion. They remained, also, without learning how to read and write.

The era approached from which dates a wholly new history for France; and it is impossible to determine accurately in what state the Revolution of 1789 found the instruction of those masses, on whom it was to confer such unbounded power. Statistics on this point almost entirely fail us. In a list of the establishments of public instruction which the Revolution found existing in France—a list given by M. Villemain in a most interesting report on secondary instruction*—there is indeed the entry, "*Écoles cantonales, écoles de village*," but opposite to this entry, where the eye looks for figures, it finds a blank, and in a foot-note the words, "The elements for this calculation are wanting." The poor of the towns had the schools of the religious congregations. It appears, too, that in the want of good elementary schools, the colleges, or grammar-schools for the middle and upper classes, to a very limited extent supplied the deficiency, by admitting to some of the numerous scholarships with which they were endowed a certain number of children from the lower classes. To this cause it is said to be attributable that, in 1789, 1 in every 31 boys of from 8 to 18 years of age was receiving in France secondary instruction, while in 1843 the proportion was but 1 in 35.† In the country, village schools existed here and there. In these no teacher could be appointed unless approved by the ecclesiastical authority; most often he was directly named by the curé. In France, as in other countries, popular tradition represents the incumbent

* *Rapport au Roi sur l'Instruction secondaire*. Paris, 1843.
† *Ibid.* p. 56.

as usually nominating to the post of schoolmaster either his sacristan or the cripple of the village. In the case of foundation schools, the founder or his representatives nominated the teacher; but here, too, the concurrence of the ecclesiastical authority was always required.* The instruction of the mass of the poor remained very nearly what it had been in the middle ages. In conversing with middle-aged working men in the French provinces, I found almost invariably that my informant himself had attended school; more rarely, that his father had attended it; that his grandfather had attended it, never.

* An edict of Louis XIV. (dated April 1695) says, "Les régens, précepteurs, maîtres et maîtresses d'écoles des petits villages seront approuvés par les curés des paroisses ou autres personnes ecclésiastiques qui ont droit de le faire."—Art. 25.

CHAPTER IV.

POPULAR EDUCATION IN FRANCE UNDER THE REVOLUTION.

THE Revolution presented itself with magnificent promises of universal education. Already, in 1775, Turgot, in his celebrated programme, had drawn the outlines of a uniform and national system, to be superintended by a Royal Council. The instructions of all three orders of the States-General loudly called for it. The clergy, while demanding a national system, insisted above all on the necessity of executing with more strictness "the regulations which tend to maintain and fortify the precious influence of the curés upon education." The nobles declared simply that "the time was come for propagating through the country districts the means of instruction for those who lived there, and for extending this instruction even to the poor." The Third Estate demanded that "public education should be so modified as to be adapted to the wants of all orders in the State; that it might form good and useful men in all classes of society." With the precision of a power which had already discerned its future means of strength, and was determined to use them, this formidable claimant suggested that the municipal and lay authorities should in future share with the Church the appointment and control of public teachers. The Constituent Assembly hastened to respond to the national wishes. A commission was appointed, which after two years of laborious inquiry appeared with a report and the project of a law. By a singular chance, as if no great public question, however alien to him, was to escape this most versatile of statesmen, the reporter of the commission was M. de Talleyrand. The Constituent Assembly received the report on the eve of its separation. It voted no plan of public instruction; but it consecrated in a single famous article the principle upon which such a plan was to repose. It decreed*: "There shall be created and organised a public instruction, common to all citizens, gratuitous in respect of those branches of tuition which are indispensable for all men. Its establishments shall be distributed gradually, in a proportion combined with the division of the kingdom."

On the 1st of October the Legislative Assembly met, and six months afterwards† it received from Condorcet another report on national education— another proposed law. But the time was no longer favourable for founding. The Convention replaced the Legislative Assembly‡; the revolutionary decrees flew thick and fast, and nearly every one of them struck down an institution without giving to it a successor. On the 8th of March, 1793, it was decreed that the property of all endowed seats of education in France

* In the *Fundamental Dispositions* of the Constitution of September 3rd, 1792. "Il sera créé et organisé une instruction publique, commune à tous les citoyens, gratuite à l'égard des parties d'enseignement indispensables pour tous les hommes, et dont les établissemens seront distribués graduellement, dans un rapport combiné avec la division du royaume."

† April 20th, 1792.

‡ September 21st, 1792.

should be sold, and that the proceeds should go to the State. On the 18th of August in the same year, the religious corporations devoted to teaching, along with all other corporations, religious and secular, were suppressed, on the ground that "a truly free state must not tolerate within itself any corporate body whatever, not even those which, having devoted themselves to public instruction, have deserved well of their country."* A little later, on the 15th of September, the abolition of all existing colleges and faculties was pronounced, and the renowned University of Paris, with a host of less distinguished institutions, fell in a common ruin. So complete was the destruction, that in the next year a warm friend of education, Fourcroy, afterwards the chief agent of the First Consul in reviving and reorganising public instruction, declared to the Convention that France was fast relapsing into barbarism. To this had come the demands of 1789, and the promises of the Constituent Assembly.

The Convention had unquestionably a sincere zeal for popular instruction, and even an exaggerated faith in it. One of its members proposed that no less than three sittings of the Assembly in every ten days should be devoted to this subject alone. It was the Convention which endowed France with two admirable institutions, of which the vitality has proved not less great than the usefulness—the Normal School and the Polytechnic School. But it would have been powerless to carry any organised instruction, even a humble one, into a region of society not then prepared to receive it; and the instruction which it dreamed of was by no

* "Considérant qu'un état vraiment libre ne doit souffrir dans son sein aucune corporation, pas même celles qui, vouées à l'enseignement public, ont bien mérité de la patrie," &c.

means humble. By decrees of the 12th of December, 1792, and of the 30th of May, 1793, it ordered the establishment of primary schools. By a decree of the 21st of October, 1793, it gave development to its plan. The primary schools were to be proportioned in number to the population. There was to be one for every 1500 inhabitants; but no place with more than 400 inhabitants was to be left without a school. The children of all classes were to receive in these schools "that first education, physical, moral, and intellectual, the best adapted to develope in them republican manners, patriotism, and the love of labour." They were to learn "those traits of virtue which most honour freemen, and particularly those traits of the French Revolution, the best adapted to elevate the soul and to render men worthy of liberty and equality." They were to be taught to speak, read, and write correctly the French language; they were to learn "some notions of the geography of France; the rights and duties of men and citizens; the first notions of natural and familiar objects; the use of numbers, the compass, the level, weights and measures, the lever, the pulley, and the measurement of time. They were to be often taken into the fields and workshops where they might see agricultural and industrial work going on, and they were to take part in it so far as their age would allow." In this manner the Convention filled up the outline traced by the Constituent Assembly. These were the "branches of tuition" which the French Revolution held to be "indispensable for all men."

A few days afterwards* it proceeded to organise the instruction decreed. A "commission of enlightened

* Decree of October 29th, 1793.

patriots and moral persons" was to be established in every district, in order to determine where the new schools should be placed, and to "*examine all citizens who proposed to devote themselves to the work of national education in the primary schools.*" The commission was to examine candidates as to their acquirements, their aptitude for teaching, their morals, and their patriotism. The examination was to be public. The commission was to form a list of the candidates who had satisfied them, and this list was to be published in each school district. On the *décadi* following its publication, such inhabitants as were parents and guardians were to meet and choose a teacher from it. Vacancies were to be filled up in the same manner. The decree was to apply to schoolmistresses as well as schoolmasters, and for the salaries of both it fixed a minimum of 1200 francs (48*l.*). But no woman of noble family, no woman who had formerly belonged to a religious order, no woman who had formerly been named to the post of teacher by a noble or by an ecclesiastic, was to be eligible for the office of schoolmistress. There was no fear that men thus circumstanced would be chosen by the local authorities; their compassion or their embarrassment might dispose them to be less severe in excluding resourceless women.

The Convention could furnish a programme of instruction, but it could not furnish schools. In despair it renounced the attempt, and addressed itself to private enterprise. On the 19th of December, 1793, appeared the startling decree which abandons abruptly the consecrated traditions of public instruction in France, and which, in the eyes of every orthodox functionary of that instruction, stands as the abomination of desolation, witnessing that the end of the world is come. *L'enseigne-*

ment est libre, begins this new voice;—"Teaching is free—it shall be public; citizens and citizenesses who desire to avail themselves of their liberty to teach" shall merely be required to inform the municipal authority of their intention to open a school, and of the matters which they propose to teach, and shall produce, besides, a "certificate of civism and good morals." Thus fortified, a teacher might open his school, and the Republic undertook to pay his scholars' fees. There was no fear lest these should be wanting; for the law provided that parents should be compelled, under pain of fine, to send their children to school, thus transferring to the scholar the control from which it exempted the teacher.

Such liberty was too novel to last; and a decree of the next year restricted it.* Freedom of instruction was maintained, in so far as it was still left to the individual to place a school where he would, without first asking the State's leave; but the teacher was subjected to a more exact superintendence. Even his charter of liberty, the decree of December, 1793, had committed him to the watchfulness "of the municipality or section, of parents and guardians, and of society at large;" any of whom might denounce him if he taught anything "contrary to the laws and to republican morality." The law of 1794 placed him in the hands of a "jury of instruction," to be chosen by the district administration from among fathers of families. This jury was to examine and elect the teacher; he had then to be approved by the district administration; afterwards he was to be superintended in the management of his school by the jury. To quicken the zeal of those

* Decree of November 17th, 1794.

parents whom the penalties of the decree of 1793 had failed to move, the new law ordered that "those young citizens who have not attended school shall be examined, in the presence of the people, at the Feast of the Young, and, if they shall then be found not to have the acquirements necessary for French citizens, shall be excluded from all public functions until they have attained them." The law fixed a minimum for the salaries of teachers, and for the proportion of schools to population, nearly at the same rate as preceding laws, but somewhat more liberally. It provided that in every commune where the clergyman's house had not been already sold for the benefit of the republic, this house should be given up to the schoolmaster for a dwelling and for a school.* It maintained the former programme of instruction, and even amplified it, adding to the course gymnastics, military exercises, and swimming. The revolutionary theory of the "acquirements indispensable for all men" here reached its fullest efflorescence.

In a year all was changed. On the 25th of October, 1795, appeared the most memorable of the revolutionary laws of public instruction, the law (as it is still called) of the 3rd of Brumaire, year IV.† This law, founded on a remarkable report by Daunou, organised the whole of instruction; it embraced primary schools, central schools, special schools, public museums, public libraries, the Institute. For primary schools it established a state of things which endured, with little change, till 1833. But at what a sacrifice! To effect the practical founda-

* This provision was repealed by a decree of August 31st, 1797.

† The first chapter of this law, which alone relates to primary instruction, is printed textually at the end of this volume.

tion of a very little, the Revolution had to renounce almost all its illusions. Popular education, which had had laws upon laws to itself, was confined, in the law of 1795, to the limits of one short chapter. The "acquirements indispensable for all men" had dwindled to reading, writing, ciphering, and the elements of republican morality. The State, which was once to give everything, was now to give nothing but a schoolhouse. The schoolmaster's salary of from 1200 to 1500 francs a year out of the public purse, descended to a salary such as he could extract out of "the local authorities." The free schooling promised to all scholars came down to a schooling which all but one-fourth of the scholars were to pay for. In compensation the youth of France might attend school or not, as they and their parents pleased. Guarantees for the efficiency of the schoolmaster were still maintained. He was still to be examined by a jury of instruction; the municipal authorities presented him for examination; the departmental authorities nominated him when examined. He was thenceforward under the superintendence of the municipal administration. The concurrence of the jury, the municipality, and the department was necessary for his dismissal. Thus the Convention atoned for its first extravagance. The day after the passing of this law, it separated.*

"What," I ventured to ask M. Guizot, "did the French Revolution contribute to the cause of popular education?" "Un déluge de mots," replied M. Guizot, "rien de plus." As regards the material establishment of popular instruction, this is unquestionably true. Yet on its future character and regulation the Revolution,

* On the 26th of October, 1795.

as unquestionably, exercised an influence which every Frenchman takes it for granted that an inquirer understands, and which we in England must not overlook. It established certain conditions under which any future system of popular education must inevitably constitute itself. It made it impossible for any government of France to found a system which was not *lay*, and which was not *national*.

CHAPTER V.

POPULAR EDUCATION IN FRANCE UNDER THE FIRST EMPIRE.

THE weak government and the exhausting wars of the Directory left, as is well known, the whole of the internal administration of France in neglect and confusion. Public instruction suffered with everything else. In 1799 Napoleon began the task, his efforts in which have shed an imperishable glory on the Consulate, and which it would have been well for him never to have forsaken for any task less pacific and less noble — the task, to use his own words, of "founding a new society, free alike from the injustice of feudalism and from the confusion of anarchy." Of his labours, modern French administration, the Concordat, the public schools for the middle and upper classes, the Legion of Honour, the Code, the University, are monuments. Primary schools did not escape his attention. But the urgent business of the moment was to deal with secondary schools; to rescue the education of the richer classes themselves, those classes in whose hands the immediate destinies of a civilised and regular society are placed, from the state of ruin into which it had fallen. To this the First Consul addressed himself. The law of the 1st of May, 1802, founded secondary instruction in France as it at this day exists. For the feeble and decaying central schools of the Convention* — mere courses of lectures,

* The law of the 3rd Brumaire, year IV., had decreed one for each department. In 1802 only thirty-two were found to have had any success. These thirty-two were the first *Lycées* under the new law.

without hold on their pupils, without discipline, and without study — the new law substituted the communal colleges and the lyceums, with boarders, with a rigid discipline, and with a sustained course of study: institutions which do not, indeed, give an education equal to that of our best public schools, but which extend to all the middle classes of France an education which our public schools give to the upper classes only. For the exclusively mathematical and scientific course of the revolutionary theorists, it substituted, but with proper enlargement, that bracing classical course which the experience of generations has consecrated, and which Napoleon, though he had not himself undergone it, had the power of mind to appreciate. Finally, by the establishment of 6400 scholarships, fairly distributed, it opened an access as wide as was possible, or even desirable, to the schools which it created.

Only the first chapter of the law of 1802 related to primary schools. This merely repeated the humble provisions of the last law of the Convention. The commune was to furnish a schoolhouse to the teacher, who still, after this was supplied to him, had to depend for his support upon the payments of his scholars. The number of these to be exempted, on the ground of poverty, from the school fee, was reduced from a fourth to a fifth. The superintendence of the teacher by the municipal authorities was confirmed. Finally, the schools were placed under the supreme charge of the newly created departmental executive, the sub prefects and the prefects.

Small as was the attention then bestowed on schools for the poor, in comparison with that which at a later time they received, it is curious to remark how strongly the inconvenience of their total disorganisation was felt in the French provinces, as long ago as the beginning of this century. It seems as if, rude and illiterate as was the village-school of France before the Revolution, its disappearance could leave a blank as serious as the blank which the disappearance of the village-school would leave now. In its endeavour to bring order out of the chaos which the Revolution had left, the Consular government invited in 1801 the practical suggestions of the council-general of each department upon the wants of the locality. The councils-general, in their replies, expressed, among other things, the greatest dissatisfaction at the state of the primary schools, and the greatest desire to see it improved. Many of them called for the re-establishment of the religious orders devoted to teaching. "The Brethren of the Christian Doctrine, the Ursulines, and the rest, are much regretted here," says the council-general of the Côte d'Or. That of the Pas de Calais begs the government "again to employ in the instruction of boys and girls the *Frères ignorantins*, and the Daughters of Charity, and of Providence." That of the Pyrenées Orientales says, "People here regret the religious associations which busied themselves in teaching the children of the poor." That of the Aisne asks, like that of the Pas de Calais, for the "reorganisation of the religious communities devoted to the elementary instruction of children of each sex." To commit the primary instruction of France to religious corporations was at no time the intention of Napoleon. To avail himself of the services of these corporations, under the control of a lay body, modern in its spirit, and national in its composition, he was abundantly willing. Such a body he designed to establish in his new University.

By a short law of the 10th of May, 1806, the University of France was called into existence. "There shall be formed," says the law, "under the name of *Imperial University*, a body with the exclusive charge of tuition and of public education throughout the empire. The members of the teaching body shall contract civil obligations of a special and temporary character." The new University was organised by a decree of the 17th of March, 1808. Under a hierarchy of grand master, councillors, inspectors-general, and rectors, was placed the whole instruction of France. The faculties, the lyceums and communal colleges, the primary schools, were alike made subject. "No school, no establishment of instruction whatsoever, can be formed outside the pale of the University, and without the authorisation of its chief."* By the imposition of dues on examinations, dues on degrees, dues on the fees paid by boarders and day scholars in grammar-schools, superior and secondary education became tributary to the new power. It was also endowed with a sum of 400,000 francs charged on the State, and with all the property of the old educational bodies of France which the Revolution had not yet alienated. It became a great civil corporation, with the power of acquiring, inheriting, and transmitting. The Grand-Master and his council represented it in the capital; twenty-six Academies, each governed by its Rector, corresponding in their districts with the ancient Courts of Appeal, represented it in the provinces.

Such was the Imperial University created by Napoleon. The powers which he conferred on it did not, at that period of disorganisation and of demand for effective government, appear exorbitant. It had at a

* Decree of March 17th, 1808, art 2

later time no fiercer enemies than the clergy; yet in 1808 a bishop writes to the Chancellor of the new University that he is rejoiced at its establishment; for "education," he says, "is at the present day in the hands of the first comer, and one has the pain of seeing it conducted by men who have neither acquirements nor principles." Created an endowed corporation, not a mere department of state, it wore a character of independence which all modern governments in France are apt to regard with suspicion, and which Napoleon himself was the last man to confer hastily. His reasons assigned for this unusual distinction are judicious, and even noble. "His Majesty," he says, in his instructions to the University Council at its first formation,—"his Majesty has organised the University as a corporate body, because a corporate body never dies, and because, in such a body, there is a perpetual transmission of organisation and spirit. It has been his Majesty's desire to realise, in a state of forty millions of people, what Sparta and Athens accomplished, what the religious orders attempted in our own day, and failed in accomplishing because they lacked unity. His Majesty wants a body whose teaching may be free from the influence of the passing gusts of fashion; a body that may keep moving, even though Government be lethargic; whose administration and statutes may be made so thoroughly national, that no one shall lightly lay his hands upon them."

These wishes have not been wholly frustrated. Disliked as a Napoleonist creation by the Bourbons, hated by the clergy, decried by the friends of liberty of instruction, ill supported by successive ministries incapable of Napoleon's elevation of views, the University of France has been unable to maintain its exclusive privileges and its corporate character. In 1824 it became a ministerial department*; in 1833 its special budget was suppressed; in 1850 its property was annexed to the State.† But the Minister of Public Instruction is still, at the same time, Rector of the Academy of Paris, and head of the University; his chief functionaries are functionaries of the University, graduated in its faculties and inspired by its traditions. That transmission of a corporate spirit, which Napoleon wished for, has been accomplished, while the exclusive privileges which the tendencies of the age would not tolerate have been withdrawn; and from this corporate spirit the members of the University derive an independence, a self-respect, and a disinterestedness, which distinguishes them from the whole body of French officials. The University of France has not the attributes of ancient universities: it has neither great estates, nor august associations, nor historic grandeur. But it has attributes, the first to which modern institutions have to aspire, and the possession of which may perhaps compensate for the absence of all others: it has intelligence, and it has equity.

Of the decree organising the University, only four articles related expressly to primary schools. The first of the four‡ specifies among the schools of which the twenty-six new Academies were to take charge, the schools for the poor, primary schools, in which are taught reading, writing, and the first notions of arithmetic. These Napoleon, like the authors of the law of 1795, pronounces to be the "elementary acquirements

* The Ministry of Public Instruction was created by an ordinance of the 26th of August, 1824.

† By a vote of the Legislative Assembly, August 22nd, 1850.

‡ Decree of March 17th, 1808, art. 5.

necessary for all men." He naturally omits from his programme the republican morality of the Convention. No special mention is made of religious instruction for the primary schools; but the decree proclaims that the whole teaching of the University is to be based upon the precepts of religion, of loyalty, and of obedience. Another article * directs the University to take care that the persons who give elementary instruction be persons capable of giving it properly. Another † prescribes the formation, in the lyceums and grammar-schools, of normal classes destined to form masters for the primary schools. In these classes are to be taught the "best methods for bringing to perfection the art of teaching children to read, write, and cipher." Finally, the decree mentions by name the religious order most concerned in popular education, the Brethren of the Christian Schools. The brethren were to be certificated by the Grand-Master, admitted to take the University oath, and specially encouraged. The Grand-Master was to examine their statutes, and to superintend their schools.

The operation of the law of 1802 had wrought little change in the primary schools. In a statistical report on the Department of Vaucluse, published in 1808 by authority of the prefect, nearly the same picture is drawn of their condition as the councils-general had drawn in 1801. Nearly one-half of the communes are without any school at all. Where schools exist, they are often under the care of teachers now old and infirm; when these teachers are gone, there is no one to take their place. Both the "Ignorantine Friars" and the old village pedagogues are greatly regretted in the

* Art. 107. † Art. 108.

country. Napoleon sincerely desired the spread of elementary instruction, although he meant to keep it within strict limits.* In establishing the University, he conceived that he established a body in whose hands the future destinies of popular education rested. The University accepted the charge. Its Grand-Master, M. de Fontanes, a man of letters, and a proficient in that florid declamation which often passes for eloquence, sincerely addressed himself to learn the facts of a system of instruction in which there was nothing academic. He directed his inspectors-general, sent in 1809 into the departments to inspect superior and secondary instruction, to examine, so far as they could, into the state of primary instruction, and to report to him on it. They reported a state of languor, degradation, death. But the establishments of the Congregation of the Christian Schools were beginning to reappear. M. de Fontanes issued a general diploma † to the brethren, authorising them to hold schools; he revised and approved their statutes; he offered to them pecuniary aid; he exerted himself to rescue them and other teachers from the conscription. He wrote to the bishops and prefects, requesting information about village schools and schoolmasters, to guide him in continuing or dismissing the latter. In one letter, written by him to a prefect in 1809, there is a passage which is valuable as showing how teachers were at that time appointed:—"The modes in which primary teachers are nominated," he says, "are extremely various; in

* By a decree of November 15th, 1811, the University was ordered to see that "les maîtres ne portassent point leur enseignement au-dessus de la lecture, l'écriture, et l'arithmétique."

† August 4th, 1810. The diploma was delivered to the Superior-General

some cantons they have to be examined before a jury; in others, the municipal council expresses its wishes; in others, again, the teacher is empowered to open school on his mere personal request, accompanied by the consent of the inhabitants, who enter into no engagement to maintain him." M. de Fontanes soon became convinced of his want of materials for immediately reconstructing primary education. He tried to use the old materials where he could. By a circular addressed in 1810 to his rectors he desired them to send him lists, for every department, of the existing schools and schoolmasters, specifying those of the latter who, in the opinion of the rector and in that of the local authorities, merited to be confirmed in their office. To these he undertook to send certificates. Meanwhile, he promised, at no distant period, a comprehensive plan of popular education.

The best criticism on the actual performance of the University is to be found in the tables of its expenditure. All that primary instruction, during the Empire, received from the public purse, was a sum of 170*l.** Even this was not contributed from the funds of the University, but from those of the Minister of the Interior. The enemies of the University were in the habit of saying that it did little for primary instruction, because from primary instruction it could draw no revenue. This was unjust. The University had, in

* 4250 fr. See *Le Budget de l'Instruction Publique*, par M. Charles Jourdain, Paris, 1857, p. 175. M. Charles Jourdain, (himself distinguished in the world of letters, to which his father rendered a signal service), is at the head of the financial department of the Ministry of Public Instruction. His work is invaluable for all that relates to the finance not only of primary, but also of superior and secondary instruction.

truth, no funds and no staff for dealing with popular education. The primary schools were in too suffering a condition to be restored by the occasional efforts of rectors and inspectors-general. The country districts of France, swept by the conscription, were too harassed and exhausted to care whether their schools were suffering or not. In more than one case the University offered funds for the assistance of such schools, and could find no one to receive and administer them. One remarkable effort in the cause of popular education, and one only, dates from the Empire. In 1810 the first normal school in France for primary teachers was founded at Strasbourg, by a prefect whose intelligent beneficence is still remembered in Alsace—M. Lezay de Marnesia. But the time for educating the French people was not yet come. Napoleon was conscious both that the work remained undone, and that it was indispensable to accomplish it. In decreeing, on the report of Carnot, the establishment of a model school, he expresses his dissatisfaction that the people should be so ill educated, his conviction that it was possible to educate them better.* But this decree dates from the very last days of his power, after his return from Elba, and six weeks before Waterloo.

* *Moniteur* of April 30th, 1815: —"Considérant l'importance de l'instruction primaire pour l'amélioration de la société; considérant que les méthodes jusqu'aujourd'hui usitées en France n'ont pas rempli le but qu'il est possible d'atteindre, desirant porter cette partie de nos institutions à la hauteur des lumières du siècle," &c.

CHAPTER VI.

POPULAR EDUCATION IN FRANCE UNDER THE RESTORATION.

To the Restoration is due the credit of having first perceived, that, in order to carry on the war with ignorance, the sinews of war were necessary. Other governments had decreed systems for the education of the people; the government of the Restoration decreed funds. An ordinance of the 29th of February 1816 charged the treasury with an annual grant of 2000*l.* for the provision of school-books and model schools, and of recompenses for deserving teachers. The sum was small; but it was the first. The same ordinance prescribed the formation of cantonal committees, to watch over the discipline, morality, and religious instruction of primary schools. These committees (which were to be unpaid) were to consist of the curé, two local officials of the government, and four notables of the canton to be nominated by the rector to whose academy the school belonged, and approved by the prefect. Above all, this ordinance instituted a certificate of three degrees, to be obtained by examination before the rector's deputy. It made special provision for the independence of Protestant schools. It may truly be said that this ordinance of 1816 presents, in germ, several of the best provisions of the law of 1833.

But in its government of public instruction, as in its government of other public interests, the Restoration was not happy. It laboured under the incurable weakness of being a traditionary monarchy working with revolutionary tools; it was placed as Charles II. would have been placed had he returned to England bound by the Commonwealth-laws instead of the Declaration of Breda. The legislation of the English Republic disappeared from the statute-book; that of the French Republic survived to hamper the Restoration. In its treatment of public instruction, as of other questions, the monarchy was perpetually striving to assert its own traditions in face of a legal situation of which it was not master, and perpetually failing. One of its first acts was to strike a blow at the University. A royal ordinance of February 17th, 1815, announced the intention of taking public instruction out of the hands of an authority "whose absolutism was incompatible with the paternal intentions and liberal spirit" of the Restoration, and which "reposed on institutions framed rather to serve the political views of the former government, than to spread among the people the benefits of a moral and useful education." Napoleon reappeared, and the University was respited. At its second return, the monarchy, more moderate or more timid, maintained provisionally a system for which it had no substitute ready.* The Grand-Master and council were replaced by a Commission of Public Instruction†; but the University was left in possession of its dues, its academies, and its exclusive privileges, of which the ordinance of February had deprived it. The friends of the monarchy urged it to decentralise as much as possible‡; to foster institutions

* By an ordinance of August 15th, 1815.

† This Commission consisted at first of five, afterwards of seven, members. M. Royer-Collard was its first president.

‡ "En France, aujourd'hui, les lois tendent à la démocratie, et l'administration tend au despotisme.—Voulez-vous ouvrir une école?

which, by their local strength, independent permanence, and conservative spirit, might serve in the country as points of support to the government. M. de Tocqueville has pointed out how, even before the Revolution, it was the constant effort of French government to overbear such institutions, because all independence was distasteful to it. But, in spite of Government, they existed in the ancient France in great numbers. They were the necessary result of the isolation of provinces, the variety of jurisdictions, the multitude of corporations. The humble Institute of the Christian Schools offered to the Restoration an opportunity of reverting to the old order of things. The moment this congregation was relieved from the Empire, it attempted to shake off the yoke of the Imperial University. The occasion was the certificate prescribed by the ordinance of 1816, and which the rectors endeavoured to enforce. The Superior-General directed the brethren to refuse to be examined. The individual certificate was calculated, he said, "to weaken the dependence of the members on their chief, and to destroy their congregation."* He boldly maintained, in defiance of the revolutionary legislation, that as his community had never ceased to have a legal existence, it ought to continue in the enjoyment of its ancient civil rights. His adversaries retorted that if the corporation of the Christian Schools had not been suppressed by the revolution, then neither had the most absurd and obsolete corporations, whom

prenez un diplôme.—L'Université ne demande qu'une chose aux Frères, c'est de dissoudre leur congrégation, pour devenir de simples instituteurs primaires dont elle disposera souverainement.—L'Université s'occupera de vous fournir le savoir, et les tribunaux s'occuperont de vos mœurs." — *Conservateur* of November, 1818.

* The Frère Gerbaud to the Minister of the Interior, July 7th, 1818.

to name was to provoke a smile, been suppressed, and they were still legally existing. We in England, with our judicious contempt of logic, should probably have contented ourselves with ignoring the monstrous decree of 1792, when a useful institution was at stake, while we left useless institutions to its operation. The government of the Restoration thought it convenient to keep the religious societies dependent on it for their existence, but it freely conceded to them exemptions and privileges. That is to say, it denied to these bodies the power of aiding it as independent forces, while it gained for itself the odium of an unjust favouritism. In July, 1818, the Commission of Public Instruction decided that the brethren of the Christian Schools should be exempted from examination, and should receive their certificates on presenting their letters of obedience. In 1824* the Minister of Public Instruction, M. de Frayssinous, remodelled the cantonal committees, so as to give the entire command of the Catholic primary schools to the bishops and clergy. Whether the Restoration was a just or an unjust steward to the French people, it cannot, at any rate, be commended for having done wisely. Without strengthening itself, it managed to offend every liberal sentiment, and to unite against its own existence the most moderate friends of liberty with the most reckless anarchists. It reimposed Latin as the language of college lectures, while it continued to refuse to fathers of families the power of disposing of their property as they pleased. It abandoned the primary schools to the clergy, while it continued to keep the Church the salaried servant of the State.

Yet, in respect to popular education, it showed uni-

* By an ordinance dated April 8th

form solicitude and occasional glimpses of liberalism. In 1828* a new Minister of Instruction, M. de Vatimesnil, restored to the cantonal committee its lay element, and to the University its control of the primary schools. He gave, for the first time, to dismissed teachers an appeal from the rector and his academic council to the Royal Council of Public Instruction at Paris. He extended the cantonal committee's right of inspection to girls' schools, which an ordinance of the 3rd of April, 1820, had subjected to the prefect alone. In 1830 † M. Guernon de Ranville, one of the ministers who signed the fatal ordinances of July, again abrogated this latter provision. The superintendence of girls' schools under sisters of the religious communities he took away from the cantonal committees, and assigned to the bishops alone. Yet this same M. Guernon de Ranville called‡ the municipal councils to deliberate on the immediate establishment of a system of communal schools which prefigures the system founded in 1833. In 1829 the State doubled the sum which since 1816 it had annually allotted to primary instruction; in 1830, on the eve of the Revolution, it increased it sixfold.§ The primary normal schools, of which the Empire had bequeathed but one to the Restoration, were thirteen in number in 1830. In more than 20,000 of the communes of France a school of some sort or other was established. Yet the reporter|| of the law of 1833 could say with truth that the monarchy of July had

* By an ordinance dated April 21st.

† Ordinance of January 6th, 1830.

‡ Ordinance of February 14th, 1830.

§ The grant in 1829 was 100,000 fr. (4000*l.*), in 1830 it was 300,000 fr. (12,000*l.*).

|| M. Cousin, in the *Moniteur* of May 22nd, 1833.

received popular education in a deplorable state from its predecessor.

In fact, the situation of primary instruction in 1830, far from brilliant as it appeared, was yet externally more specious than internally sound. The ordinance of 1816 imposed on teachers the necessity of being examined and certificated; it thus established the best and only guarantee for the efficiency of that agent on whom a school's whole fortune hangs: but the guarantee was illusory. The reader has seen how the religious corporations were allowed to evade it, by presenting their letters of obedience in lieu of a certificate. There remained the lay teachers. They had to undergo an examination before the rector's delegate. But the rector had at his disposal no proper staff to which to commit such functions. Inspection did not then exist. In nine cases out of ten the rector named as his delegate the curé of the parish for which a schoolmaster was required; the curé named the man of his own choice with or without examination; and the rector bestowed the certificate which his delegate demanded. Even the legal power of control over the choice of incompetent teachers the University lost in 1824. Catholics themselves confessed the injury which Catholic schools had suffered by the exemption of their teachers from the most salutary of tests.* Nor was the communal school in many cases more of a reality than the schoolmaster's certificate. Of the 20,000 communes provided with schools barely one half possessed, even in 1834, school-premises of their own; in the other half the school was held in a barn, in a cellar, in a stable, in the church-porch, in the open air, in a room which served at the

* *Rapport au Roi*, by the Duke of Broglie, October 16th, 1830, in the *Bulletin Universitaire*, vol. ii. p. 174.

same time as the sole dwelling-place of the schoolmaster and his family, where his meals were cooked and his children born.* Where school-premises existed, they were often no better than their less pretentious substitutes: they were often hovels, dilapidated, windowless, fireless, reeking with damp; where, in a space of twelve feet square, eighty children were crowded together; where the ravages of an epidemic swept the school every year.† The state of things reported by the inspectors, nearly 500 in number, whom M. Guizot, at the end of 1833, sent through the length and breadth of France to determine accurately the condition of elementary schools with which the law of 1833 at the outset had to deal, is probably the same state of things which a similar inquest, had the happy thought of making it arisen, would have revealed in every country in Europe when popular instruction first began to be closely scanned. Here the teacher was a petty tradesman, leaving his class every moment to sell tobacco to a customer; there he was a drunkard; in another place he was a cripple. The clergy were often found at war with the schoolmaster; but then the schoolmaster was often such that this state of war was not wonderful. "In what condition is the moral and religious instruction in your school?" one of M. Guizot's inspectors asked a schoolmaster. "*Je n'enseigne pas ces bêtises-là,*" was the answer. Another inspector found the schoolmaster parading, at the head of his school, the town where he lived; drums beating, the scholars singing the Marseillaise; and the procession halting before the clergyman's house to shout at the top of their

* *Tableau de l'Instruction primaire en France*, par M. Lorain, Paris, 1837, p. 3.

† *Ibid.* p. 3, 162.

lungs, "Down with the Jesuits!" * The apathy of the local authorities, too, was disheartening. "We counted on meeting with gratitude," said the inspectors; "instead of that, we have met, almost everywhere, with resistance." An inspector arrived on a November evening, wet and tired, at a remote commune to which he brought the promise of a school; he sought out the mayor, on whose hospitality, (for there was no inn,) he reckoned; instead of hospitality he received from the mayor this greeting:—"You would have done a great deal better, Sir, if you had brought us money to mend our roads; as for schools, we don't want 'em;"—and, late as it was, the unfortunate inspector had to cross a ford, and seek refuge in another village.†

* *Tableau de l'Instruction primaire en France*, p. 11.

† *Ibid.* p. 15. M. Lorain, distinguished in the service of public instruction in France, was one of the agents employed by M. Guizot in the inspection of 1833; his most interesting book is a summary of the results of the whole inspection.

CHAPTER VII.

POPULAR EDUCATION IN FRANCE UNDER THE MONARCHY OF JULY 1830.—LAW OF 1833.

THE monarchy of July contained among its chief supporters men who had long revolved the problem of popular education, and who were determined to try to work it out. Brought up in the nurture of the University and imbued with its spirit, they soon made it manifest that education was to be seriously superintended by an educational authority. An ordinance of October 1[illegible], 1830, had finally destroyed ecclesiastical preponderance in the local committees; an ordinance of April 1[illegible], 1831, did away with all exemptions from the certificate. In the two years from 1831 to 1833 thirty new normal schools were created. An order from the Royal Council of Public Instruction minutely regulated them.* The grant for primary education rose in 18[illegible] to 28,000*l.*, in 1832 to 40,000*l.* Meanwhile a great and comprehensive measure was maturing. It was brought before the Chambers in the spring of 1833. The reporter of the commission which examined it was M. Cousin; the Minister of Public Instruction who proposed it was M. Guizot. It became law on the 28th of June, 1833.

This law of 1833 is so important, it is so truly the root of the present system of primary instruction in

* December 14th, 1832.

France, that I have thought it desirable to reprint it in the original at the end of this report. It had the great merit of being full of good sense, full of fruitful ideas, full of toleration, full of equity; but it had the still greater merit of attaining the object which it had in view. It founded in France for the first time a national elementary education. Succeeding legislation has subverted many important provisions of it; but its all-important provisions remain standing. What was previously, to use a French expression, *facultative* to the communes, what the law only recommended to them, and they did or not as they liked, this measure made *obligatory*; and it provided means for the fulfilment of this obligation. I proceed to give a short sketch of it.

The first chapter of the law determined the objects which primary instruction was to embrace. The second and third determined the nature of the schools which were to give this instruction. The fourth and last established the authorities who were to govern it. A fifth chapter had extended to girls' schools the provisions of the law; but it was found premature to deal at that moment with girls' schools; they were first regulated by legislation in 1836.

The Convention had at first exaggerated what was indispensable in primary instruction; it had afterwards too much reduced it. Napoleon had maintained the reduction. In consequence, a numerous class, needing something more than reading, writing, and arithmetic, but not needing Greek and Latin, was left unprovided for. It remained uninstructed, or it was driven into the communal colleges, where it received an education

* By an ordonnance dated June 23rd

which it did not want, and which left it unfitted for its position in life. For this class the law of 1833 created *a superior* primary instruction, not properly embracing foreign languages, ancient or modern, but embracing all that constitutes what may be called a good French education. For the immense class below, for the mass of the French people, it established an *elementary* primary instruction.

This instruction, the indispensable minimum of knowledge, the "bare debt of a country towards all its offspring," "sufficient to make him who receives it a human being, and at the same time so limited that it may be everywhere realised," * added something to the scanty programme of 1795 and 1802. In the first place it was religious. "Moral and religious teaching" formed a part of it. It added, besides, the elements of French grammar; and, for a purpose of national convenience, the legal but imperfectly received system of weights and measures.

The Charter had proclaimed liberty of teaching; private schools, therefore, were free to compete with public schools in giving this primary instruction. To establish them there was no longer needed, as heretofore, the authorisation of a rector. The only guarantee which the State demanded of them was the possession by the teacher of a certificate of morality, and of a certificate of capacity. Liberty of teaching was thus secured to all competent persons who claimed it. Liberty to incompetence is not an article of faith with French liberalism.

But by far the greatest part of primary instruction must of necessity be given in public schools. "The

* *Exposé des Motifs de la Loi du 28 Juin* 1833, by M. Guizot, Jan. 2nd, 1833.

principle of liberty, admitted as an only principle, would be," says M. Cousin, "an invincible obstacle to the *universality* of instruction, since it is precisely the most necessitous districts that private adventure visits least."* Every commune, therefore, either by itself or in conjunction with adjacent communes, was to maintain at least one elementary school.† To this school all the indigent children of the commune, no longer a fourth of them or a fifth, but *all*, were to be admitted without fee. These national schools must respect that religious liberty which the nation professed. The wishes of parents were to be ascertained and followed in all that concerned their children's attendance at the religious instruction.‡

The elementary schools were to respect religious liberty, and they were to be planted in every commune; but how were they to be planted? Preceding laws had not answered this question, and they had remained a dead letter. The law of 1833 answered it thus:—*By a joint action of the commune, the department, and the State.*

If the commune possessed sufficient resources of its own to maintain its elementary school, well and good. Some had foundations, gifts, and legacies, for the maintenance of schools; some had large communal property. In the Vosges, for instance, there are communes possessing great tracts of the beech forests with which those mountains are clothed, whose annual income

* See M. Cousin's report in the *Moniteur* of May 22nd, 1833. M. Guizot, in his *Exposé des Motifs*, speaks to the same effect: "Les lieux où l'instruction primaire serait le plus nécessaire sont précisément ceux qui tentent le moins l'industrie."

† *Loi sur l'Instruction primaire*, June 28th, 1833, Art. 9.

‡ *Ibid.* Art. 2

amounts to several thousand pounds sterling. Where the existing resources of the commune were insufficient, it was to tax itself to an amount not exceeding three centimes in addition to its ordinary direct taxation. If this was insufficient, the department was to tax itself, in order to aid this and similarly placed schools, to an amount not exceeding two centimes in addition to its ordinary direct taxation. If this was still insufficient, the Minister of Public Instruction was to supply the deficiency out of funds annually voted by the Chambers for the support of education.*

A machinery for providing schools was thus established. It remained to provide for these schools proper teachers. A master's house and a fixed salary for him of not less than 8*l.* a year the commune was bound to supply. The residue of his income was to proceed from school fees. The rate of these was to be determined by the municipal council of the commune. They were to be charged for monthly periods, and to be collected, like other public dues, by the ordinary tax-gatherer. A fund for retiring pensions for teachers was to be formed by a yearly drawback on their fixed salaries.† Their maintenance was thus provided for; to provide them with a proper intellectual and moral training every department was bound to furnish a normal school. Certificates of capacity and morality

* *Loi sur l'Instruction primaire*, &c., Art. 13. An ordinance of July 16th, 1833, provided that where a commune or department neglected to provide for charges which the law imposed on them, the amount due should be levied by royal ordinance.

† In consequence of the law of June 9th, 1853, regulating civil pensions, the schoolmaster's pension, like that of all other civil servants in France, is now paid by the Treasury from the general funds of the State.

were exacted from them, with precautions to render that of capacity no longer illusory.*

It remained to appoint the authorities with whom was to rest the supervision of the school. They were two, a parish committee and a district committee; the first supplied by the commune, the second by the arrondissement. In both, the chief authorities of the locality, clerical as well as lay, were members by virtue of their office; but in both there was a decided preponderance of the lay element. These committees were to meet once a month. The immediate inspection and superintendence of the schools rested with the communal committee. But the Chamber of Deputies, more zealous than the minister for the action of the Executive, had refused to this committee all voice in the nomination of the teacher. He was presented by the municipal council, nominated, on this presentation, by the district committee †, instituted by the Minister of Public Instruction. The district committee not only nominated the teacher, but also dismissed him; he had, however, an appeal to the Minister in Council.

Such was the law of 1833, not more remarkable for the judgment with which it was framed than for the energy with which it was executed. As if he had foreseen the weak point of his law, the inadequacy of the local authorities to discharge the trust committed to their hands, M. Guizot multiplied his efforts to stimulate and to enlighten them. In successive circulars to prefects, to rectors, to directors of normal schools, to inspectors, he endeavoured to procure the active co-operation of all his agents in the designs of the Government, and to inspire in all of them the zeal with which

* *Loi sur l'Instruction primaire*, &c., Art. 25.

† Comité d'arrondissement.

he himself was animated. On behalf of the elementary schools, he strove to awaken that spirit of local interest and independent activity which he and his friends have never ceased to invoke for their country, and the want of which has, since the Revolution, been the great want of France. He succeeded imperfectly in inspiring his countrymen with a faith in habits of local exertion; and the elementary schools of France have suffered from his want of success. But he succeeded in founding the schools; and he succeeded in inspiring faith in his own zeal for them. In the chamber of the Frère Philippe or of the Père Étienne, as among the Protestant populations of Nismes and of Strasbourg; in the palaces of bishops and in the manses of pastors; in the villages of Brittany and in the villages of the Cevennes — everywhere I found M. Guizot's name held in honour for the justice and wisdom of his direction of popular education when it was in fashion, for his fidelity to it now that it is no longer talked of. Singular confidence inspired in quarters the most various upon the most delicate of questions! which insincere ability can never conciliate, which even sincere ability cannot always conciliate; only ability united with that heartfelt devotion to a great cause, which friends of the cause instinctively recognise, and warm towards it because they share it.

The results of the law of 1833 were prodigious. The thirteen normal schools of 1830 had grown in 1838 to seventy-six; more than 2500 students were, in the latter year, under training in them. In the four years from 1834 to 1838, 4557 public schools, the property of the communes, had been added to the 10,316 which existed in 1834. In 1847 the number of elementary schools for boys had risen from 33,695, which it reached in 1834, to 13,514; the number of scholars attending them from 1,654,828 to 2,176,079.* In 1849, the elementary schools were giving instruction to 3,530,135 children of the two sexes.† In 1851, out of the 37,000 communes of France, 2,500 only were without schools; through the remainder there were distributed primary schools of all kinds, to the number of 61,481.‡ The charge borne by the communes in the support of their schools was nearly 300,000*l.* in 1834, the first year after the passing of the new law. In 1849 it had risen to nearly 400,000*l.* The charge borne by the departments was in 1835 nearly 111,000*l.*; in 1847 it was more than 180,000*l.* The sum contributed by the State, only 2,000*l.* in 1816, 4,000*l.* in 1829, 40,000*l.* in 1830, had risen in 1847 to 96,000*l.*§ The great inspection of 1834 had been a special effort. But in 1835, primary inspectors, those "sinews of public instruction," were permanently established, one for each department, by royal ordinance.∥ In 1847 two inspectors-general and 153 inspectors and sub-inspectors had been already appointed. An ordinance of June the 23rd, 1836, extended to girls' schools, so far as was possible, the provisions of the law of 1833. It did not impose on the communes the obligation of raising funds for their support; but it subjected them all alike to the authority of the communal and district committees¶, who were to delegate inspectresses to

* *Mémoires pour servir à l'Histoire de mon Temps*, par M. Guizot, vol. iii. p. 81.

† President's message of June 6th, 1849.

‡ President's message of November 4th, 1851.

§ *Budget de l'Instruction Publique*, pp. 181-2.

∥ February 26th.

¶ Ever since the ordinance of February 9th, 1830, schools under mistresses who belonged to religious communities had been ex-

visit them; and it required from their teachers the certificate of capacity. From members of the female religious orders, however, their letters of obedience were still accepted as a substitute for the certificate. Normal schools for the training of lay schoolmistresses were at the same time formed. A year and a half afterwards* a similar ordinance regulated infant schools, which ever since 1827, when M. Cochin, the benevolent mayor of the twelfth arrondissement of Paris, founded a model infant school in his own district, had attracted interest and found voluntary supporters. The pecuniary aid given by the State to these institutions was small; the first grant, in 1840, a grant which they had to share with girls' schools, was but 2,000*l*. They multiplied, nevertheless; their number rose from 555 in 1840 to 1489 in 1843, and to 1861 in 1848. Primary teachers had been empowered† to establish classes for adults in connection with their schools. In 1837 there existed 1856 of these classes, giving instruction to 36,965 working people. In 1843 there were 6434 of them, with an attendance of 95,064 pupils; in 1848 the classes were 6877 in number, the pupils 115,164. Public instruction was not only founded, it was in operation.

Two defects in the system soon became visible. One was in the authorities charged to superintend it. Neither the communal committee nor that of the district performed its functions satisfactorily. The communal or parish committee, composed of the mayor, the clergyman, and one or more principal inhabitants

empted from all supervision but that of the ecclesiastical authority and the prefect.

* December 22nd, 1837.

† By a *Règlement sur les Classes d'Adultes*, issued by the Royal Council of Public Instruction, March 22nd, 1836.

nominated by the district committee, was not disinclined to meddle in the management of the school, but neither its fairness nor its intelligence could be safely trusted. So strongly had this been felt, that the Chamber of Deputies in 1833 had refused to intrust to this committee the powers which the Minister, in his zeal for local action, had destined for it, and had insisted on giving to the Minister the power of dissolving it on the report of the district committee. The district committee, composed of the principal personages, ecclesiastical and civil, of each sub prefecture, was generally deficient neither in fairness nor in intelligence; but it was distant, it was hard to set in motion, it was disinclined to decisive measures. In truth, a due supply of zealous and respectable persons, both able and willing to superintend primary schools, is wanting in the country districts of France. It was to form such a class that M. Guizot had framed measures and written circulars; for this he had solicited prefects and rectors; for this he had directed every inspector to forego, at first, his right of inspecting schools without notice, to convoke committees and municipalities to meet him, to multiply his communications with them, to invite their confidence and to keep them informed of the views of the government, to make his inspections fully and patiently, not to neglect his rural schools, however humble or however remote, in order that the rural population might itself learn to take interest in its schools, when it saw that "neither distance, nor hardship of season, nor difficulty of access, prevented the government from bestowing active care on them." * He had not succeeded. In England such

* See M. Guizot's circular to the inspectors on their appointment, August 13th, 1835, in the *Bulletin Universitaire*, vol. iii. p. 275. The whole circular is well worth reading.

persons exist in almost every locality; the one thing needful is to choose them.

The other defect was in the position of the teachers. The miserable fixed salary of 8*l.* a year, supplemented by the small fees of the scholars, was wholly insufficient for their maintenance. Fully indoctrinated with a sense of the magnitude of their office, they were transferred from the normal school, where their life was one of comfort; they were planted in a village where they were considerable personages, in constant relations with the mayor and the curé, and obliged to keep up a certain appearance; and there they were left to exist on a pittance which just kept them from starvation. Their position was one of cruel suffering, and their discontent was extreme.

The Government determined to relieve them. In 1847, a measure was introduced by M. de Salvandy, then Minister of Instruction, which fixed three classes of teachers and a minimum of salary for each class: for the lowest class, 24*l.* a year; for the second, 36*l.*; for the highest, 48*l.* In Paris itself the lowest salary of a teacher of the first class was to be 60*l.*

To English schoolmasters in 1860 these salaries will appear despicable; to the French schoolmaster in 1847 they would have been a great boon. But the Revolution of 1848 arrested the measure which promised them.

CHAPTER VIII.

POPULAR EDUCATION IN FRANCE UNDER THE REVOLUTION OF 1848 AND THE SECOND EMPIRE. LEGISLATION OF 1850, 1853, AND 1854.

THE Revolution of 1848, however, had great designs for the primary teachers. They were to be the agents to popularise and consolidate it. The portentous circular* by which M. Carnot exhorted the schoolmasters of France, on the eve of the elections, to use all their influence to promote the return of sincere republicans, and to combat the popular prejudice which preferred the "rich and lettered citizen, a stranger to the peasant's life, and blinded by interests at variance with the peasant's interests," to the "honest peasant endowed with natural good sense, and whose practical experience of life was better than all the book-learning in the world," is still in every one's memory. The schoolmasters of the department of the Seine had not waited for M. Carnot's invitation to open gratuitous evening classes for the instruction of adults in the "rights and duties of citizens." The Minister applauded their zeal. But satisfactions more solid than applause were due to a class from which so much was expected. The grant of the State for primary education rose in the year after the Revolution to 5,920,000 francs. In 1847 it had been but 2,399,808 francs. The whole addition was destined to augment the salaries of primary teachers.

* March 9th, 1848.

The Revolution fell; and its conquerors did not forget that it had made the schoolmasters its missionaries. A commission was appointed* to report on the state of primary instruction throughout the country, and on the operation of the law of 1833. Upon its report the main law which now governs public instruction in France, the law of March 15th, 1850, was founded. This commission judged the primary teachers very severely. It condemned their training as ill-planned, their teaching as over-ambitious, their conduct to spiritual and temporal authorities as disrespectful.† A disclosure which took place about this time in the Nièvre, one of the most ignorant and backward departments of France, shook esteem for their morality. Every voice was raised for a repression of their pretensions, and a strict control of their conduct. The religious congregations devoted to teaching were visited by a great increase of public favour. The heads of the principal communities of each sex, the Superior-General of the Brethren of the Christian Schools, the Superior-General of the Lazarists,- were examined before the commission as to the operations and wishes of their societies. They were consulted as to the requirement from teachers belonging to religious orders of the certificate of capacity. For reasons which speak with equal eloquence for his own serenity of judgment and

* When M. de Falloux became Minister of Public Instruction, December 10th, 1848. The commission which reported on primary instruction was a sub-commission of that which, under the presidency of M. Thiers, inquired into the whole public education of France.

† *Rapport fait au nom de la Sous-Commission chargé par M. le Ministre de l'Instruction Publique de préparer un Projet de Loi sur l'Instruction primaire*; Paris, April, 1849, pp. 2, 6, 8, 10, 18, 20.

for the usefulness of the certificate test, the Frère Philippe desired for the brethren its continuance. For reasons which prevailed with the commission, which he did me the honour to repeat to me, and which seem to me full of weight, the Père Étienne deprecated for the sisterhoods its imposition. One of the most eminent liberals in France told me that, for his part, ever since 1848 he had wished to confide the whole primary instruction of the country to the religious communities. It was declared that the public morals were proved by the statistics of crime not to have improved since the law of 1833, but on the contrary to have deteriorated*, and that recourse must be had to religion to cure a state of disorder which mere instruction had perhaps aggravated, certainly not corrected. Sentences of suspension and dismissal were launched by the prefects right and left against the lay primary teachers. But the misdeeds of these functionaries were extravagantly exaggerated. The alarm and irritation of the revolutionary year made their accusers intemperate and unjust. In every quarter of France which I visited, rectors and inspectors united to assure me that grounds for serious complaint against the lay teachers had been very scarce indeed: that the foolish profession of strong republican opinions (to which, besides, the circular of the Minister directly called them) had been the sole fault of the great majority of those who offended; that it was astonishing that a class, so poor and so stimulated, should have, on the whole, behaved so well. On dispassionate inquiry, made at the instance of the University functionaries, a great number of teachers who had been summarily dismissed were

* *Rapport fait au nom de la Commission*, &c., p. 8. But on this question of the increase of crime, see the interesting criminal statistics at the end of this volume.

reinstated. The loud complaints against their over-training and against the normal schools gradually died away, and a few years afterwards the Government itself proclaimed how unjust had been the imputations against these latter. "For a time," says the minister, M. Fortoul, in 1854, "people may have made the normal schools responsible for the faults of a few young men whose errors were caused far more by the culpable promptings addressed to them than by the education received in these schools; but on all sides people are now beginning to appreciate them more justly." Under the hostile impressions of 1849, however, the law of March 15th, 1850, was conceived and promulgated.

This law, with the organic decree of March 9th, 1852, and the law of June the 14th, 1854, forms the body of legislation now actually in force in France on the subject of public instruction. The design of the two last-named acts is to complete and to make more stringent the main law of 1850.

The new legislation swept away much of the law of 1833. It changed the authorities in whom the control of primary instruction was vested. It abolished the communal committee and the district committee. In the bodies which it substituted it eradicated the elective principle. It gave to the mayor and the minister of religion in every commune the supervision and moral direction of primary instruction.* The old committees were replaced, as to some of their functions, by delegates from each canton. The canton is a division larger than the commune, smaller than the arrondissement. But these cantonal delegates are the nominees of the departmental council. They inspect the primary

* Law of March 15th, 1850, Art. 44.

schools of their canton; but their powers only enable them to address representations on the results of their inspection to the departmental council or the inspector, and they have no real authority over the schools or teachers. The departmental council meets twice a month at the chief town of the department. It consists of thirteen members, presided over by the prefect. At first a majority of the members proceeded from election. At present every member, except the prefect, the procureur-général, the bishop, and an ecclesiastical nominee of the bishop, who sit of right, is nominated by the Minister. This council has very extensive powers. It nominates the cantonal delegates and the commissions charged with the examination for certificates. It has the regulation of the public primary schools, fixes the rate of school fees to be paid in them, draws up the list of teachers admissible to the office of communal teacher in the department, is the judge of teachers in matters of discipline, can even interdict them for ever from the exercise of their profession, subject to an appeal to the Imperial Council of Public Instruction in Paris. It can refuse to any teacher, without right of appeal *, that permission to open a private primary school which the law of 1833 accorded to all teachers provided with certificates of morality and capacity. But it cannot nominate, suspend, or dismiss a teacher. This power, after some fluctuation, has been confided to the promptest, the sternest, the strongest of public functionaries—the functionary on whose firm hand the Chamber of Deputies, in 1833, in its zeal for a more stringent control of public instruction, had in vain cast longing eyes—the prefect. Even the ministerial insti-

* Law of March 15th, 1850, Art. 28.

tution is no longer necessary for the teacher. The prefect names, changes, reprimands, suspends, and dismisses all public primary teachers of every grade.* To interdict them absolutely and for ever from the exercise of their profession is alone beyond his power. It has even been decided that a clause in the decree of 1852 †, giving to municipal councils the right to be heard respecting the nomination of their communal teacher, means merely that they are at liberty to inform the prefect whether they prefer a layman or a member of a religious association.

But the prefect exercises his authority "on the report of the Academy-Inspector."

This introduces us to a new wheel in the machinery of French public instruction. The academies of France, the constituent members of the University, have been at different times twenty-six, twenty-seven, and eighty-six in number. They are now but sixteen. Each academy has a district embracing several departments. The rectors of academies, who under the first Empire and the Restoration were the rulers of primary instruction, have now in their charge only its normal schools, and in elementary schools the methods of teaching and course of study. But attached to every rector, for each of the departments composing his district, is a functionary called an academy-inspector.‡ This official's chief concern is with secondary instruction, but he has also the general supervision of primary instruction; it is to him that the primary inspector makes his reports, and by his representations the prefect, in dealing with the primary teachers, is mainly guided.

* Law of June 14th, 1854, Art. 1.
† Art. 4.
‡ Inspecteur d'Académie.

One other authority remains to be noticed. It is the Imperial Council of Public Instruction. This council is the latest development of the Council of the University, of the Commission, Council Royal, and Superior Council of Public Instruction. Its composition has undergone many changes. The Minister has always presided at it; but of its members the majority were formerly chosen by the great ecclesiastical, judicial, or learned bodies whom they respectively represented, and it had a permanent section composed of members named for life. Every member is now named by the Emperor; the permanent section is abolished, and members are appointed for one year only. Before this council the Minister, if he thinks fit, brings for discussion projected laws and decrees on public education. He is bound to consult it respecting the programmes of study, methods, and books, to be adopted in public schools. To watch in the provinces over the due observance of its regulations on these matters is the business of the rectors and their academic councils. Finally, the Imperial Council has to hear and judge the appeals of teachers on whom departmental councils have laid their interdict.

Thus the French public teacher, in place of the general supervision of the communal council, in which the prepossessions of one member often neutralised those of another, is now put under the individual supervision of two persons, the mayor and the curé. These watch over the morality and religion of his school; the cantonal delegates watch over its instruction. Above these, in place of the easy district-committee, armed with power indeed to reprimand, suspend, or dismiss him, but slow to exercise this power, and liable to have its extreme sentence, that of dismissal, reversed by an appeal to a higher authority *, he has the ever-wakeful executive, the prefect himself, armed with powers which he is prepared to use, and against which there is no appeal. Finally, his scholastic career may be closed altogether by the departmental council.†

But the new legislation, though thus tightening the reins of control for the teacher, could not possibly leave his salary unimproved. His pecuniary condition was so lamentable as to call pity even from his enemies; many thought, indeed, that to the misery of this condition were due nearly all the faults which had made enemies for him. The fixed salary of 8*l.* a year was retained; but it was provided that where the school fees added to this did not make up an income of 24*l.* a year, what was wanted to complete this sum should be paid by the public. This was, in fact, to increase the charges of the State; for no additional taxation was imposed on the commune or the department. With so vast an army of public teachers, to increase the pittance of each even a little was formidably expensive. A new law ‡ provided a class of "supplying teachers," *instituteurs suppléants*, less costly than the regular communal teacher. In future no one could be appointed communal teacher who had not served for three years since his twenty-first year as an assistant (*adjoint*) or as a supplying teacher. The same decree permitted public mixed schools, where the scholars were not more than forty in number, to be placed under the charge of women, whose salary was to be that of supplying masters. These new teachers were divided into two classes; the

* The Minister in Council Royal. — *Loi sur l'Instruction primaire*, 28 Juin 1833, Art. 23.

† But with appeal to the Imperial Council. See above.

‡ Decree of December 31st, 1853.

minimum of salary for the first was fixed at 20*l.* a year, for the second at 16*l.* a year. They were only to be employed in communes where the number of inhabitants did not exceed 500, or temporarily to fill vacancies in larger places. But, on one pretence or other, large as well as small communes in considerable numbers soon managed to confide their schools to these cheaper teachers. The sufferings which the law of 1850 had sought to alleviate reappeared. By a decree * due to the present Minister of Public Instruction, M. Rouland, the lower class of *suppléants* was abolished, and there is now but one class of supplying teachers, and one minimum of salary for them, 20*l.*

This is grievously insufficient: but the reader is not to suppose that all the public schools of France are starving their teachers on 20*l.* or 24*l.* a year. These are *minima* of salary, frequently exceeded by the free will of communes, and for which no good and experienced teacher can be obtained. The law permits a commune, if it pleases, to establish schools entirely gratuitous: only it must support these schools out of its own resources. In all the principal towns of France this is done, as there is not one communal school in Paris, for instance, in which a scholar pays anything. The teachers of these schools have therefore no school fees to trust to; but they receive from the municipality salaries far exceeding the bare legal rate, salaries which, though not equal to those of similar teachers in England or Holland, are sufficient to maintain them in comfort. It is in the villages and hamlets of France that the privations of underpaid schoolmasters are to be witnessed.

* Decree of July 29th, 1858.

The new legislation has thus altered the law of 1833 in all which concerns the supervision of primary schools. It has attempted, not very successfully, to amend the pecuniary situation which M. Guizot's law created for the primary teacher. But the grand and fruitful provision of M. Guizot's law, the money clause, the happy distribution of the cost of public schools between the commune, the department, and the State, victoriously endured the test of hostile criticism. It remained unassailed and unassailable, modified only in an insignificant point of detail.

Another important provision of M. Guizot's law remained untouched, that which guaranteed religious liberty in public schools. It is the happiness of France, indeed, that this liberty is so firmly established that no legislation is likely to try to shake it. Among the many interesting instructions written by M. Guizot between 1833 and 1837, none are more interesting than those which relate to this vital question. The text of the law of 1833, and the tolerant disposition of M. Guizot himself, tended to make denominational schools, as we should call them, the exception, and common schools the rule. "In certain cases," says the law *, "the Minister of Public Instruction may authorise as communal schools, schools more particularly appropriated to one of the religious denominations recognised by the State." "It is in general desirable," writes M. Guizot†, "that children whose families do not profess the same creed should early contract, by frequenting the same schools, those habits of reciprocal friendship and mutual tolerance which may ripen later, when

* *Loi sur l'Instruction primaire*, 28 Juin 1833, Art. 9.

† In a circular to the prefects, July 24th, 1833. See "Bulletin Universitaire," vol. iii. p. 293.

they live together as grown-up citizens, into justice and harmony." But the dangers to which religious liberty was sometimes exposed in these common schools did not escape him. He wished the religious instruction to be, above all things, real; not "a series of lessons and practices apparently capable of being used by all denominations in common."* Such vague abstractions, he said, "satisfied the requirements neither of parents nor of the law; they tended to banish all positive and efficacious religious teaching from the schools." But, the more the religion of the majority is taught positively and really in a school, the more it becomes necessary to guard the liberty of the minority. There is danger either that the minority will be made to participate in the religious instruction of the majority, or else that its own religious instruction will be left uncared for. Against both dangers M. Guizot endeavoured to provide. Rectors were charged to see that in public schools no child of a different religious profession from that of the majority was constrained to take part in the religious teaching and observances of his fellow-scholars. They were to permit and to request the parents of such children to cause them to receive suitable religious instruction from a minister of their own communion, or from a layman regularly appointed for the purpose. They were to take care that in every week, at fixed hours to be agreed upon between the minister of religion, the parents, and the local committee, such children were conducted from the school to the Protestant temple, or any other edifice frequented by members of their communion, there to take part in the lessons and practices of the faith in which they had

* See his excellent circular to the rectors, November 12th, 1835. *Bulletin Universitaire*, vol. iv. p. 382.

been brought up. Inspectors and local committees were strictly enjoined to see these regulations observed. Similar provision was made for religious instruction and religious freedom in the normal schools. Finally, where the minority had cause to desire a school to itself, and reasonable numbers to fill it, the authorities were to be very heedful that its demand was not unjustly refused by the municipal councils.

The event proved that religious instruction in common schools presented grave practical difficulties. The new law profited by the lessons of experience. Under the dominion of the new law denominational schools are the rule, common schools are the exception. In those communes where more than one of the forms of worship recognised by the State is publicly professed, each form is to have its separate school.* But the departmental council has power to authorise the union, in a common school, of children belonging to different communions.† Of children thus united, however, the religious liberty is sedulously guarded. It is provided that ministers of each communion shall have free and equal access to the school, at separate times, in order to watch over the religious instruction of members of their own flock.‡ Where the school is appropriated to one denomination, no child of another denomination is admitted except at the express demand of his parents or guardians, signified in writing to the teacher. Of such demands the teacher is bound to keep a register, to be produced to all the school authorities. I confidently affirm, in contradiction to much ignorant assertion, that the liberty thus proclaimed by the law is

* *Loi du* 15 *Mars* 1850, Art. 36. † *Ibid.* Art. 15.

‡ *Loi du* 15 *Mars* 1850, Art. 44; *Décret du* 7 *Octobre* 1850, Art. 11.

maintained in practice. The venerable chiefs of the principal Protestant communities of the French provinces the president of the Consistory of Nismes, the president of the Consistory of Strasbourg—individually assured me, that, as regarded the treatment of their schools by the authorities, they had nothing whatever to complain of: that Protestant schools came into collision with the authorities no otherwise than as Catholic schools came; that such collision, when it happened, was, in nine cases out of ten, on matters wholly unconnected with religion. In Languedoc, indeed, the embers of religious animosities still smoulder: but it is among the lower orders of the population. It is not that the State persecutes the Protestants; it is that the Protestant and Catholic mobs have still sometimes the impulse to persecute each other, and that the State has hard work to keep the peace between them.

The law of 1833 had proclaimed the right of all indigent children to free instruction. Many who were not indigent had usurped this boon designed only for the poor. The law of 1850, to prevent this abuse, directed the mayor and the ministers of religion to draw up yearly, for each commune, a list of children having a real claim to the privilege; but it was soon found that the mayor and the ministers were far too easy. In fact, the moment a commune had levied its three centimes, all motive for economy on the part of the communal authorities ceased; all further school expenses must be at the charge of the department or the State. At the expense of the department and the State, therefore, the parish authorities freely enlarged their list of claimants for free schooling. As a last resource, the never-failing prefect* has been charged to determine annually, for

* *Décret du* 31 *Décembre* 1853, Art. 13.

every public school of his department, the highest number of free scholars to be admitted into that school; the free admissions granted by the mayor and his colleagues must in no case exceed this number. Nor can any free scholar be admitted into a communal school unless he brings with him a ticket for free admission granted by the mayor: this last provision applies even to schools entirely gratuitous.

Finally, the law of 1833 had attempted to establish for the benefit of the lower middling classes of France a superior grade of primary instruction, which, without assuming a classical and scientific character, might yet carry its recipients much beyond the instruction of the elementary schools. It had imposed upon every urban commune, which either was the chief town of a department, or contained more than 6,000 inhabitants, the obligation of establishing, besides its elementary schools, a "superior primary school."* It had instituted two grades of certificates, corresponding to the two grades of instruction. M. Guizot desired† that "as there was to be no commune without its primary school, and no department without its normal school, so there might be no town of 8000 or 10,000 inhabitants without its 'middle school' to crown the edifice of public instruction, and to stop only where the learned studies of classical schools commence." He provided that in these middle schools a certain number of free admissions should be reserved for the best scholars of the elementary school, to be presented, after a competitive examination, by the communal committee.‡ The design seemed admirable, yet

* *Loi sur l'Instruction primaire*, 28 Juin 1833, Art. 10.

† See his circular to the rectors on his appointment, October 17th, 1832; *Bulletin Universitaire*, vol. iii. p. 99.

‡ *Loi sur l'Instruction primaire*, 28 Juin 1833, Art 11.

it had not well succeeded. Not that the obligation of the law was eluded: in 1843, out of 290 communes bound to establish superior primary schools, 222 possessed them; 103 communes, not bound to provide such schools, had voluntarily established them; but they did not much attract the population. In 1837, the average attendance of scholars in the whole number of superior primary schools, public and private, then existing in France, did not exceed twenty-eight in each school.* The lower class of the population remained satisfied with the primary schools; the class above them continued, where the primary schools did not satisfy it, to struggle into the communal colleges.

My limits forbid me to do more than touch on this great subject of secondary instruction; yet to touch on it for one moment in passing I cannot forbear. I saw something of it; I inquired much about it; had I not done so, I should have comprehended the subject of French primary instruction very imperfectly. Let me, then, be permitted to call the English reader's attention to the advantage France possesses in its vast system of public secondary instruction; in its 63 lyceums and 244 communal colleges, inspected by the State, aided by the State†, drawing from this connection with the State both efficiency and dignity; and to which, in concert with the State, the departments, the communes, private benevolence, all co-operate to provide free admission for poor and deserving scholars. M. de Talleyrand truly

* *Manuel Législatif et Administratif de l'Instruction primaire*, par M. Kilian, chef de bureau au Ministère de l'Instruction Publique; Paris, 1838-39, p. 116.

† In 1855 the grant from the State to the lyceums was 1,300,000 fr.; to the communal colleges, 98,080 fr. 86 c.—*Budget de l'Instruction Publique*, pp. 164, 167.

said that the education of the great English public schools was the best in the world. He added, to be sure, that even this was detestable. But allowing it all its merits, how small a portion of the population does it embrace! It embraces the aristocratic class; it embraces the higher professional class; it embraces a few of the richest and most successful of the commercial class; of the great body of the commercial class and of the immense middle classes of this country, it embraces not one. They are left to an education which, though among its professors are many excellent and honourable men, is deplorable. Our middle classes are nearly the worst educated in the world. But it is not this only; although, when I consider this, all the French commonplaces about the duty of the State to protect its children from the charlatanism and cupidity of individual speculation seem to me to be justified. It is far more that a great opportunity is missed of fusing all the upper and middle classes into one powerful whole, elevating and refining the middle classes by the contact, and stimulating the upper. In France this is what the system of public education effects; it effaces between the middle and upper classes the sense of social alienation; it raises the middle without dragging down the upper; it gives to the boy of the middle class the studies, the superior teaching, the proud sense of belonging to a great school, which the Eton or Harrow boy has with us; it tends to give to the middle classes precisely what they most want, and their want of which is the great gulf between them and the upper; it tends to give them personal dignity. The power of such an education is seen in what it has done for the professional classes in England. The clergy and barristers, who are generally educated in the great public schools, are nearly identified in thought, feeling, and manners with the aristocratic class. They have not been unmixed gainers by this identification; it has too much isolated them from a class to which by income and social position they, after all, naturally belong, while towards the highest class it has made them, not vulgarly servile certainly, but intellectually too deferential — too little apt to maintain perfect mental independence on questions where the prepossessions of that class are concerned. Nevertheless, they have, as a class, acquired the unspeakable benefit of that elevation of the mind and feelings which it is the best office of superior education to confer. But they have bought this elevation at an immense money-price—at a price which they can no better than the commercial classes afford to pay; which they who have paid it long, and who know what it has bought for them, will continue to pay while they must, but which the middle classes will never even begin to pay. When I told the French University authorities of the amount paid for a boy's education at the great English schools, and paid often out of very moderate incomes, they exclaimed with one voice that to demand such sacrifices of French parents would be vain. It would be equally vain to demand them of the English middle classes. Either their education must remain what it is, vulgar and unsound; or the State must create by its authorisation, its aid—above all, by its inspection institutions honourable because of their public character, and cheap because nationally frequented, in which they may receive a better. If the former happens, then this great English middle class, growing wealthier, more powerful, more stirring every year, will every year grow more and more isolated in sentiment from the professional and aristocratic classes. If the latter, then not only will the whole richer part of our rich community be united by the strong bond of a common culture, but the establishment of a national system of instruction for the poorer part of the community will have been rendered infinitely easier. In fact, the French middle classes may well submit to be taxed for the education of the poor, for the State has already provided for their own. But already there are loud complaints among the lower middling classes of this country that the Committee of Council is providing the poor with better schools than those to which they themselves have access; and we may be very sure that any new measure which proposes to do much for the instruction of the poor, and nothing for that of the middling classes, will meet with discontent and opposition from the latter. It is impossible to overrate the magnitude of this question. English superior instruction is perhaps intelligent enough to be left to take care of itself. Oxford and Cambridge are popularising themselves: with little noise and in the shade, the London University is performing a work of great national benefit. At any rate, superior instruction is the efflorescence and luxury of education; it is comparatively of limited importance. Secondary instruction, on the other hand, is of the widest importance; and it is neither organised enough nor intelligent enough to take care of itself. The Education Commissioners would excite, I am convinced, in thousands of hearts a gratitude of which they little dream, if, in presenting the result of their labours on primary instruction, they were at the same time to say to the Government, "Regard the necessities of a not distant future, and *organise your secondary instruction.*"

The new French legislation recognised the visible fact that the superior primary school was an unprosperous invention. With much good result, with some inconveniences, the communal colleges continued to attract those for whom M. Guizot had destined his middle schools. These schools, therefore, are no longer maintained. But the new law retains the old programme of superior primary instruction, and has introduced it into the elementary schools*, where the instruction certainly needed raising. This superior programme, however, is but *facultative* in the primary schools, and the old elementary programme is alone obligatory. But any commune may, with the authorisation of the departmental council, insist that the whole or part of the *facultative matters*, as they are called, shall be taught in its school.†

For girls' schools the new legislation continued the provisions of 1836 nearly unchanged. For girls the two grades of primary instruction were still maintained, because for girls there was no secondary instruction, like that of the communal colleges, to compete with the superior primary school.‡ All public schools for girls, whether kept by lay teachers or by sisters of some religious order, and all private schools not being boarding-schools, were subjected to the supervision of the authorities charged with that of boys' schools. Lay boarding-schools are inspected by ladies delegated by

* *Loi du 15 Mars* 1850, Art. 23.

† *Loi du 15 Mars* 1850, Art. 36. The *matières facultatives* are as follows:—L'arithmétique appliquée aux opérations pratiques; les éléments de l'histoire et de la géographie; des notions des sciences physiques et de l'histoire naturelle applicables aux usages de la vie; des instructions élémentaires sur l'agriculture, l'industrie, et l'hygiène; l'arpentage, le nivellement, le dessin linéaire; le chant, et la gymnastique.

‡ Called by the new law *école de premier ordre*, not *école primaire supérieure*.—*Décret du* 31 *Décembre* 1853, Art. 6.

the prefect; boarding-schools belonging to religious associations by ecclesiastics nominated, on the presentation of the bishop of the diocese, by the Minister of Public Instruction. The certificate of capacity must, as before, be obtained by lay schoolmistresses; and, for the sisters, their letters of obedience still suffice. Such, in its main provisions, is the legislation by which primary instruction in France is at this moment regulated.

CHAPTER IX.

PRESENT MATERIAL AND FINANCIAL CONDITION OF POPULAR EDUCATION IN FRANCE.

THE reader will desire to know what result is produced by this legislation. I will endeavour to show both the material and the moral result produced. The material result in money raised, schools founded, scholars under instruction; the moral result in the quality of the instruction, the proficiency of the scholars, the effect, so far as that can be ascertained, on the nation. I begin with the former.

The task is not easy. For the last eight years no report on the state of primary instruction has been published by the French Government. In the financial report yearly issued by the Department of Public Instruction, the sums raised for primary schools by their most important contributor, the communes, are not returned. Vast preparations were made in 1858 for a detailed report, to be accompanied by full statistics. At the last moment the Government recoiled before the expense of its publication. The invaluable materials collected for it, and still lying in the archives of the Ministry of Public Instruction, I have had, thanks to M. Magin's kindness, an opportunity of examining. But I owe to M. Rapet the following statistics for the years 1856 and 1857, compiled with great labour from the original returns, many of which are unpublished, and supplying information which no printed official documents contain.* The returns relating to the number of schools and scholars are given in round numbers. I should premise that schools belonging to religious associations are designated by the title of Congreganist Schools—*Écoles Congréganistes.*

Total number of primary schools existing in France in 1857 - - - - - -	65,100
Number of boys' or mixed schools - - -	39,600
" girls' schools - - - -	25,500
	65,100

These numbers are divided as follows:—

Public boys' schools - -	- 36,200	
Private boys' schools - -	- 3,400	
		39,600
Public girls' schools - -	- 13,900	
Private girls' schools - -	- 11,600	
		25,500
		65,100

Among the 39,600 public boys' schools, 17,000 are mixed, that is, they admit girls as well as boys. The number of mixed schools tends continually to diminish, by the creation of separate schools for girls. Although M. Cousin, in his report† of 1833, calls the objection to mixed schools a "wide-spread error which makes female education on a great scale an almost insoluble problem," and directs against it the whole weight of his authority, the objection has not ceased to gain strength, and is at the present day, in France,

* But see also Tables I., II., III., and IV., at the end of this volume.

† *Moniteur*, May 22nd, 1833.

almost universal. Upon no point, I am bound to say, have I found all those connected with education in that country more unanimous. In Holland, on the other hand, there prevails an equal unanimity in favour of mixed schools.

Of the 17,000 mixed schools of France, 2250 are taught by women, of whom the greater number belong to religious orders. The remaining mixed schools are under masters.

Dividing the primary schools of France according to the lay or ecclesiastical character of their teachers, we have the following numbers:—

Public lay boys' schools - -	34,100		
" Congreganist " - -	2,100		
		36,200	
Private lay boys' schools - -	2,900		
" Congreganist " - -	500		
		3,400	
			39,600
Public lay girls' schools - -	4,700		
" Congreganist " - -	9,200		
		13,900	
Private lay girls' schools -	3,200		
" Congreganist " - -	8,400		
		11,600	
			25,500
			65,100

The number of children under instruction in these schools is 3,850,000, divided as follows:—

Boys, in boys' or mixed schools	2,450,000
Girls, in girls' schools - -	1,150,000
Girls, in mixed schools - -	250,000
	3,850,000

Of these children, 2,600,000 paid for their schooling: 1,250,000 were free scholars.

I now come to the chapter of expense.

The total expense of primary instruction in France for the year 1856 was 42,506,012*f.* 46 *c.* This is, in round numbers, 1,700,000*l.*

The items of this expenditure are in part *ordinary* and *obligatory*, (as they are called,) recurring every year; in part *extraordinary* and *facultative*.

	f.	*c.*
Total ordinary and obligatory expenditure -	29,202,243	52
" extraordinary and facultative expenditure	12,581,591	61
" cost of inspection - - -	722,177	33
	42,506,012	46

Certain obligatory charges the law regards as belonging properly to the commune, and the families which compose the commune; others as belonging to the department; others to the State.

	f.	*c.*	*f.*	*c.*
Obligatory Charges properly belonging to the Communes and Families.				
Teachers' salaries - -	26,197,503	53		
Rent of school-houses -	1,488,307	51		
Printing forms for the collection of the school-fee	107,741	30		
			27,793,552	34
Obligatory Charges properly belonging to the Department and State.				
Ordinary expenses of normal schools - - -	1,360,155	87		
Expenses of examination commissions and cantonal delegacies - -	48,535	31		
Inspection (paid by the State)	722,177	33		
			2,130,868	51
			29,924,420	85

CHARGES borne by the Department and State.

	f.	c.		
Normal schools for young women, and extraordinary expenses for normal schools - - -	391,321	85		
Grants to communes for the erection, purchase, and repair of school-houses and fittings - -	961,112	42		
Books for poor scholars - -	32,444	53		
Special grants for girls' instruction	319,319	57		
Grants for classes of adults and apprentices - - -	68,186	25		
Grants for infants' schools and needlework - - -	472,620	74		
Reward and relief to teachers -	206,613	36		
Grants to private schools and charitable establishments - -	61,369	00		
Printing and sandries - -	167,209	89		
			2,681,397	61
			12,581,397	61

Making, in the year 1856, a total extraordinary expenditure, in round numbers, of 503,000*l*. The items of this expenditure vary from year to year, but its general amount remains much the same.

To meet this expenditure, the following sums were received:—

	f.	*c.*	*f.*	*c.*
From donations and legacies - - -			184,320	86
From families:—				
By fees from scholars -	9,301,552	56		
By payments from normal school students for board, &c.	513,327	38		
			9,814,879	94
From communes:—				
By obligatory school taxation	11,955,063	15		
By voluntary school taxation	9,900,000	00		
			21,855,063	15
From departments:—				
For ordinary expenses -	4,101,213	55		
For extraordinary expenses -	1,171,916	59		
			5,273,130	14
From the State:—				
For ordinary expenses -	3,660,093	40		
For extraordinary expenses -	1,509,844	52		
			5,169,937	92
			42,297,332	01

So that the amount received nearly equalled the amount expended.

It appears from the above figures that had the communes borne the full ordinary expenses of their schools, as well as the extraordinary expenses actually contributed by them, they would have had to find a sum of, in round numbers, 1,507,740*l.* They actually bore a charge of 874,200*l.*; but of this they were legally bound to bear but 478,200*l.* They voluntarily undertook a burden of 396,000*l.* Families and private persons contributed, in school-fees, board, and donations, about 423,900*l.* The departments bore a charge of 210,920*l.*; of this, the obligations of the law imposed on them 164,040*l.*; they voluntarily taxed themselves for 46,880*l.* Finally, the State directly contributed about 206,800*l.* (nearly the same amount as the departments): to defray regular charges which it had undertaken to make good, it paid 146,400*l.*; while for the additional expenses which have been detailed it granted 60,400*l.*

The expenses of primary instruction above enumerated do not include the expense of the central administration in Paris. This, for 1856, was 659,018 *f.* 57 *c.**; in round numbers, 26,360*l.* Not more than one third of this charge, which embraces the services of superior, secondary, and primary instruction, belongs to primary instruction. We must add the salaries of four inspectors general at 8,000 *f.* each, 32,000 *f.* (1,280*l.*), and their travelling allowances, 10,000 *f.* (400*l.*) This will give a total of, in round numbers, 10,170*l.*, to be added to the general expense of primary instruction in 1856. The general total will then, instead of 1,700,000*l.*, become 1,710,470*l.*; considerably less than one million and three-quarters sterling.†

Public primary instruction in France, then, cost in the year 1856 about 1,710,500*l.*; of this, parish taxation (as we should say) contributed somewhat less than nine-seventeenths; county taxation about two-seventeenths; the consolidated fund about two seventeenths; and school fees and private benevolence somewhat more than four-seventeenths. Taxation, obligatory and

* Thus divided: — *Personnel*, 472,257 *f.* 50 *c.*; *Matériel*, 180,711 *f.* 11 *c.*; *Indemnités à des employés supprimés*, 6,099 *f.* 96 *c.* See the *Compte définitif des Dépenses de l'Exercice* 1856 (*Service de l'Instruction publique*); Paris, 1858.

† The services of rectors and academy-inspectors (taking, under the head of *Administration académique*, a sum of 817,523 *f.* 32 *c.* in the estimates of 1856) are in part given to primary instruction; but as these functionaries strictly belong to superior and secondary instruction, I charge primary instruction with no share in this item

voluntary, produced altogether nearly 1,295,000*l.*; that is to say, it produced more than three-fourths of the whole amount expended.

What will, I think, most strike the reader in considering these figures will be this—the immense number of schools maintained in proportion to the money spent. France possessed, in 1856, 65,100 primary schools. Of this number all but 15,000 were, not *aided*, but *maintained*, out of an expenditure of considerably less than one million and three-quarters sterling: the 15,000 private schools received amongst them some assistance out of it, but the 50,100 public schools were, I repeat, *maintained*. Nor does the total of 65,000 primary schools include infant schools, numbering 2,684 in 1859*, and receiving 262,000 infants. Neither does it include adult schools, apprentice schools, needlework schools, educating among them a great number of pupils, and nearly all assisted, some supported, out of this expenditure, but for which, unfortunately, there are no collected statistics of as recent a date as 1856.† If added, these would certainly carry the number of places of instruction for the poorer classes in France to 75,000, and the number of learners in them to above four millions. But, omitting these,

* Infant schools in France are now regulated by the decree of March the 21st, 1855, which places them under the immediate patronage of the Empress and of a central committee. The decree establishes inspectresses of infant schools, one for each of the sixteen academies of France; these ladies are named by the Minister, and paid by the State; they each receive 80*l.* a year, and allowances for travelling.

† In 1848 there were 6877 adult schools in France, with 115,164 pupils. In 1843 there were 36 apprentice schools, with 1268 scholars; and 115 *ouvroirs*, or needlework schools, with 5908 girls attending them.

omitting the private schools, for 1,710,000*l.* a year more than 50,000 schools are entirely maintained, and more than three millions and a half of children are instructed. Assume the whole expenditure to contribute equally to this result; then, to the three-fourths raised by taxation, three-fourths of the school-result effected are due. In other words, for 1,295,000*l.*, more than 37,500 schools are maintained, and more than two millions and a half of children are taught.

In Great Britain, according to the latest returns, the annual expenditure on primary instruction, properly so called, was about 800,000*l.* Putting out of sight, as we have put out of sight in the case of France, the value received for this expenditure in the shape of administration, inspection, &c., let us ask what it achieved for schools and scholars. It *maintained* no schools, but it aided, we will assume, in one way or other, all the schools liable to inspection; and on this estimate, which is exaggerated, it aided 8,461 primary schools, giving instruction to 934,000 scholars: that is to say, it helped, at the outside, 8,461 schools to exist, and it helped 934,040 children to receive instruction. In France, the same grant would have entirely maintained nearly 25,000 schools, and to more than a million and a half of children it would have entirely given instruction.

The reader will also, I think, be interested to observe, that in France taxation for schools does not appear to extinguish voluntary effort for their support. Certainly, in France, the local interest about schools, the local knowledge about school matters, does not approach to that which we find in England. Yet, in spite of this, it appears that the French communes—already compulsorily taxed, whether they send their children to school or not, to the amount of 478,200*l.* for primary instruction—already compulsorily taxed, if they send their children to school, to the amount of 372,000*l.* for school fees—voluntarily impose on themselves an additional taxation of 396,000*l.* a year, in order to make their boys' schools better, in order to provide themselves with girls' schools and infant schools, the establishment of which the law does not make obligatory. It appears that the departments, having already undergone a compulsory rate of 164,040*l.* for the establishment of the departmental normal schools, and for the assistance of the communal primary schools, voluntarily rate themselves to the amount of 46,880*l.* more, in order to train schoolmistresses, to improve school-buildings, to furnish school-books to the poor, to supply other wants for which the law does not provide. The truth is, that a school system, once established in a locality, inevitably renders school matters a subject of interest and occupation with the inhabitants of that locality, even though they may not all be very ardent or very enlightened school-promoters; and a normal or a village school in France, which local zeal would probably never have been strong enough to found, local attachment is generally strong enough to maintain and improve when founded.

These schools, indeed, would look humble enough beside an Elizabethan normal college in England, or the elaborate Gothic edifice with which the liberality of the Committee of Council enables an English rector to adorn his village. English certificated schoolmasters would reject with disdain the salaries of their teachers. English normal-college students, accustomed each to his separate room, would look with contempt on the vast dormitories, rigidly plain though scrupulously neat, in which French students sleep by companies, under the charge of an overlooker, like the inmates of an hospital or a barrack. The English Privy Council Office would regard with contempt a certificate examination which occupies but a few hours, and which leaves conic sections unexplored. English inspectors would never quit their fellowships for posts the occupant of which has the salary of an exciseman. This service of inspection, indeed, in which I could not but feel a sympathetic and friendly interest, is, of all the cheap services of French public instruction, the very cheapest. Till recently a primary inspector's salary was such as to appear, even to French officials, cruelly insufficient; intolerably out of proportion with the importance of his functions. It was such as to reduce him to live by what he could borrow, not unfrequently having recourse for his loans to the teachers under his inspection.* But even now that their position is improved †, even now that their salary is raised nearly to the highest point which, in 1857, their compassionate friends thought possible, what is it that French inspectors receive? The highest class of them receives 96*l.* a year; the second class 80*l.*; the third, and infinitely the most numerous, 64*l.* They have besides this, while actually engaged, away from home, in the business of inspection, a personal allowance of 5*s.* 6*d.* a day, with 6*d.* (it is almost incredible) for every school which they visit. Out of this allowance they have to defray their own travelling expenses. Compared with this, the incomes of the officials of the

* *Budget de l'Instruction publique*, p. 132.

† By a decree of June 21st, 1858, due to M. Rouland, the present Minister. There are at present 275 primary inspectors; 30 in the highest class, 60 in the second, 185 in the lowest. There is, besides, for Paris, a special class of inspectors, with salaries of 100*l.* a year. The total yearly cost of inspection is 28,887*l.*

central administration are princely. But compared with our standard, they are, with one single exception, very low. The divisional chief, answering to the secretary to our Education Committee, receives, when his salary has reached its highest point, 480*l.* a year; the two *chefs de bureau*, corresponding to our assistant secretaries, receive 240*l.*; the lower officials in a like proportion. The four inspectors-general of primary instruction, the corner-stone of the administrative fabric, and the employment of whom makes it possible to employ with profit an army of inspectors of a lower grade, receive but 320*l.* a year. Vice-president or vice-minister there is none; indeed, the French officials thought the post of this functionary, when I explained it to them, a very curious invention. "Your vice-presidency," they said, "must generally have for its occupant one who would not have been designated chief minister of public instruction; yet it is he who, under the shadow of a nominal chief's authority, will inevitably transact nine-tenths of your educational business, and give the guidance to your system." Such was their criticism, whether it be sound or not; at all events they have not the office. Alone, amid his host of inferior functionaries, with unapproachable brilliancy, *velut inter ignes Luna minores*, shines the Minister. He has a salary of 4000*l.* a year, with a house and allowances, which raise the value of his post much higher. This enormous disproportion between the chief's salary and that of even his highest functionaries strikes an English observer as strange. Perhaps French subordinates console themselves with the reflection that in their country any educated man may aspire to be Minister of Public Instruction, as any common soldier may aspire to be a Marshal of France.

The habits of our country are hardly compatible with official salaries so low as those of France; and to have our schoolmasters' means reduced to the French standard would be a serious misfortune. But there can be no doubt that a certain plainness and cheapness is an indispensable element of a plan of education which is to be very widely extended; that a national system is at this price. In operations on a really vast scale, that rigid economy, even in the smallest matters, which in very limited operations may be thought overstrained, becomes an imperious necessity. The department to which I have the honour to belong is perhaps the most rigidly administered of any of the English public departments; it is of very recent date, it has grown up under the broad daylight of publicity. But its habits were formed when the schools under its supervision might be counted on the fingers. *On ne dote pas une armée*, mournfully cries M. Eugène Rendu, contrasting the condition of French inspectors with that of their English brethren: but an army the English school-inspectors must become if they are to meet the exigences of a national school-system. Yet what nation can afford to employ, in such a service, 275 highly trained diplomatists, selected to conduct delicate negotiations with influential rectors? The thing is impossible; a vast body like that of the French inspectors must necessarily be taken from a larger class, paid at a lower rate, and recruited in part, as the French inspectors are with eminent advantage recruited, from among the masters of elementary schools. "Should you not gain in some respects by having your inspectors drawn from a higher class in society?" I asked M. Magin. He said that the work of primary inspection was perfectly well done by the present staff, and, so far as I had the means of observing, I entirely agree with him; but even had the actual results been less satisfactory, he would not allow that it was possible to entertain the question for a moment. The number, he said, was too overwhelming. Again, with respect to what may seem small matters of expenditure, it is impossible to over-estimate the saving which is effected in France, where administration is on so vast a scale, by a scrupulous economy in respect to these. Royal and imperial ordinances limit the privilege, and guard against the abuse, of official postage. Stationery and printing, those great administrative agents, are under severe control. "*La paperasserie administrative est le fléau de l'administration Française*," said a distinguished official one day to me, — "French administration is bepapered to death:" — in English administration, also, paper plays no small part; but on how much more extravagant a scale! I have before me the form of report used by French inspectors when they visit a school. It is a single note-sheet of ordinary paper, containing printed questions, over against which the answers have to be written. Within these iron bounds is the ill-appreciated but irrepressible eloquence of inspectors confined. An English inspector's visit to any elementary school expends six sheets and a half of excellent foolscap. These appear insignificant matters; but when you come to provide for the inspection of 65,000 schools, it makes a difference whether you devote to each six sheets and a half of good foolscap, or a single sheet of very ordinary note-paper. Again, I take the item of certificate examinations. The charge for these in France is borne by the departments: under one sum is included the outlay for these, the outlay for the cantonal delegacies, the outlay for premises for savings-banks; all three being at the charge of the department. In 1856 this item for the whole of France was under 2000*l.* For this sum, besides the other expenses just mentioned, the certificate examinations requisite to meet the wants of a system of 47,000 schools employing certificated teachers, were provided for. What, in the same year, was the cost of our certificate examinations for a system of some 6000 schools? I am very curious to know, but unfortunately I cannot ascertain. The French, who are the best account-keepers in the world, have an excellent plan of crediting each department with the cost of its own printing. It would be well, perhaps, if we followed their example; at present an English department has its printing executed, its stationery provided, and in its estimates makes no sign. But I remember the five days' paper-work of our examinations — I remember the supplies of stationery — I remember the crowning operations of the Department of Science and Art. Again, with respect to a far greater source of expense, the building and fitting of schools. In Paris are to be seen school buildings very handsome, very elaborately fitted; but in the country districts they will not bear comparison, for completeness and architectural decoration, with those in the country districts in England. Buildings are very commonly adapted to school purposes instead of being expressly erected for them; but these school-rooms are quite good enough to be exceedingly useful, and by condescending to use them an education system can carry its schools and teachers into poor and remote communes, which must else have remained strangers to them. I am bound to say that great good sense seemed to me to characterise French administration both in its requirements and in its forbearance when dealing with schools: to take the much disputed article of boarded floors for instance; recommended generally in all schools, these have never been inflexibly required but for infant schools. Perhaps we may one day have to take a lesson from France in some of these respects. Not without doing violence to some crotchets, not without lopping off some elegant but superfluous branches of expenditure, will the plaything of philanthropists be converted into the machine of a nation.

CHAPTER X.

PRESENT INTELLECTUAL AND MORAL CONDITION OF POPULAR EDUCATION IN FRANCE. — SCHOOLS IN PARIS.

THE reader is now informed of the number and cost of the French primary schools. He will naturally ask next: What are these numerous schools of France like? what sort of an education do they give to their scholars? To this question I shall endeavour to reply by giving an account of a few of the schools which I myself visited, and I will select those which may serve as representatives of the class to which they belong.

This is not difficult. M. Rouland, the Minister of Public Instruction, in an interview with which he honoured me while I was in Paris, assured me, on hearing that I proposed to visit schools in all parts of France, that I was giving myself a great deal of very unnecessary trouble; that when I had seen a few schools anywhere, I had seen enough to enable me to judge of all. It would have been improper for me to accept this assurance, even upon such eminent authority, without verifying it by my own experience. I therefore proceeded on my enterprise, for which M. Rouland obligingly furnished me with the most ample facilities; and I visited schools in all quarters of France. I learned much which, without visiting the localities, I never should have known: but I also learned that M. Rouland had good reasons for his assertion, and that schools in France differed one from another much less than schools in England. Having learned this, I am at least enabled to spare the reader repeated descriptions of the same thing.

On the 17th of April I visited, in company with M. Rapet, a public lay school in the Rue du Faubourg Montmartre. It was a good specimen of its class. Held in a large and imposing building, in a good street, it contained a boys' school and a girls' school, with about 200 scholars in each. The schoolrooms are built over each other, the ceilings being, in all the best and newest schools, so constructed that there is no noise. The rooms were less lofty than our best schoolrooms, but quite as well ventilated; in general I found the ventilation of schools better in France than it is in England. Each school had its covered playground as well as its open-air playground. This covered playground, very rare in England, is a noticeable feature of all the best schools in the French towns; it is generally a large room on the same floor with the schoolroom; its use is to afford to the children a place for recreation in bad weather, and for their meals in the middle of every day. The parents are glad of an arrangement which relieves them throughout the day from the charge of their children, who also are thus saved two journeys in the crowded streets. I saw, in the covered playground of this school, the children, after a game of play, ranged at their dinners, which they bring with them from home; an assistant teacher was present, and the greatest order prevailed. The fittings of the schoolrooms were good, much on the same plan as that formerly followed in our British schools, but with better desks; the walls were barer than with us, and, indeed, it is rare to see on the walls of a French schoolroom the abundant supply of maps so common in English schoolrooms; but there is generally to be found the map of France and the map of Europe. Conspicuous were the crucifix and the bust of the Emperor—the indispensable ornaments of French public schoolrooms. The boys' school occupied two good rooms; one under the charge of the master, a well mannered and intelligent man; the other under the charge of an assistant master, or *adjoint*. These *adjoints* play an important part in French primary instruction; they are young men not yet arrived at the age when they may be full communal teachers*; the law does not oblige them to be certificated, but all those employed in Paris and in the large towns are certificated, because the municipalities of these towns will employ no other; the departmental council decides whether a school needs an *adjoint* or not; the head-master names him. Monitors were employed in the lower section, which was that under the assistant's care, and much the largest. The appearance of the boys was very much the same as that of the boys whom I see constantly in British and Wesleyan schools; there were very many whom I could not have distinguished from English children. Their instruction † also, was much on a par with that of the scholars of a good British or Wesleyan school in London; their reading was somewhat better; their writing, to my eye, not so good, but the French style of handwriting is different from ours; their grammar and dictation about equal; their arithmetic better; their history

* To be full communal teacher in France a man must be 21 years old, and have served three years after the age of 21 as *adjoint* or as *suppléant*. See *Décret du* 31 *Décembre* 1853.

† For the present time-table (by authority) of the lay public schools of Paris, see the end of this Report.

and geography not so good. The same is true, I think, of nearly all the French primary schools; the reading and arithmetic are better than ours, the arithmetic in particular being in general much more intelligently taught by their masters, and much more intelligently apprehended by their children; the information about geography and history is decidedly inferior. I must notice, however, that in the schools of Nancy, and in the excellent Jewish schools of Paris, to which M. Albert Cohn, the president of the Jewish Beneficent Society, kindly conducted me, the boys answered my questions on geography, and, still more, on history, as well as the best instructed scholars whom I have ever found in an English school.

The girls were all collected in one large room. The city of Paris is about to institute *adjointes*, or assistant mistresses, for girls' schools; in the mean time, the schoolmistress here has the aid of fourteen monitresses, who receive a small sum, the highest of them eight francs a month. The order, both here and in the boys' school, was excellent. The instruction in both, as in all the communal schools of Paris and of every large town in France, is entirely gratuitous. Books, as well as schooling, are given gratuitously by the city of Paris, which spends on popular instruction nearly 100,000*l.* a year. Parents, even the well-circumstanced, receive gladly and without a shadow of scruple this boon of free education for their children. The best judges, however, are of opinion that the urban municipalities have not done well in bestowing it so indiscriminately; the law certainly contemplated the exaction of school-fees from those who can afford to pay them; and, it is said, the want of the funds without difficulty thus obtainable prevents the establishment of new schools which are needed.

The law, indeed, prescribes that no child shall be admitted gratuitously into a public school unless he produces a ticket of admission signed by the mayor: and if this ticket of admission were given with proper caution, scholars who can afford to pay for their schooling would, no doubt, be excluded from schools not intended for them. But, in point of fact, this ticket is given at Paris with great laxity; mayors very generally authorise the teachers of well-conducted schools to make out their own lists of candidates for admission, and this list, when presented, is accepted without further inquiry. But in the teachers, both of lay and congreganist schools, there is an invariable tendency to prefer the better trained, better dressed, more creditable child of well-circumstanced parents, to the ill-conditioned offspring of the poor. A teacher's pardonable pride in having his school respectable, and in winning, through his scholars, an influence with their influential parents, explains well enough this tendency, even if it cannot, in the disciples of the Abbé de Lasalle, entirely excuse it. The deserved popularity of the schools of the Brethren, and the undoubted preference for them of the most respectable part of the urban populations, give them ample opportunities of thus offending. To the Sisters they are yet more abundantly offered, and as seldom resistible. There are communes where, out of five Sisters engaged for the service of public education, one Sister alone devotes her labours to the poor. Under this one Sister all the poor children of the parish, of all ages, are taught in a single free class, often numbering as many as eighty scholars. The four remaining Sisters devote themselves to the diversified instruction of two classes of about fifteen girls each, drawn from the well-circumstanced families of the commune, who pay from three to five francs a month for a daughter's schooling. It is undoubtedly true that in this way the instruction of the poor often suffers; sometimes by the actual exclusion of poor children from public schools where their places are improperly occupied by the rich, sometimes by the undue subordination of their instruction to that of richer scholars.

Yet I could not discover that even in the great towns, where population is thickest, masses of poor children anywhere remained without instruction. There are cases of hardship, such as those which I have mentioned; but I should mislead the English reader if I allowed him to think that I found in any French city educational destitution such as that of the 21,025 schoolless children of Glasgow, such as that of the 17,177 schoolless children of Manchester.* I should mislead him if I let him think that I found in France, or that I believe to exist in France, a schoolless multitude like the 2,250,000 of England. I endeavoured without success to obtain returns showing the number of children in France between the ages of five and thirteen years who remain without schooling. Inquiries have been for the last few years in prosecution with a view to obtain accurate information on this matter; but those conducting them avowed to me that they were not yet sufficiently complete to enable them to give me statistics which might be relied on. It would be well, perhaps,

* See *The State of our Educational Enterprises*, by the Rev. Wm. Fraser, Glasgow, 1858, p. 116. I do not agree with Mr. Fraser's conclusions; but it is impossible to value too highly either the information which he has collected, or the spirit in which he writes.

if the statisticians of all countries were equally cautious or equally candid. But in all the large towns which I visited, the inspectors united in assuring me that, irregularly as the schools might be frequented, feeble as might be the result which they produced, no considerable class of children remained out of the reach of their operations. In Paris, where I made special inquiries, M. Rapet—whose assurances, in every case where I could verify them, I never failed to find true, who is not inexperienced, who is not of a sanguine temper, who does not by any means see French public education in a rosy light—assured me of the same thing. Other officials unconnected with education, and with the fullest opportunities for learning the habits of the poor, repeated his assurances. My own observation of the streets and schools in the most destitute and populous quarters of Paris confirmed them. I believe that in the great cities of France industry is organised down to a much lower stage than in those of England; that the number of families without any recognised and regular mode of living is far smaller; that the number of children, therefore, left by parents, who themselves hang loose upon society, to run as wild through the world as themselves, is comparatively restricted.

A few days later I visited a school in the Rue de la Sourdière, kept by the Sisters. There is here a girls' school with 200 scholars, held in three good and well fitted rooms, each under the care of a Sister; there is also an infant school of 100, under the care of two other Sisters. These Sisters belong to a community of sixteen, who live in the same house under a superior; five are charged with the care of the schools, the remainder devote themselves to visiting the poor, tending the sick, preparing medicaments for them, and similar works of charity. The premises where the school was formerly held were very bad; two years ago the city of Paris bought the present house, and arranged it excellently for its actual purpose. The order in both schools was admirable; the instruction in the girls' school moderate. The arithmetic, however, was good; nearly all the girls in the upper class could work correctly sums in interest and in vulgar and decimal fractions: in a similar school in England this would seldom be the case. On the other hand, few girls in this class could tell how many departments France contained, or had even an elementary knowledge of geography: the upper class of a girls' school in England is generally fairly informed on geography—certainly has almost always learned the number of the English counties. In Paris, the instruction in the schools of the Sisters is commonly inferior, the inspectors told me, to that of the lay girls' schools. In the provinces it is not so; not, perhaps, that the Sisters' schools are there better, but that the lay schools are worse. Apart from the mere instruction, however, there is, even in Paris, something in the Sisters' schools which pleases both the eye and the mind, and which is more rarely found elsewhere. There is the fresh, neat schoolroom, almost always cheerfuller, cleaner, more decorated than a lay schoolroom. There is the orderliness and attachment of the children. Finally, there is the aspect of the Sisters themselves, in general of a refinement beyond that of their rank in life; of a gentleness which even beauty in France mostly lacks; of a tranquillity which is evidence that their blameless lives are not less happy than useful. If ever I have beheld serious yet cheerful benevolence, and the serenity of the mind pictured on the face, it is her Is it then impossible—I perpetually asked myself in regarding them—is it then impossible for people no longer under the world's charm, or who have never felt it, to associate themselves together, and to work happily, combinedly, and effectually, unless they have first adhered to the doctrines of the Council of Trent?

The law of France does not recognise perpetual vows; but it is extremely rare—it is so rare as to be almost without example, and an indelible stigma—for a Sister to quit the religious life when she has once embraced it. She may quit, indeed—fatigue or ill health may often compel her to quit—the laborious profession of a teacher; but it is only to engage in some other charitable service of her calling. If she ceases to be a schoolmistress, she becomes a visitress or a nurse, or she gives her labours in the dispensary. To the end of her life she remains the servant of the necessitous and of the afflicted. This sustained religious character secures to her the unfeigned respect of the common people, and enables her to render invaluable services to society.

Attached to the same establishment is an *asile ouvroir*, or needlework school, which I visited. These schools are open after or between the ordinary school-hours; they are attended by girls from mixed schools under masters, to which they are often annexed; by girls from ordinary girls' schools, of which the teacher is not particularly skilled in needlework; finally, by girls who attend no other school at all. For the benefit of the latter a little instruction in reading, arithmetic, and religious knowledge is added to the lessons in sewing, knitting, and marking. Embroidery and ornamental work are proscribed by law, except in those districts of France where they form an important branch of female industry. As the schools are open only for a few hours in each day, the services of skilful teachers can be secured for a very moderate remuneration. These establishments, which are of great use, and which have had no small share in giving to French needlewomen their superiority, are unknown as a school institution in England.

The next day I visited two establishments kept by Brethren of the Christian Schools. The first, situated in the Rue St. Lazare, contained 250 boys, and was conducted by three of the brethren. It is not a public, but a private school (*école libre*); but it is a private school in a condition in which many private schools in France actually find themselves, and therefore I mention it. It was founded by private subscriptions, and it was intended to be a kind of parochial school, under the superintendence of the local clergy. Subscriptions fell off, and the city of Paris at the present moment pays the rent of the building where the school is held, and will sooner or later end by taking upon itself the whole expense of the institution, and by converting it into a communal school. Hardly anywhere in France, (in this the reports of all the inspectors concur), can the private boys' schools, whether they be lay or congreganist, hold their own in the competition with the public schools. The private girls' schools kept by the Sisters are more fortunate. But for their boys—although even in the private school the teacher has the indispensable guarantee of the certificate of capacity, without which, in France, no man may teach parents undoubtedly prefer the public school with its additional guarantees of a public character and a more detailed inspection. To State inspection all private schools are subject; but only in what concerns their provision for the bodily health and comfort of the pupils, and their maintenance of due morality. So strongly do these establishments feel the advantage conferred by the publicity and stimulant of thorough inspection, that they constantly request the inspector to extend his examination from their school premises to their school instruction. Generally he refuses, and for reasons which his English brethren would do well to remember. "If I find the instruction ever so bad and injudicious," he says, "I have no power to get it changed; and I am bound to give public service where I know it can have results." Many an English squire, in like manner, wishes for the stimulant of inspection, while he is determined to keep his school entirely independent. In other words, he wishes to have an inspector down from London occasionally, as he would have a landscape-gardener or an architect, to talk to him about his school, to hear his advice, and to be free to dismiss him, as he might dismiss the landscape-gardener or the architect, the moment his advice becomes unpalatable. He wishes to have a public functionary to act as show-man to his school once a year. But it is not for this that the State pays its servants. State-supervision is useless if it can be rejected the moment it becomes a reality, the moment it tends to enforce general reason against individual caprice. The counsels of inspection, to be of any real worth, must be in some way or other authoritative.

As the school in the Rue St. Lazare presented in other respects little that was remarkable, I shall pass on from it to another school kept by the Brethren, which I saw on the same morning, a public school in the Rue du Rocher. Here not less than four Brethren were employed; one for each of the four classes into which this large school, containing 400 boys, was divided. The Schools of the Brethren have a decided advantage over the lay schools in the number of their teachers. A lay school in Paris has a master and an *adjoint*, two efficient teachers; a school of the Brethren has never less than three; always, when the school is large, a greater number. For the evening or adult school a fresh relay of Brethren is ready, while the lay teacher has the toil of evening and day alike. A sick or overworked Brother is sent to recover, in perfect rest of body and mind, at one of the houses of residence of his order, while another of his community is sent to take his place, without disturbance or detriment to the school. The illness of a lay schoolmaster agitates him with apprehension, mulcts him in salary, and deranges his school. Such are the advantages which a great association like that of the Brethren confers on its members. But even such an association is not numerous enough to supply to elementary schools an adequate force of teaching power. It supplies more than its lay competitors in France; it has thus a great advantage over them. But what were even four teachers among these 400 boys of the Rue du Rocher, with 110 boys to be controlled and taught in a single room by one brother, 80 by a second, the remainder in two other rooms by the third and fourth? I here touch the weak point of the French schools. The Brethren, it is true, do not employ monitors; but the value of monitors is by this time pretty accurately appreciated. Under certain circumstances the employment of them is indispensable. M. de Lasalle, in his *Manual**, laid

* See his remarkable words quoted by M. Ambroise Rendu in his *Essai sur l'Instruction publique*, vol. i. p. 81.

down a plan for the division and subdivision of the school work by means of the use of monitors, and is, in truth, the earliest inventor of the mutual or monitorial system. In the war between the simultaneous and mutual systems, which raged so hotly in France from 1815 to 1830, the Brethren, like the clergy, naturally took part against a system extolled by their enemies and directed against their influence. The brethren were partisans of the simultaneous system, which centred the whole system in the head teacher, that is, in one of themselves. The French liberals were partisans of the mutual system, which, as they hoped, would substitute innumerable neutral influences for the one influence of the ecclesiastical head-teacher. But all this is past. The battle between lay and clerical influence is no longer fought with the weapons of the mutual and simultaneous systems. Clergy and laymen alike confess the imperfections of both. I talked little to my friends among the French inspectors about the pupil-teachers of Holland and England. I was in France that I might learn what they knew, and not that I might teach them what I knew. But if these lines ever meet the eye of any one of them, let me assure him that popular education in France will gain more by the introduction of pupil-teachers into a single school, than by libraries of discussion upon the mutual and simultaneous systems.

Pupil-teachers — the sinews of English primary instruction, whose institution is the grand merit of our English State system, and its chief title to public respect: this, and, I will boldly say, the honesty with which that system has been administered. Pupil-teachers — the conception, for England, of the founder of English popular education, of the administrator whose conceptions have been as fruitful as his services were unworthily maligned, of Sir James Shuttleworth. In naming them, I pause to implore all friends of education to use their best efforts to preserve this institution to us unimpaired. Let them entreat ministerial economy to respect a pensioner who has repaid the outlay upon him a thousand times; let them entreat Chancellors of the Exchequer to lay their retrenching hands anywhere but here; let them entreat the Privy Council Office to propose for sacrifice some less precious victim. Forms less multiplied, examinations less elaborate, inspectors of a lower grade—let all these reductions be endured rather than that the number of pupil-teachers should be lessened. If these are insufficient, a far graver retrenchment, the retrenchment of the grants paid to holders of our certificates of merit, would be yet far less grave than a considerable loss of pupil-teachers. A certificate, indeed, is properly a guarantee of capacity, and not an order for money. There is no more reason that it should entitle its possessor to 20*l.* than that it should entitle him to a box at the opera. Private liberality can repair the salaries of the schoolmasters, but no private liberality can create a body like the pupil-teachers. Neither can a few of them do the work of many. "Classes of twenty-five or thirty, and an efficient teacher to each class:" that school-system is the best which inscribes these words on its banners.

The overwhelming size of their classes has naturally an exhausting effect on French teachers. In none of them is this effect more apparent than in the Brethren, originally in many cases the feebler and less robust members of a poor family, who have sought in the career of tuition not only a field of pious labour, but an exemption from military service* and from the rude life of a tiller of the ground. They have often, the younger ones more especially, a languid and apathetic air, and go through their work as if they had strength to go through it only by routine. They speak as little as possible, and to save their voices have invented a machine like a rattle, peculiar to the schools of the brethren, with which they give all the signals that another teacher would give with his voice. They keep their scholars writing, an English teacher would say, perpetually; in all the French schools, indeed, lay as well as congreganist, the written bear to the oral exercises an exorbitant proportion, but in no schools so exorbitant as in those of the brethren. As some compensation, the caligraphy of their pupils is celebrated. But the habit of oral questioning, (and on this point M. Rapet entirely agreed with me,) is far too little practised.

The Brother who has the principal charge of a school must be certificated. On the Brethren who assist him there is imposed no such obligation. One often finds, therefore, in one of these schools, a great difference between the vigour, confidence, and acquirements of the chief teacher, and those of his assistants. But they live very harmoniously together, and the youthful Brother, in time, obtains his certificate, and qualifies himself to take the principal charge of a school. The superior of the house of residence which furnishes teachers to a school exercises very constantly and very thoroughly his right of inspection of it.

* Ever since 1818 the engagement to remain for ten years in the service of public instruction frees him who takes it from the obligation of military service.

In the Schools of the Brethren there is the same want of maps which is observable in the lay schools, but the nakedness of the walls is generally relieved by religious pictures and religious sentences. The instruction differs in no important particular from that of lay schools. That of the best lay schools, however, is unquestionably, on the whole, somewhat more advanced.* In lay and congreganist schools alike, drawing and music are more systematically taught than in our schools, and taught, in general, by special masters. The communities of the Brethren furnish them with a suppy of trained labour in all departments of teaching. I was greatly struck with the appearance of the young Brother who taught drawing in the school of the Rue du Rocher; he had a genuine vocation for his art, and his face expressed the animation and happiness which the exercise of a genuine vocation always confers. I visited him and his brethren in their house of residence; their chapel had been elaborately decorated by his sole industry: it must have been a labour of months, but a labour of love.

The Brethren are far less constant than the Sisters to the religious life. For the Sisters the religious life is the principal object of their association, the profession of teaching but the accessory: for the Brethren the career of teaching is the principal, the rest the accessory. Their vows as members of their own community are for three or five years; but as public functionaries in the

* As long ago as 1818, the Rector of the Academy of Strasbourg gives as a reason why there were no schools of the brethren in Alsace, then as now one of the best-educated districts in France, that "dans les endroits plus populeux et plus riches, on exige un enseignement supérieur à celui des Frères."—See *Essai sur l'Instruction publique*, vol. iii. p. 213.

service of public instruction, and, as such, exempt from the conscription, their engagement is for ten years, and for this term they actually serve in schools. At the end of this time it is not unusual for them to depart at once out of the career of teaching and the pale of their community, and to return to the garb and professions of civil life. Some of them marry and become fathers of families. Their association, therefore, is by no means invested in the eyes of the people with the same religious and sacred character as that of the Sisters.

This is true; and it is probably true, also, that the motives which determine their entrance into their order are often not religious. It is probably true that, as the best-informed persons assert, many a young peasant becomes a Brother of the Christian Schools because he can commence his duties and cease to be a charge to his parents two years sooner than if he embrace the career of a lay teacher. He cannot be admitted into a normal school before the age of 18; the fraternity will receive him at 16. If slow at learning, he dreads the certificate-examination; but without the certificate he cannot earn his bread as a lay teacher, while the fraternity can employ him as one of their numerous under masters though he be uncertificated. Many of the French inspectors, therefore, eye the schools of the Brethren a little severely. They regard them, certainly, with far less indulgence than the schools of the Sisters; they regard their teachers as wearing a character of religious vocation which often really belongs to them no more than to the teacher of a common lay school; they are fond of maintaining that the congreganist boys' schools afford to parents no better guarantee than the lay schools for the religion and morality of their children; they are eager to prove that parents have really no preference for the former over the latter. The Brethren, on the other hand, are not unwilling to have it understood that they suffer from the hands of authority unmerited obstruction; that their Christian devotedness has its difficulties to contend with; that if their success is great, it is because their merits are irresistible.

Conscious, upon this question, of the most absolute impartiality, I shall frankly state the conclusion at which I have arrived. On the one hand, it is unquestionable that the religious associations have hitherto had rather to bless the favour than to complain of the obstruction of the civil authorities. If they sometimes have the primary inspector a little against them, they almost always have had the primary inspector's masters, the prefect and the Minister, on their side. From the day when a Protestant Minister, M. Guizot, offered to the Superior* of the Christian Schools the decoration of the Legion of Honour—a distinction which its proposed object, with a modesty not less prudent than pious, respectfully declined—to the present time, when Ministers say to a functionary, who reports some infraction of school law by the Sisters, *Vous me faites des difficultés: laissez cela*—when inspectors tell me with their own lips, *Si nous avons quelque chose à reprocher aux frères, nous y regardons à deux fois avant de la dire; cela nous attirerait des misères; c'est extrêmement redoutable*—the religious associations have been to all governments an object of favour and respect, sometimes sincere, sometimes interested. Of this there can be no question.

On the other hand I am profoundly convinced that

* The Père Anaclet, in 1833.

in the quarters where they are numerous, and certain districts which may be called great centres of lay feeling—Normandy, Lorraine, Alsace—being excluded, the population generally prefers the schools of religious associations to lay schools. With respect to girls' schools there cannot be a moment's doubt; the Sisters' advantage is utterly beyond the reach of competition. With respect to the Brethren's schools also, however, I feel entire certainty. In Paris it is even a bad sign of the respectability and religious character of a family when it prefers for its boys a lay school to a congreganist. In the country, wherever I had the means of making personal inquiry, I found the same thing; if a school of the Brethren was accessible, the more decent, the better conducted a family was, the more certainly it sent its boys there. It was commonly thought that there the children would be under a better influence; that the moral tone, as it is called, of such a school was superior.* I add, with some hesitation on this point, which is not so easy of proof, that I believe the common opinion was right.

* Comparisons have often been instituted between the lay and congreganist schools as to their success in combating the revolutionary tendency; but it seems impossible to arrive at any clear conclusion. At Bordeaux, in 1848-9, the youth trained in lay, and those trained in congreganist schools, were observed to be equally quiet and well conducted; at Bazas, Libourne, and Blaye, (in the same academy district,) where the schools had long been in the hands of the Brethren, the population was turbulent. In the Landes, where few schools are in the hands of the Brethren, the conduct of the population was perfectly orderly. It was thought to be the relations of the rich with the poor in any locality, (at Bordeaux these are particularly good,) which made the difference as to the behaviour of the working people in that locality. In the academy-district of Paris, the Socialist and revolutionary spirit was observed (say the inspectors) to be as rife in quarters where the religious had the schools as in those where they were taught by laymen.

The reader must recollect, however, that the schools of the Brethren, although constantly on the increase, are not and cannot be very numerous. The Sisters are everywhere, because teaching is with them but one of many functions, for some of which almost every locality desires them. But the Brethren, who perform no function but that of teaching, who go out in parties of not less than three, who cost a commune 1500 or 1600 francs, instead of the 500 or 600 francs which a common lay teacher costs, and whose schools, being inevitably gratuitous, fail to contribute in aid of their teacher's maintenance the resource of school-fees, cannot be generally introduced into small and poor communes. Among the various associations, more than twenty in number, which devote themselves to the instruction of the poor, there are some indeed which are less costly than the Brethren of the Christian Schools. There are the Brethren of Marie, in the regions about Lyons* and Bordeaux, who go out as teachers in parties

* Lyons is also the original seat of the *Société d'Instruction élémentaire*, the most considerable lay association which has in France made popular education its object. In 1826 a few persons in Lyons, about 20 in number, who wished to introduce more lay influence into the management of schools for the poor, formed themselves into a society, which in 1829 was authorised by royal ordinance. The society began with eight or nine schools under its direction; it has now 39 in Lyons and the immediate neighbourhood. It has its own inspector and its executive commission, and assembles monthly to meet its teachers, in presence of the inspector, who then makes his report. The society raises about 10,000 fr. a year by private subscription. At first it was quite independent; but as its operations extended, the municipality of Lyons came to its aid, and now pays the difference between the 10,000 fr. which the society annually raises by subscription, and the 80,000 fr. which it actually spends. But this aid makes the schools of the society *public* and *municipal* schools. As such, they now have their teachers appointed

of two: there are in Brittany the Brethren of Lamennais, founded by a brother of the celebrated writer of that name, who go out singly. But none of them enjoy the same favour as the Brethren of the Christian Schools, or can compare with them in success. The Bishop of Quimper told me that the Brethren of Lamennais, who are quartered upon the curé of the parish whither they are sent, and who cost very little, were irksome inmates to the curés, and not willingly accepted by them.* In fact, the moment a Brother goes singly, and can therefore be employed by any poor commune, he loses the virtue which religious association confers upon its members, and which is the source of half their strength. How unlike to the lonely teacher, isolated in his labour, isolated in his weariness, isolated in his joy, isolated in his temptation, is the little company of three devised by M. de Lasalle, meeting after the toil of the day in their common home, a society for themselves in the most unsocial spots, at once a solace to each other, and a salutary check!

If the English reader must not think that this excellent association can reach all the poor of France, so neither must he think that to put instruction in its hands is, so far as its action extends, to put it entirely in the hands of the clergy. Their schools are public schools, as the lay schools are; they are subjected to the same authorities as the lay schools; the clergyman has no

by the prefect, and all the authority left to the society is a right of inspection, and of drawing up for their schools a programme of instruction, which, however, cannot be adopted unless approved by the academy-inspector of the district.

* I found in the department of Finistère but twenty one primary schools conducted by the Brethren of this order; sixteen public schools and five private. This was in 1859. The whole number of primary boys' schools in the department was 265.

more power to name or dismiss a teacher, or to interfere with the instruction, (except so far as to satisfy himself that the religious instruction is properly cared for,) in the one than in the other. Undoubtedly, the Brethren are felt by the curé to be more akin to him than the lay teacher is; undoubtedly he prefers them to the lay teacher, and procures their introduction into his parish when he can.* But the school is not really under the clergyman's hand, like the National school of an English parish: it is under the hand of the ordinary civil authorities, the mayor, the cantonal delegates, the inspectors, the prefect. What really resembles our National school is the parochial school of France (*école paroissiale*), generally taught by the religious, but a *private* school, founded expressly that it may be in ecclesiastical hands, and not in civil. But these schools are very rare in France, difficult to maintain, not acceptable to the population. The public school taught by the religious is a school under teachers in general sympathy with the clergy, but not clergy themselves, nor able to become so; and, as members of a great association, having a spirit of their own, an independence of their own, and dealing with the curé nearly as equal to equal. If the National schools of England were taught by an order of lay deacons, nearly equal to the clergyman of the parish in their social position, and legally independent of him, they would then be in the position of the public congreganist schools of France. The National schoolmaster would then stand towards the rector, not as now, much on the same footing as his gardener, but on the same footing as a

* The hostility of the clergy to lay schools for boys is perhaps diminishing; but they use all their efforts to get the education of girls exclusively into the hands of the Sisters.

brother clergyman unattached. The English National schools would then be in the hands of a body which, though with strong clerical affinities, would be a body perfectly distinct from the clergy, and incapable of blending with it; a body with a spirit and power of its own; a body by its very essence more scholastic than priestly; whereas a clergy, however admirable, as a body never forgets that it was priest before it was schoolmaster.

It was important to call the reader's attention to this wide difference between a system of private schools in the hands of the parish clergyman, and a system of public schools in the hands of a religious association and of the State. But I hasten to add, that were the religious associations of France a thousand times more devoted to the clergy than they are, the population would still continue to prefer their schools; and yet the clerical influence would not be a whit the gainer. It is to morality and religion that the French people, in sending its children to the congreganist schools, does homage*, not to any ultramontane theories. For the supremacy of a clerical party in the State it has not the slightest favour; nor, indeed, since the Revolution, does it even dream of such supremacy as possible. I have said this elsewhere, when to many it seemed a matter of question; I repeat it more boldly now, when facts have come to give to it their confirmation. The clergy have no deep-rooted influence with the French masses. They may agitate families. They may frighten

* "The *religieux* and *religieuses* are the natural people to teach the poor."—I found this sentiment almost everywhere. At the same time the superiority of the lay boys'-schools in secular instruction was generally admitted.

governments into making concessions to them: they may induce the State (happy result of the fears of rulers!) to rebuild their churches. They may constrain the attendance at church of Voltairian officials. But no priesthood will at the present day rule the French nation.

CHAPTER XI.

PRESENT INTELLECTUAL AND MORAL CONDITION OF POPULAR EDUCATION IN FRANCE.—SCHOOLS IN THE PROVINCES.

MINDFUL of M. Rouland's saying, I must not carry the reader with me to too many schools; but I must still ask him, after seeing the schools of Paris, to accompany me to one or two in the country. On the morning of the 13th of May, I found myself in the office of the academy inspector of the Gironde, M. Dauzat, whose conversation, full of shrewdness and fine remark, I had been enjoying the day before; the primary inspector of the district, M. Benoît, was there to meet me. I said to the two inspectors, that having visited many institutions by official selection, I had a desire to choose a school to visit, and a country school, for myself. A map of the department hung upon the wall, and they told me to choose where I would. I fixed upon Blanquefort, a place six or seven miles from Bordeaux, and recalling by its castle the memory of the mediæval wars and of the Black Prince. They assured me I could not have chosen more happily; that the schools of Blanquefort were neither better nor worse than the schools of most places of the same class; and that they presented an instructive variety. A little after twelve, accordingly, M. Benoît and I set out in an open carriage for Blanquefort. The day was beautiful; our road lay, at first, among gardens and country houses, but after a mile or two passed into a quiet and rural country. The environs of Bordeaux have not the movement of those of Manchester or Lyons; it is a rich and stately, but somewhat stagnant city. As we drove along, M. Benoît told me what his life was, and how a French inspector in the Gironde passed his year. He had served in the army when almost a boy, had been present with his father at the battle of Vimieiro, and had been included in the Convention of Cintra. At the peace of 1815 he found himself a lieutenant on half-pay, with small prospect of military advancement: having some turn for teaching, he had opened a private school, had been tolerably successful, and finally had been made a primary inspector. It is from the functionaries of secondary instruction, from the principals and professors of communal colleges and of private schools, that the majority of the primary inspectors are taken. They must have either the degree of bachelor of arts, or the complete certificate embracing all the subjects, both obligatory and facultative, of primary instruction; they must also have exercised some educational function for two years. Unless this function has been of a certain rank, they have further to undergo, previous to their actual appointment, a special examination in the laws which regulate French primary instruction, and in pedagogy; this examination takes place before a commission nominated by the rector to whose academy the school-district assigned to the new inspector belongs. A certain number of inspectorships is reserved for the most successful of the primary schoolmasters, and of the lecturers in normal schools; the director of a normal school would not accept the office. His post is worth considerably more than that of a primary inspector, and is the highest prize to which a schoolmaster can aspire.* A few of the best of the primary inspectors are advanced to the rank of academy inspector: it is the academy inspector who, in each department, is at the head of primary instruction; who receives the reports of the primary inspectors, advises the prefect, receives the inspector general on his rounds, and communicates with the central authority in Paris. Among the most efficient of these functionaries are those promoted from primary inspectorships. M. Benoit seemed satisfied with his present position; he had, as most Frenchmen have, some little property of his own; and the department of the Gironde, like other rich departments, gives its primary inspectors a yearly allowance† in addition to their salary from the State. He had under his inspection not less than 646 schools, with 38,250 children; but he lived in Bordeaux, and great part of his work was either in the town itself or in the immediate neighbourhood. While M. Benoit was telling me all this, the carriage rolled on, and presently he pointed out to me the church and village of Blanquefort, upon its vine-covered hill. We drove to the boys' school, and reached it just as the children were assembled for their afternoon lessons.

It was the only boys' school of the place, which is a large, well-built village of about 2000 inhabitants. The master told me that he had 60 boys in ordinary attendance; I found present but 13. Many are absent

* The salary of a normal school director of the highest class is from 2500 fr. to 3000 fr. a year, of the lowest class from 2200 fr. to 3000 fr. a year. Lecturers have from 1000 fr. to 1800 fr. See *Décret du 26 Décembre* 1855, Art. 1.

† In the Gironde this allowance is 400 fr. a year. In 1857 a sum of 23,638 fr. 87 c. was thus spent by the departments in gratuities to primary inspectors.

at this season, (just the old story in England), for field labour; but the field labour of Médoc, not of England —to clear the vineyards of snails and caterpillars, and to gather the strawberry harvest. The schoolroom was large, clean, airy, and well lighted; it was fitted with desks on the old British plan, and the children were at work under monitors. On the walls was one large map of France, and several small ones of other countries. The highest class was reading a lesson on the ostrich, similar to the lessons on natural history in the third Irish reading-book; they read well. We sat down among them, and M. Benoit questioned them in a natural kindly manner, which proved his long experience of children. At his request I examined them in grammar; they parsed a sentence well, better than I should expect to find it parsed in a country school in England. Then I questioned them in geography; they could name the capitals of Europe, its principal mountains, its principal lakes, the seas connected by the Straits of Gibraltar, &c. The chief towns of the French departments they also gave with perfect readiness and accuracy. Of history they knew nothing. In arithmetic M. Benoit examined them, setting them problem after problem; and I really hardly knew which most to admire, the goodness of the examination or the quickness of the children. Their writing was such as in an English school an inspector would describe as very fair. All but fourteen of those present were reading in books. The school-books were of the kind ordinarily used in French lay schools; not good, but not, perhaps, worse than ours. The Brethren, who publish their own school-books, and sell them to all but their poorest scholars, who receive them gratuitously, are not more successful. I generally found their classes reading a series of moral lessons, without substance and without style, and repulsive by their sterile monotony. According to strict rule all books used in the French schools ought to be chosen from a list sanctioned by the Minister of Public Instruction; but there is much laxity. In fact, with them, as with us, there exists no thoroughly good school-series to choose.*

The Blanquefort boys were well disciplined, and their appearance was cheerful and healthy. Five or six of them were without shoes and stockings; but M. Benoit told me, (and the look of the children confirmed what he said,) that this was not because these children were poorer than others; many parents in the South of France, he said, the well-circumstanced as well as the poor, let their children go barefoot in the hot weather for the sake of coolness. There was some poverty, however: of the sixty children in ordinary attendance, one sixth had free schooling because they were poor; they were chosen by the mayor and curé, approved by the municipal council, and their admission finally sanctioned by the prefect. The rest pay a uniform fee of two francs a month. From April to November the attendance is thin, but never falls below forty scholars.

Attached to the school was the master's house. It was, M. Benoit told me, an unusually good one; it had six rooms, all of them well furnished; in one of them were books and a piano: at the back of the house was a large garden, to which the school playground adjoined. The law prescribes for a schoolmaster's accommodation a three-roomed house and a garden. The salary of the master was 1200 francs a year: of this sum 200 francs were furnished by the commune, the school pence sup-

* The above was written in 1859. Since then, one excellent series of reading books has been published in this country.

plied the rest. He was an intelligent, well-mannered man, of about thirty years of age.

From hence we went on to the girls' school, distant but a few paces. The reader will remember that the law does not impose upon communes the obligation of providing girls' schools. The one in question was held in a bad, ill-ventilated building, without playground, and was taught by the master's wife. Forty-eight girls had their names on the books; twenty-eight were present. The girls of Blanquefort were distinguished by wearing no covering on their hair; the country girls from the neighbourhood wore a handkerchief. None of them, I was told, (and they themselves confirmed it to me,) were likely to become domestic servants. For service they avowed a great distaste; their ambition was to live by their needle. For this they are well prepared at school, two hours in every afternoon being devoted to needlework. They read very well indeed, and worked problems in arithmetic with much cleverness and facility. Their stock of general information was small. Fifteen of them were free scholars on the ground of poverty, the rest paid from one to two francs a month. The mistress has a salary of 800 francs a year; 200 francs of this the commune pays—voluntarily, the reader will remember: the school-fees come to 600 francs.

The schoolmaster of Blanquefort, therefore, has from his own and his wife's salary an income of 80*l.* a year. He is besides secretary to the municipality, an office almost always held by the village schoolmaster*, and

* He is often, besides, clerk and organist. He is thus at once the man of the mayor and the man of the curé. When they get on well together his position is comfortable; when they quarrel, as they often do, it is difficult enough.

which the authorities encourage him to accept. This gives him 300 francs (12*l.*) more. He has also a good house and garden.

There is general ease among the population of the Gironde, and its villages and incomes must not be taken as samples of villages and incomes in the Cantal or the Creuse; but Blanquefort is a fair sample of the villages or little towns of its class in any thriving French department, and the reader will, I think, be struck, as I was, to remark how many things practically here come in to ameliorate the meagre part created for the teacher by the law, and in remote and indigent districts* actually sustained by him.

We had not yet done with Blanquefort. M. Benoit told me that there was a girls' school kept by the Sisters, which I ought to see: and thither, accordingly, we repaired. These Sisters, six in number, belong to a local order; they rent the houses which they occupy. The commune gives them nothing, but the department gives them 100 francs (4*l.*) a year towards the expenses of their infant school. Two Sisters have charge of the infant school, four of the girls' school. The moment I approached the premises, which stood a little out of the main street of the village, I was struck with the air of propriety, neatness, and order which reigned there. We first entered the girls' school. The cleanliness of the room, the discipline of the children, were really beautiful; flowers stood everywhere, and the open windows admitted the sweet air of the country

* Even in these districts his position is now somewhat better than the law of 1850 made it. On the favourable report of the prefect, the Minister of Public Instruction is now authorised to augment, from the public funds, the annual salaries of deserving schoolmasters to 700 fr. after six years' service, and to 800 fr. after ten years' service. See *Décret du* 31 *Décembre* 1853, Art. 5.

in May. The furniture and school-fittings were as fresh as those of the lay girls' school were shabby and worn. The walls were well furnished with boards and maps. The girls were at their needlework, which M. Benoît told me enjoyed a high reputation; I saw their copy-books, and I heard their reading, and in any English school I should have highly commended both. Forty-three girls were present, seventy-five had their names on the books. Of these, fifteen are admitted free, as indigent children; the rest pay from one to two francs a month. We passed into the infant school; this school-room also was brilliantly clean. The infants, forty-eight in number, (eighty were on the books,) were arranged on the gallery, the girls, even here, being separated from the boys. Boards and Bible-pictures covered the walls as in a well-provided infant school in England. From one of the pictures a Sister was giving a gallery lesson on the story of Joseph. Her little pupils in the gallery looked clean and happy, and the treatment of them was evidently affectionate and even tender. Their instruction did not go far—why, indeed, should it?—but they knew their letters well, they went through their exercises and their singing regularly and prettily, and their discipline was perfect. Play-ground, passages, and offices were as neat and as beautifully clean as the schoolrooms themselves.

I have just touched on the religious instruction; I may add that in the French schools generally, lay as well as congreganist, I found the children well instructed in the catechism and well acquainted with Scripture history. Sunday schools teach them these; they teach them little besides, but they teach them these very fairly. I passed an hour or two at Toulouse in going from chapel to chapel in the cathedral church of

St. Stephen, to watch the Sunday classes under their priests; they were crowded but orderly, and work was carried on very diligently. These catechism classes in the churches are, in fact, the French Sunday school; the Protestants have carried the institution somewhat further; but, as an instrument of secular as well as of religious instruction, it is not of much importance in France.

I do not know if the reader will think, as I do, that this visit made without notice to the schools of a country place of my own selection was very satisfactory. I would not have exchanged it for a week of visits made at the choice of the local inspectors. It showed me the everyday life of thousands of spots in the many departments of France; in her thriving departments certainly, but not more thriving than Warwickshire and Lincolnshire are thriving. Of this life it left me with a pleasant impression; an impression which, amidst the many mournful sights and mournful stories of the general life of humanity, I shall not easily lose. We left the Sisters, to whose door the schoolmaster, who, like every one else in the place, lived on good terms with them, had come to join us. I entered the church; there, too, were flowers everywhere, and grateful coolness and shade. We sent the carriage round by the road, and the schoolmaster guided us up and down slopes of grass and vineyards, across a clear brook, to the old castle. The masonry of its keep rises still fresh and unworn out of the reed-grown moat; but all within the walls is a ruin, over which cluster the wild roses. A peasant has made his dwelling where once was the grand entrance; but he has nothing to tell of the castle's history and of the Black Prince. The ploughshare of the Revolution has passed over that feudal age; they are gone, the leopards of England from the gateway, the name of the Black Prince from the memories of the population. Even in the reminiscences of the excellent M. Benoît himself, it did not, I think, hold a very prominent place. Through a thicket of brushwood I climbed to the top of the ruin; around me, beneath the luminous air, stretched the pleasant country of southern France; on the horizon were the towers and spires of Bordeaux, and its smoke hanging in the clear sky. We rejoined the carriage, and reached Bordeaux before nightfall.

A few days afterwards, at Toulouse, I expressed to the obliging inspectors who did the honours to me of that city, my wish, after having seen an average specimen of a French country school at Blanquefort, to see a school which was decidedly below the average, a school which was, from whatever cause, in a somewhat suffering condition. They promised to gratify me; and the next day the primary inspector drove with me to the public lay school of St. Martin de Touche, a village of 800 souls, a few miles from Toulouse. As we entered the village I remarked the handsome church, quite new, and was told that it had just been entirely rebuilt. The school had certainly not been rebuilt: it was a poor building, ill ventilated, with an uneven brick floor and no playground. The master looked depressed and without energy to struggle against his difficulties; he was no longer young, and weighed down with the charge of what is less common in France than in England, a very large family. But the moment I came to talk with him I was struck with his superiority; and the inspector told me that he was a man of very considerable cultivation and mental power, who had been educated for the priesthood, but had married and been driven to turn schoolmaster. His salary was 1000 fr. (40*l.*) a year; all the children had free schooling, but bought their own books. It is the city of Toulouse which pays the master's salary and gives to the village a free school; like the other great cities of France, it does the same for all the villages in its environs. Perhaps it would aid the cause of popular education more efficiently if it spent its money upon it in a somewhat different manner*; but its liberality is unquestionable. There were twenty-eight boys present; forty-five had their names on the books. I was told that there were generally about thirty in attendance through the summer; in winter the school is quite full. All the boys were wearing wooden shoes without stockings, though the children, almost all of them, of small proprietors pretty well off; they wear shoes and stockings on Sundays only. In general, unless their parents are in great destitution, boys here

* The effect of free schooling fills a school, but *[illegible]* — this is the nearly universal testimony of the French inspectors. In the Bas Rhin (a very well-educated district) free schooling is being gradually suppressed, with the acquiescence of the parents; and in this department there were in 1855 but 750 children, of an age to attend school, who did not attend it. In the adjoining department of the Haut Rhin, there were 1000. But in the academy district of Besançon (also well-educated) the inspectors declare that the attendance at schools which have been made free has doubled, tripled, and even quadrupled; and that the scholars are kept at such schools more steadily. At Lyons, again, "free schooling is not disliked by the population," say the inspectors; "it is rather regarded as a debt which the State owes to them;" and at Lyons, as in Paris, all the public schools are free. But the majority of the reports show that, while free schools are generally filled and even over-filled, and often at the expense of paying schools, the poor are careless about their children's attendance and progress in them, as they value little what they pay nothing f[illegible]

do not begin to work regularly till the age of thirteen, but in summer their occasional help is often wanted by their parents. The instruction in this school was better than I expected from its unpromising aspect; the reading was very fair, though sing-song, like rustic reading in England; there was little geography (though the walls were not ill furnished with maps) and less history: the grammar and arithmetic were good; the handwriting and dictation very good indeed. The latter lesson amused me; the master was dictating to his pupils, from the *Journal des Instituteurs*, M. Rouland's letter to the bishops desiring their prayers for the success of France in the Italian war. This newspaper, published under the auspices of the Minister of Public Instruction, and taken in by almost every schoolmaster in France, by no means confines itself to scholastic information. A copy of it lies before me *: of fourteen pages which, exclusive of those occupied by advertisements and commercial intelligence, it contains, seven are devoted to *Politique*, and seven to *Pédagogie* and *Sciences usuelles.* Politics have naturally the post of honour. The number commences: *On lit dans le* Moniteur. *On cherche en Angleterre à attribuer à la France la cause des charges que l'on impose au peuple Anglais pour les défenses nationales.* Then follows the rest of the well-known article of the *Moniteur.* A little further on England figures once more: — *La Tamise, dit le* Times, *qui baigne les murs du palais de Westminster, est véritablement en décomposition.* The remainder of the first seven pages is full of news from the seat of war, notices of the countries engaged in it, appreciations of their policy; all undeniably interest-

* The number for July 31st, 1859.

ing, all irreproachably national, but not the least in the world pedagogic.

We smile: it is thus that M. Rouland fulfils the duty of government to "enlighten public opinion, and not to leave it at the mercy of personal passions and party hatreds." * Yet, perhaps, nothing is wholly ridiculous, which tends to foster that admirable unity of patriotic spirit which pervades France from one end to the other, and which is the great force of the nation.

The master's wife had a class of six little boys in an adjoining room. She had formerly taught the girls of the village, but the Sisters had opened a school, and, as almost always happens, all the girls had been drawn off to them. This school of the Sisters had present, on the day of my visit, forty scholars.

Before quitting elementary schools, I must conduct the reader to a genuine private school. I could not select a better example than the British school in Paris. This is entirely supported by voluntary contributions, and all the State has to do with it is to exercise its legal right of inspection, extending only to matters of what our neighbours call "hygiene, salubrity, and morality." † The boys' school had forty two children present on the day of my visit; they were very young, the children of British parents, but many of them speaking French better than English; the British school course is followed. The master, a certificated student

* His own words, in a warning to a newspaper: "Éclairer "l'opinion publique, et ne pas la livrer aux entraînements des passions personnelles et des haines de parti."

† See *Loi du* 15 *Mars* 1850, Art 21. "L'inspection des écoles "libres porte sur la moralité, l'hygiène, et la salubrité. Elle ne peut "porter sur l'enseignement que pour vérifier s'il n'est pas contraire à "la morale, à la constitution, et aux lois."

from the Borough Road Training College, whom I remember to have seen there, is an undoubtedly able and intelligent young man; but he seemed to me to be somewhat out of spirits about his school, and to feel his solitude in Paris a good deal. The girls' school was more thriving. The children were older, the mistress, a former student of the Home and Colonial Institution, appeared sanguine about the success of her school, and in cheerful spirits. In this school I felt myself to be indeed on British ground, for there was a committee. The excellent lady who represented them was there, not in anticipation of my visit, for I had not announced it, but on an habitual errand of kindness to advise and encourage the teacher. Like many British committees in England she seemed to have no ardent fondness for government control; she was somewhat impatient of authoritative visits, even when directed solely to matters of "hygiene, salubrity, and morality;" she lamented that her school should be under the supervision of "bigoted Roman Catholic inspectors." Her fears were vain; for her inspector was M. Rapet, no more a bigoted Roman Catholic than I am. But how many friends of popular education have I seen on British committees in England, during my tours of inspection through nearly all its counties, haunted with the same apprehensions as this benevolent lady; not exactly hostile, but agitated by a susceptibility which never slumbered. *Cœlum non animum mutant*:—it was impossible to forbear smiling.

I had intended to describe a Protestant public school in France; but really such a school differs so little from a Roman Catholic lay school in the same locality, that I forbear. Yet the grown-up Protestant population has certainly throughout France a general superiority over the Roman Catholic, in conduct, industry, and success in life. To what is their superiority owing? It is in great measure, I believe, owing to this, that the French Protestants have the unspeakable advantage, for the character, of finding themselves a small minority in presence of a vast majority; and in order to hold its own and to succeed in life, the minority has to put forth its strength and to do its best.

CHAPTER XII.

PRESENT INTELLECTUAL AND MORAL CONDITION OF POPULAR EDUCATION IN FRANCE.—NORMAL SCHOOLS.

From elementary I pass to normal schools *; and before I speak of the ministerial orders which regulate these I will describe what I actually saw in them. Strange to say, in Paris there is no public normal school for primary teachers; there is an institution at Courbevoie for the training of Protestant teachers, and at Versailles there is a departmental normal school; but the capital trusts to the provinces for its supply of teachers, and so powerful are its attractions that it never fails to obtain the best of them. I saw the most efficient, perhaps, of the provincial normal schools; that of Bordeaux, that of Nancy, that of Strasbourg. I will describe that of Bordeaux.

The department of the Gironde and that of the Lot and Garonne unite to maintain this institution, each establishing scholarships in it for its own students. The director has been very successful, and has recently been rewarded with the decoration of the Legion of

* In 1859 there were in France seventy normal schools for laymen, with 2,750 students in training in them. There were thirty-four normal institutions for the training of lay schoolmistresses; but the Department of Public Instruction possesses no returns of the present number of students in these. There are, besides, the noviciates in which the religious are trained.

Homon. In his training school there are fifty-one students. The course is now for three years, having previously to 1851 been for two years only: and considering that the students arrive quite without the previous training of the pupil teachers by whom our normal schools are peopled, considering that they often have almost everything to learn, three years is not a longer period than is required to form them. The students whom I saw were certainly more rustic and undeveloped than ours; later in life the experience of the world and the natural quickness of their race enable them to present themselves with at least as much advantage as our schoolmasters. Most of them are the sons of country teachers; hardly any of them were town-bred. The class of the third year, consisting of thirteen students, was receiving a mathematical lecture when I visited the institution. They do not go far in mathematics; no student in the institution was advanced as high as quadratic equations, no student was reading Euclid; they were taught, however, the elements of practical geometry. The object is to teach them what is needed for a primary school; the programme of the normal college exactly corresponds to the programme of the primary school; the student is not allowed to pass, at the end of his first year, from the obligatory matters of primary instruction to the facultative, unless he has given proof of his thorough knowledge of the former, and not of his knowledge of them merely, but also of his skill to teach them. The teaching of *method*;—it is on this that circular after circular of the Minister * insists, it is

* "Ne les excitez pas à sortir de ce cercle (that of the *obligatory* "part of primary instruction) qui est encore assez vaste, et faites en "sorte que ceux qui le franchiront cèdent à des dispositions naturelles . .

on this that the reports of the commissioners who superintend normal schools perpetually dilate, it is to this that principals and lecturers address all their efforts. Practising schools are annexed to each training college, and in them the French students pass a great deal of their time; much more, in proportion to that spent in the lecture-room, than ours. And with what success? Undoubtedly, a knowledge of method is of the highest importance to the schoolmaster; *donner c'est acquérir*, says a French poet most truly; to teach is to learn; and to give a man, therefore, the power of teaching well is to give him the power of learning much. Undoubtedly, too, the attention to method in the French training schools has resulted in the establishment of improved modes of teaching particular subjects; the teaching of arithmetic, for instance, the teaching of reading, have been facilitated and simplified. Yet I doubt whether, in all this zeal for method, in this exclusive thought for the bare needs of the primary school, in this jealous apprehension lest the normal college pupil should become more of a student than a schoolmaster, the range of study has not been made unduly narrow, and a risk incurred of developing the student's mental power so insufficiently that he will be thoroughly effective neither as student nor schoolmaster. The question is a most difficult one: I have little doubt that we in England have fallen into the contrary extreme; that we crowd so much and so

"et non à des prétentions peu justifiées. À vrai dire, ce qui fait le "véritable instituteur, ce n'est pas le brevet, que tout le monde peut "conquérir, c'est l'art de diriger les esprits et la pratique de l'éducation." — *Instruction générale sur les Attributions des Recteurs concernant l'Instruction primaire*, by M. Fortoul; October 31st, 1854.

various book-learning into our normal school course that the student, unless a very able man indeed, is left at the end of it stupefied rather than developed; not in the condition of one trained to bring, for all his future work, his faculties into full and easy play, but of one crammed so full and so fast, that, in order to begin his real intellectual life, he must, like Themistocles, seek to learn how to forget. Perhaps, in this matter of normal school training, as in others, common sense, usually the last voice suffered to make itself heard, will be heard at last; will suggest some middle way between the tenuity of the French programme and the extravagance of ours; will devise, for the future masters of our village-schools, some course which neither stints them to the beggarly elements of reading and writing, nor occupies them with the differential calculus and the pedigree of Sesostris.

The staff of a French training school consists of a director, two lecturers, and a chaplain. The director is personally charged with the main part of the tuition. The system of accounts is very exact, and rigidly inspected; so vast and complicated is the machine of public instruction that it can be kept from falling into disorder only by perfect precision on the part of its lower functionaries, and, on the part of the Minister, by unsparing severity to irregularities. The economy of the Bordeaux establishment was austere; the students all slept in one vast common dormitory, but the neatness and cleanliness, in France so far better practised in public establishments than in private, were exemplary. The dietary is regulated by a ministerial decree. Students of the first year pay from their own resources 100 francs, one fourth of the yearly charge of a student here*;

* The annual value of an entire scholarship, or student's fee, is in no French training school higher than 1000 fr., in none lower than [illegible]00 fr.

after the first year and the examination which follows it the best students complete their training free of charge, the rest continue to pay their fourth. About one-third of the whole number are thus free students. The department supplies the funds for the whole or partial scholarships thus bestowed. A good garden is attached to the establishment; and lessons in horticulture and agriculture, an idle pretence in most of the elementary schools which profess them, are in most of the normal schools of France a reality, and are greatly enjoyed by the students.

Under the legislation of M. Guizot, the admission to normal schools was by competitive examination. In the suspicion which fell on these establishments in 1848, not only the competitive examination, but all examination at entrance, was abolished; and the prefect in departmental council admitted candidates by his own nomination, on their production of certificates of morality and good conduct. It was soon found that candidates who could produce excellent certificates of morality often turned out utterly incapable students.* The normal schools gradually recovered themselves in public estimation, and the jealousy of their over-ambitious studies abated. The Minister, M. Fortoul, found himself constrained to re-establish some examination at entrance†; but that which he instituted was no longer competitive, and bore only on the most elementary branches of knowledge. This examination still subsists; it is conducted

* "Beaucoup arrivaient possédant à peine les premiers éléments de l'instruction, et nullement préparés pour suivre avec fruit les cours de l'école. Il en résultait un affaiblissement des études dangereux pour l'avenir de l'instruction primaire." — *Manuel de Législation et d'Administration de l'Instruction primaire*, p. 157.

† See his circular to the rectors, February 2nd, 1855.

by the academy inspector of the district, and excludes from the normal school the utterly incompetent. Those who pass it successfully, who are not less than eighteen years old and not more than twenty-two, who produce good certificates of conduct, and who take an engagement to continue for at least ten years in the service of public primary instruction, are then, as before, nominated by the prefect if he thinks fit, within the limits of the numbers fixed by the Minister for each normal school. It is the prefect, also, who nominates to scholarships and to portions of scholarships on the favourable report of the *Commission de Surveillance*, which, named by the rector on the proposition of the departmental council, has in each normal school the special charge of the discipline and progress of the students. A student who at the end of the year is judged unfit to pass to the course of the following year, is discharged* from the training school.

The training school examinations are not those which determine the award of the certificate of capacity. To adjudge these, there sits twice a year, in the chief town of every department, an examination commission† named by the departmental council, and consisting of seven members, of whom one must be a primary inspector of the department, one a minister of the same religious persuasion as the candidate, and two functionaries of public or private instruction. The examination, like the normal school course, is limited to the programme of primary school instruction. Any person

* The prefect dismisses, *sur l'avis du directeur, la commission de surveillance entendue*. See *Décret du 26 Décembre* 1855, Art. 24, 25.

† Law of March 15th, 1850, Art. 46. Regulated by a ministerial arrêté of February 15th, 1850.

aged not less than eighteen years may appear as a candidate, giving a month's notice of such intention. The examination is oral and written. Exercises in dictation and grammar, handwriting, the four rules of arithmetic (including vulgar and decimal fractions), and in the composition of a narrative or a school-report, are performed by the candidates. For each of these four exercises is allowed a space of time not exceeding three-quarters of an hour. The commission collects and judges these written exercises; the candidate who has failed in them is not allowed to continue his examination any further. Those who have performed them satisfactorily are called up in turn before the commission, and examined orally in reading, religious knowledge, grammar, and arithmetic. The religious examination is always conducted by the minister of the candidate's own persuasion. A quarter of an hour is allowed for each of these oral exercises, and the proper certificate-examination is concluded.*

Those who desire to be examined in all or any of the optional or *facultative* branches of primary instruction, now make known their wishes. A candidate who has passed the obligatory examination with difficulty is not allowed to be examined any further. The others are examined in those subjects which they select. Teachers who have obtained the simple certificate on a former occasion may present themselves for examination in the facultative subjects; but they must take all of them. In each subject the examination is oral, and lasts but a quarter of an hour. When all is concluded, the com-

* Women-candidates are also examined in needlework by ladies delegated for this office by the rector. The oral examination of men is public, that of women private.

missioners draw up a list, in order of merit, of the candidates who have satisfied them; if they differ in opinion respecting a candidate, the majority decides. This list is then forwarded to the rector, who issues the certificate. There is but one grade of certificate; but on the simple instrument is entered a special mention of those facultative subjects in which the candidate may have elected to be examined, and of the degree of satisfaction which he has given to the examiners.

Fortified with this document, the future teacher, if a member of a religious association, awaits his appointment to a public school of his order by the prefect, on the presentation of his superior. If a layman, he has his name entered on the list of admissibility*, drawn up yearly for each department by the departmental council, and from which the prefect makes his nominations to lay schools. This list contains notes respecting each name borne on it, and here the students of normal schools reap the benefit of favourable reports on their ability and conduct by the commission of their normal school.

The legislation of 1850, in its hostility to the normal schools and their high training, provided† that a *certificate of stage*, issued by the departmental council to persons who had taught satisfactorily for three years as assistants in public schools authorised to receive them, might henceforth replace the certificate of capacity. This certificate of stage involved no examination, and its introduction threatened to lower the standard of attainment in public teachers. Happily few departmental

* Decree of October 7th, 1850, Art. 13.

† Law of March 15th, 1850, Art. 47.

councils consented to authorise any *stagiary schools* at all; in the few departments where they were established, they proved failures, and they have now been generally abandoned. At the present moment, for the chief teachers of the public schools in France, the obligation of the certificate may be said to be universal.*

I fear I may have wearied the general reader by these details, but for English inspectors and schoolmasters they will not, I think, be without interest. I will remind these, if they are disposed to make light of such an examination as I have described, that the French certificate is not a prize, but an obligation; that it carries no money with it; that it is a negative not a positive test of merit. I will remind our Privy Council Office that it is greatly to be doubted whether, if the State imposes the certificate-test on the whole body of its schoolmasters, the negative form be not the most advisable, and even the sole possible. When the test is of this kind, it will generally happen, as I found in the French schools, that the pitch of the master's instruction to his best scholars is higher than that of his certificate examination. So too, in England, the pitch of a master's instruction, in the upper forms of Rugby or Harrow, is higher than that of the bare degree examination obligatory upon himself. But in our elementary schools the whole instruction is pitched immeasurably below

* In lieu of the regular certificate, the law accepts, besides the certificate of stage above mentioned, the diploma of bachelor of arts, the certificate of entrance from one of the *écoles spéciales*, and the title of actual minister of one of the recognised religious persuasions.—Law of March 15th, 1850. Ministers of religion hardly ever in France become primary schoolmasters; and the degree of bachelor, or the certificate of entrance into an *école spéciale*, involves a much severer examination than the regular certificate of capacity.

the scale of attainment demanded as indispensable from our certificated masters; and every stranger who had read our teachers' examination questions, would inevitably be disappointed in our elementary schools. In truth, we impose an examination for honours as our schoolmasters' only access to a bare degree.

CHAPTER XIII.

THE POPULAR EDUCATION OF FRANCE AND ENGLAND COMPARED. LEGISLATION.

I HAVE now briefly to sum up the main points of the French system; and I will then in conclusion attempt, although with great diffidence, to give some estimate of its effects upon the French people.

First, then, with respect to a question which meets every system of education upon the threshold — the great question, shall it be secular, or shall it be religious? The French system is religious; not in the sense in which all systems profess to be more or less religious, in inculcating the precepts of a certain universal and indisputable morality: it inculcates the doctrines of morality in the only way in which the masses of mankind ever admit them, in their connection with the doctrines of religion. I believe that the French system is right. When I come to speak of Holland I shall have more to say of this matter, and shall perhaps be able to give some important information concerning it; at present I content myself with saying that this side the French system has chosen. Here it coincides with the systems of England and Germany. Morality—but dignified, but sublimed by being taught in connection with religious sentiment; but legalised, but empowered by being taught in connection with religious dogma — this is what the French system makes the indispensable basis of its primary instruction.

But what dogma? Secular education is one; it would be well if religious education could be one also. It would be well, unquestionably, if there reigned everywhere one truly catholic religious faith, embracing all the faithful in a common bond. But the spirit of sect exists; it has committed its ravages; it is necessary to take account of them. Forcibly to repress it is impossible, except by evoking a spirit more noxious than even the spirit of sect — the spirit of religious persecution. But the French system does not seek divisions; it accepts those that are radical, irreconcilable. All minor shades of division that are not incurably separate, that may without violence to their nature combine, it leaves to combine, it does not deepen by distinguishing them. Protestantism and Roman Catholicism, the great rival systems of authority and inquiry;—Judaism, inveterate in its fated isolation; these it recognises as necessary, irreconcilable, religious divisions in a modern State of Western Europe. It recognises these, but it recognises no other. In an empire of thirty-six millions it recognises no other.

Here the English system diverges. In Great Britain, in a population of 21,000,000, it recognises no less than seven religious incompatibilities. If it followed the French example, it would accept, as denominations essentially distinct, at most only Anglicanism, non-Anglican Protestantism, Roman Catholicism, Judaism. As it is, it distinguishes Anglican Protestantism, the Biblicalism of the British and Foreign School Society, the Protestantism of Wesleyan Methodism, the Protestantism of the Orthodox Church of Scotland, the Protestantism of the Free Church of Scotland, the Pro testantism of the Episcopalian Church of Scotland, and Roman Catholicism.*

But the divergence does not stop here. The French system recognises certain religious divisions in the population; but it does not divide itself in order to meet them. It maintains its own unity, its own impartiality; in their relations with the State, with the civil power, all denominations have to meet upon a common ground; the State does not make itself denominational, they have to make themselves national. When the Concordat was under discussion, neither supplication nor adroitness could prevail with Napoleon to give to the State itself an exclusive denominational character; he steadily refused to call the Roman Catholic religion the religion of the State; he would only consent to call it, what it undoubtedly was, the religion of the majority of the French nation. State-inspection represents the unity of the civil power, not the divisions of rival sects. It takes care that children learn, in the public schools, each the doctrines of his own religion; but it protects each, in learning these, from the intolerance of the other, and itself remains neutral, that it may check intolerance the better. The State, therefore, owes no account to any man of the religious persuasion of its inspectors: for it is not as religious sectaries they have to discharge their duties, but as civil servants; and the moment they begin to discharge them as religious sectaries, they discharge them ill.

In England the State makes itself denominational with the denominations. It offers to them no example of a civil unity in which religious divisions are lost;

* We have an eighth class of schools in Poor-law Union Schools; but here the distinction (though perhaps needless), is at any rate based on administrative, not on religious, grounds.

in which they meet as citizens, though estranged as sectaries. It makes its inspectors Anglican with the Anglicans, Roman Catholic with the Roman Catholics, Orthodox Presbyterian with the Old Church of Scotland, Free Church with the New. It does not hold itself aloof from the religious divisions of the population; it enters into them.

What has been the result? By dint of concession to the denominational spirit, by dint of not maintaining an impartial and unsectarian character, the State, in England, has been betrayed into a thousand anomalies, and has created a system far more irritating to sectarian susceptibilities than if it had regarded none of them. More than four fifths of the population of France profess Roman Catholicism, and about one three hundredth part of French inspection is in the hands of Roman Catholic ecclesiastics. One half of the population of England profess Anglicanism, and more than three-fourths of English inspection is in the hands of Anglican ecclesiastics. I heard the other day of an English National school aided by public money, the only school in the place, which had for one of its regulations that no child of dissenting parents should be admitted unless he consented to be rebaptized. I saw with my own eyes, the other day, in a British school aided by public money, a printed placard stuck up in a conspicuous place in the schoolroom, offering a reward of 10*l.* to any Roman Catholic who could prove, by text, ten propositions; such as, that we ought to adore the Virgin Mary, that we ought to pray for the dead, that St. Peter was unmarried, that he ever was Bishop of Rome, and so on. Is it tolerable that such antics should be played in schools on which the grant of public money confers a public character? Would it be possible that they should be played in a public school in France, where the State permits liberty of conscience, but not liberty of persecution? But it is said that the State, in England, has bound itself not to interfere with the management of the schools which it aids. True; but whom does this answer excuse? It excuses the functionaries who administer the system, not the State which made and maintains it. No State has the right thus to shackle its own reason and its own equity.

The French system, having undertaken to put the means of education within its people's reach, has to provide schools and teachers. Here, again, it altogether diverges from ours, which has by no means undertaken to put the means of education within the people's reach, but only to make the best and richest elementary schools better and richer. Should it ever undertake what the French system has undertaken, perhaps it is in the plan for the provision of schools that it will find its predecessor happiest. Where everything is left to be done by voluntary effort, schools where most needed are not established at all. Where everything, again, is left to be done by the State, there is wasteful extravagance and local apathy. Where everything, finally, is left to be done by the parish, there is niggardly pinching. I read the other day that in Canada the great difficulty in the rating system there followed is that the local boards starve their schools. The French plan places its schools chiefly, but not absolutely, in the hands of local boards; it tempers the parsimony of the parish with the more liberal views of the central power; and between the parish contributor and the State contributor it places a third contributor of less narrow spirit than the first, of more economical spirit than the second,—the Department or County.

I am bound to add, however, that in one most important particular, its provision for teachers, the French system has recoiled, through fear of expense, from making adequate use of the machinery at its disposal. The best authorities are all agreed that the fixed salary of the teacher was put by the law of 1833 too low, and that the law of 1850 ought to have raised it directly, instead of attempting, in a circuitous manner, to provide a palliative for its insufficiency. At present the lay teachers tend to quit their profession as soon as they can for some more profitable career; if it were not for the inducement offered by the exemption from military service, it would be difficult to recruit their ranks. It is in vain that the State offers to them the lure of honourable mentions, medals of bronze and of silver*, and even the rank of academic officer, with the privilege of wearing an official coat with a palm embroidered on the collar†: these public distinctions to the teacher are excellent, but they are of no avail so long as he is utterly underpaid.

The State has provided schools and teachers; under what authority shall it place them? Of inspection, the great guarantee of efficiency, it has abundance; it has first inspectors-general, then rectors and academy inspectors, then primary inspectors, then cantonal delegates, then the parish authorities, the mayor and the minister of the persuasion followed by the scholars. But what authority shall give effect to the representations of all this inspection? Local school committees, said the law of 1833; rectors of academies, representing the Department of Public Instruction, said the law

* In the year 1857 (the latest for which I have any returns), the sum spent by the State on medals for teachers was 2728 fr. 70 c.

† *Décret du 9 Décembre* 1850.

of 1852; the prefect, representing the Home Department, says the present law. The local school-committees had undoubtedly performed their work ill. Perhaps in England a well-chosen county committee might safely be intrusted with the functions which in France, under the law of 1833, the district committee performed so unsatisfactorily; but to give them to the more narrowly local body, to the communal committee, to the parish vestry, would be to destroy your school-system, however promising. The Canadian report which I just now quoted says that another of the great difficulties with which the public school-system of Canada has to contend, is the utter unfitness of the local school-commissioners for their functions. To superintend the actual expenditure of money voted, to inspect, and to report to a higher authority, is the proper province of the parochial committee. It cannot safely be trusted with full powers over the teacher. The most liberal persons in France consider it proved, by the working of the law of 1833, that, for public schools, it is expedient to give the ultimate power of confirming or dismissing the teacher to some central authority. With us, indeed, the central Government has no power to get rid of a schoolmaster, the most destructive or the most negligent. It can dismiss a school inspector, but it cannot dismiss a school teacher. Our system provides its chief educational shepherd with abundant resources against his own watch-dogs; with none against the wolf. In France, the local committees no longer retain powers which they showed themselves unfit to exercise. But from the local committees to the prefect is a prodigious step. The prefect and the Home Department, stern authorities of police and public order, are scarcely the proper authorities for dealing with schools and teachers, unless some actual breach of the law has been committed. The Ministry of Public Instruction, with its academies and rectors, is in some sort a literary department of State; and with this character it has something of the humanity of letters. The teachers themselves would prefer the government of the rector to that of the prefect. It is true that the prefect generally acts on the advice of the rector's representative, the academy-inspector; but the rector himself, and the Minister his superior, are much the fittest persons to act upon this advice, and would act upon it with quite sufficient stringency.

The machinery of French inspection is perhaps a little redundant. It is found impossible to obtain from the cantonal delegates, unpaid and with occupations of their own, that regular intervention in the details of primary instruction which the Government solicits from them. Possibly, if they gave it, it might be found to bring with it as many difficulties as advantages. A general supervision, with the office of keeping the higher school authorities informed, so that the teacher may feel that neither his efforts nor his negligence escape notice,—this is, perhaps, all that can be judiciously asked of the local authorities, or that they can properly give. All above the cantonal delegates is excellent. The primary inspectors are the very life of the school system; their inspection is a reality, because made when not expected: the Nancy inspector who went round the schools of that town with me, had a pass-key by which he let himself into any one of them when he pleased, and he told me that he entered every public school in the town fifty times in the year. The academy-inspectors, receiving the reports of the primary inspectors, and themselves in connection with the sixteen academies of France, supply local centres for dealing with the mass of details received from the primary inspectors and thus relieve the central office in Paris. The four inspectors-general, in personal communication with the school-authorities, the primary inspectors, and the Minister, preserve the latter from the danger of falling a victim to the routine of his own bureaux, while he also obtains from four picked and superior men a unity of appreciation of school-matters which he would seek for in vain from the 275 primary inspectors, chosen necessarily with less advantage of selection. If I were asked to name the four deficiencies most unanimously remarked in our system by the most competent foreign judges whom I met, they would be these:—first, the want of district-centres for managing the current details of school business, and the consequent inundation of our London office with the whole of them; secondly, the inconceivable prohibition to our primary inspectors to inspect without previous notice; thirdly, the denial of access into the ranks of the primary inspectors to the most capable public schoolmasters; fourthly, and above all, the want of inspectors-general.

Having established schools with due safeguards, does the French system compel the children of France to enter them? It does not; in France, education is not compulsory. A few advocates for making it so I met with; but, in the opinion of most of those with whom I conversed, the difficulties are insuperable. Perhaps, for a government to be able to force its people to school, that people must either be generally well-off, as in America; or placid and docile, as in Germany; or ardently desirous of knowledge, as in Greece. But the masses in France, like the masses in England, are by no means well-off, are stirring and self-willed, are not the least in the world bookish. The gradual rise in their wealth and comfort is the only obligation which can be safely relied on to draw such people to school. What Government can do, is to provide sufficient and proper schools to receive them as they arrive.

CHAPTER XIV.

THE POPULAR EDUCATION OF FRANCE AND ENGLAND COMPARED. RESULTS ON THE PEOPLE.

In what numbers has the population yet, in France, actually arrived in the public schools? What proportion of it remains wholly untaught? What sort of education do those who are taught carry away with them? These are questions which, as I have already said, cannot all of them at present be satisfactorily answered. I believe, however, that the great mass of the population now passes, at some time or other, through the schools. It is an indisputable fact that the attendance in the schools for adults has been for some time falling off, because the actual adult population has grown up in possession of the elementary knowledge which these schools offer. It is a great thing that the primary schools do actually exist almost everywhere in France; they are there, they are always at the population's service, without long journeys, without high fees, without unjust conditions. It is something that the demand for children's labour is as yet considerably less in agricultural France than in manufacturing England. But I should be deceiving the reader if I led him to suppose that the French people exhibits any real ardour in seeking education for its children, or that the bait of the gain to be drawn from his child's labour is, when offered, one whit better resisted by a French than by an English parent. Nay, in the great manufacturing region of France, in the Department of the North*, public opinion and positive law prove far less powerful than in England to contend with the cupidity of the employer, the necessities of the employed. The French law prescribes that the child's day, in a manufactory, shall be of ten hours; the law is not observed; the child works habitually for twelve. Of these ten hours the law commands that two at least shall be given to schooling: when these two hours are given at all, the master habitually makes the child's day, already of twelve hours in defiance of the law, of fourteen hours, in order not to lose the time taken for schooling. In hardly any of the manufactories is there a school for the children employed.† In the towns without great manufactures, and in the agricultural districts, more children do, I believe, attend school than in similar places in England. But even these attend very irregularly, and are very easily withdrawn: there are just

* Even from the well educated Alsace the inspectors report that the public schools are far too few in number, and that the manufacturers employ children in defiance of the law. But in the Gard I found that the manufacturers [illegible] very generally established schools for their workmen's children. There are very good schools of this kind at Nîmes. They are private schools, [illegible] and the schooling is free; some of the children are [illegible], as they do not go to work till they are fourteen. The teachers are well paid, receiving 70l. or 80l. a year; and the best teachers [illegible] the public schools to take charge of these [illegible] private [illegible].

† I have great pleasure in saying that M. Mason mentioned to me, as a signal exception, a manufactory at Coudekerke Branche, near Dunkirk, belonging to [illegible], in which there is an excellent school for both the girls and the boys employed in the establishment.

the same complaints from the French inspectors as from the English, of the desertion of schools in summer and autumn. I have looked through the returns, for a number of departments, of the declarations made by conscripts when drawn for the army, as to their own ability to read and write; the number of those declaring themselves unable to do either is remarkable*, and contrasts strangely with the alleged attendance of the primary schools. It is true that conscripts show almost always an impulse, upon these occasions, to cheapen themselves as much as possible, and to acknowledge nothing which may make them more eligible objects for a service which they try to escape. Officers have assured me that men often turned out to be able to read and write perfectly well, who when drawn had declared themselves incapable of doing either. But it is true, also, that many a peasant-boy does actually lose

* Even here, however, there is progress. In the Drôme (academy of Grenoble) 12 per cent. of the conscripts drawn in 1842 declared themselves unable to read and write; of those drawn in 1855, only 26 per cent. In the Aube (academy of Dijon) the conscripts declaring themselves unable to read and write were 21 per cent. in 1845, 13 per cent. in 1854. In the Haute Marne (in the same academy-district) they were 27 per cent. in 1828, only 7 per cent. in 1855. In the Doubs (academy of Besançon) they were, even in 1837, but 6 per cent.; in 1855 they were 3 per cent. In the Haute Saone, 21 per cent. in 1835, 9 per cent. in 1855. In the district of the Academy of Paris, there were drawn in 1835, for the department of the Eure and Loir, 738 conscripts unable to read and write; in 1855, 522. For the Seine and Marne, 727 in 1835, 380 in 1855.

Even in the most backward part of the Paris district, the department of the Cher, the number of schools has more than doubled in the last twenty years, the number of scholars more than tripled; the number of girl-scholars has sextupled. In the most backward department of all France, the Nievre, the number of inhabitants able to read and write is declared to have nearly tripled in the twenty years from 1835 to 1855.

all his school learning between the day when he leaves school, and the day when he is drawn for the army; he is not the least studious by nature, and his class are not the least studious; they have an incorrigible preference for the knowledge to be acquired at the cabaret, at the village-ball, in the great world, over that to be acquired in solitude and from books. Even when fully retained, the instruction carried away from a French primary school is also, undoubtedly, most elementary; although, as I have before said, not quite so elementary as one who merely reads the programme in the law would think*, and although not, in my opinion, more elementary than, at present, the instruction offered by a state like France or like England to all its people, ought to be and must be. Still, unquestionably, as regards the actual school learning of the French peasant, the merit of the French system is more in its probable future than in its actual past or present:—the schools are there.

Yet—and I now come to the last of the topics which I undertook to treat—I am convinced that, small as may be the result yet produced in actual school learning by the school legislation of France, the result which it has produced upon the temper and intelligence of the population has not been unimportant. But I shall have need of all the reader's indulgence while I attempt to exhibit this important but somewhat impalpable result.

* Taking at hazard 120 communal schools in the department of the Haute Garonne, I found that, of the optional matters of primary instruction, history and geography were taught in 37 of them, geometry in 28, drawing in 24, singing in 19, physical science in 1, agriculture in none. Much is said in France about agricultural instruction for the elementary and normal schools; but up to the present time next to nothing has been done.

The intelligence of the French people is well known; in spite of their serious faults, in spite of their almost incredible ignorance, it places them among the very foremost of ancient or modern nations. It is the source of their highest virtue, (for the bravery of this people is rather a physical than a moral virtue), of a certain natural equity of spirit in matters where most other nations are intolerant and fanatical. I suppose that this intelligence is a thing not altogether peculiar and innate in the people of France; if it were, the upper classes, adding high culture to this exclusive natural gift, would exhibit over the upper classes of other nations a superiority of which they certainly have not given proof. If it is culture which developes this intelligence in the higher ranks of all nations, then of some culture or other the French masses, in spite of their want of book-learning, must be feeling the beneficent operation, if they show an intelligence which the masses of other nations do not possess. This culture they do actually receive; many influences are at work in France which tend to impart it to them; amongst these influences I number their school-legislation.

This works partly by its form, partly by its spirit. By its form it educates the national intelligence, no otherwise than as all French legislation tends thus to educate it; but even this is worth noticing. It is not a light thing that the law, which speaks to all men, should speak an intelligible human language, and speak it well. Reason delights in rigorous order, lucid clearness, and simple statement. Reason abhors devious intricacy, confused obscurity, and prolix repetition. It is not unimportant to the reason of a nation, whether the form and text of its laws present the characters which reason delights in, or the characters which reason abhors. Certainly the text of an English Act of Parliament never carried to an uneducated English mind anything but bewilderment. I have myself heard a French peasant quote the Code Napoleon; it is in every one's hands; it is its rational form, hardly less than its rational spirit, that the Code has to thank for a popularity which makes half the nations of Europe desirous to adopt it. If English law breathed in its spirit the wisdom of angels, its form would make it to foreign nations inaccessible. The style and diction of all the modern legislation of France are the same as those of the Code. Let the English reader compare, in their style and diction alone, M. Guizot's education law, printed at the end of this volume, with the well known bill of a most sincere and intelligent friend of English education, Sir John Pakington. Certainly neither was the French law drawn by M. Guizot himself, nor the English bill by Sir John Pakington; each speaks the current language of its national legislation. But the French law, (with a little necessary formality, it is true,) speaks the language of modern Europe, the English bill speaks the language of the Middle Ages, and speaks it ill. I assert that the rational intelligible speech of this great public voice of her laws has a directly favourable effect upon the general reason and intelligence of France.

From the form I pass to the spirit. With still more confidence I say—It is not a light thing for the reason and equity of a nation that her laws should boldly utter prescriptions which are reasonable and equitable. It is not a light thing for the spread, among the French masses, of a wise and moderate spirit on the vital and vexed questions of religion and education, that the law of 1833 should say firmly, *Le vœu des pères de famille sera toujours consulté et suivi en ce qui concerne la* *participation de leurs enfants à l'instruction religieuse.* It is not a light thing that the whole body of modern French legislation on these critical questions should hold a language equally firm, equally liberal. To this it is owing that in a sphere where the popular cry, in other countries, either cannot be relied on or is sure to be wrong, there exists in France a genial current of sound public opinion, blowing steadily in the right quarter. To this it is owing that from dangers which perpetually thwart and threaten intellectual growth in other countries, intellectual growth in France is comparatively secure. To this, finally, it is owing that even on questions beyond this sphere—if they assume a sufficient generality and do not demand a large knowledge of particular facts, of which the mass of Frenchmen is deplorably ignorant — the habit of intelligence continues in the French people to be active and to enlighten. It is with truth that M. Guizot says in his latest work: "C'est la grandeur de notre pays que *les esprits ont besoin d'être satisfaits en même temps que les intérêts.*"*

I wish to make perfectly clear to the reader what I mean. I am by no means praising the whole legislation of the French State. I am by no means praising the general principle of action by which the State, in France, has been guided. There are many points on which it has not informed its people at all; there are many points on which it has informed them ill. It is possible (this is a fair matter for discussion), that, even although on some points it has informed them well, it may have made them pay for that information too high a price. What I say is, that on certain capital points the State in France has by its legislation and administration exercised a directly educative influence upon the reason and equity of

* *Mémoires*, vol. ii. p. 235.

its people*, and that of this influence the mental temper of the French people does actually show the fruits.

It would be an interesting, but far too lengthy task, to inquire into the causes which have prevented the State, in England, from performing these educative functions for the intelligence of its people. The State in England has shown neither taste nor aptitude for the practice of government as a profound and elaborate art; it has done what was absolutely indispensable, and has left its people to do the rest, if it could, for itself.

Its people has willingly acquiesced in a non-interference agreeable to its independent spirit, and in great measure imposed by its mistrust. Doubtless, the vigour of the national character has under this state of things greatly benefited. Yet it has its inconveniences. The State in England administers so little, so much dreads the suspicion of undue usurpation, that, when occasionally called upon to administer on a great scale, it finds its organism cramped by disuse and apprehension; it

* To give a curious practical instance. In Corsica, the condition of the woman had for years been that of a mere beast of burden. In order to raise it, the French Government determined to put the elementary schools of the island in her hands. Under M. Fortoul's administration a normal school for young women was established at Ajaccio, and 18,000 francs a year granted for its support. Wherever it was possible, the charge of the primary school was given to a mistress. At first the men strenuously resisted for their children the degradation of being taught by that inferior creature, a woman; but the Government stood firm. Women are now established in charge of a great number of the schools of Corsica, and the consideration and respect paid to the sex has notably increased.

Again: Corsican vengeance is proverbial. In the hope of creating in the young generation a better sentiment, the Government has, in all the schools of the island, covered the walls with texts inculcating forgiveness of injuries, and against private revenge.

moves as a man, whose limbs had been bound for years, would move when first set free and told to walk. The people, with no help from a power greater than its own, with no suggestions from an intelligence higher than its own, fails in functions for which the intelligence and power of an ordinary individual are not sufficient. How often one is forced to say of it, when one sees it attempting these functions, that it seems, *propter* libertatem libertatis *perdere causas*;— to have won the mechanism of free institutions through its energy, to lack the means of turning them to good account through its ignorance! How often may one observe, in any local community in England, that almost everything which individual energy has to do, is well done; almost everything which the collective reason of the community has to do, is ill done! Still, there are some remarkable instances in which, even in England, the national intelligence has been positively influenced by the action of Government. The legislation of free trade—at first established, not in virtue of an irresistible national conviction, but by the initiative of a great Minister and by the exertions of an active party which, though numerous and intelligent, was still a party—has ended by itself creating in its own favour that national sentiment which it did not find, and by educating public opinion on political economy in a sense which the best judges pronounce sound, and to a height to which the public opinion of no other nation has yet been educated. But matters of trade and commerce concern the direct material interests of a nation. With these every government must perforce deal; and here, besides, the English State is on a ground which it imagines solid and secure. With the moral and spiritual interests of a nation, governments find themselves less imperiously called to deal; and here, besides, the English State is on a ground which it imagines shifting and unsafe. It deals with them as little as it can; it sometimes deals with them as if it was the organ of the popular clamour which shouts one thing to-day and another to-morrow; it hardly ever deals with them as if it was *the organ of the national reason.*

It even appears unconscious or incredulous that on these matters a national reason exists. It treats all opinions as of an equal value, and seems to think that the irrational, if expressed as loudly as the rational, must weigh with it as much. It seems not to believe that an opinion has any inherent weakness by virtue of being absurd; or that, in confronting it, the strength of superior reason is really any strength at all. Its proceedings in this respect are in very remarkable contrast with those of the State in France. I will give an example of what I mean, and to find it I will not go beyond the subject of education.

In dealing with education, a government must often meet with questions on which there are two opposite opinions, and both rational. If it is wise, it will invariably treat such opinions with due respect, and will be guided, in deciding between them, by the character of the times, the state of the circumstances, the dispositions of its people. Shall public education be in the hands of the clergy or in the hands of the laity?—shall the instruction given in primary schools be exclusively secular, or shall it be also religious?—here are two questions, upon each of which opposite opinions, both having a ground of reason, may fairly be maintained. In inclining to either, in abandoning its own inclinations on the side of either, a government may be taking a course which reason sanctions; at any rate it is giving victory or defeat to arguments of which reason can take cognisance. The national intelligence can at least follow it in its operations. But a government, in dealing with education, will also sometimes meet with opinions which have no ground in reason, which are mere crotchets, or mere prejudices, or mere passions. Will it have the clearness of vision to discern whether they are such, or the courage, if they are, to treat them as such?—that is the question. Will it encourage and illuminate the national intelligence by firmly treating what is unintelligent as unintelligent, what is fanatical as fanatical, in spite of the loudness with which it may be clamoured? or will it wound and baffle and confuse the national intelligence by treating what is unintelligent as if it were intelligent, as if it were a real power, as respectfully to be parleyed with, as possible to be inclined to, as reason herself. The reader will be conscious that the State has sometimes followed, in England, the latter course.

It will be rejoined, I know, that in France the State is absolute, and can crush alike unreason or reason as it pleases. But this is an error. Among the many remarkable words recorded of the first Napoleon, none are more remarkable than those in which, on more than one occasion, he pointed out the limits to the power of the State in France, the limits even to a power such as his own. Of representative institutions, he said, he might allow as little as he pleased; after the anarchy of the Revolution, the nation was demanding a strong government. With the spirit of revolution, with the spirit of reaction, with all party-spirit, he might, with firmness, deal as he pleased; priestly intolerance, Voltairian intolerance, he was strong enough to disregard; only one force even *he* was not strong enough to disregard, and that was a great force of rational and respectable sentiment in the mass of the French people. Happy for him had he always remembered his own words! Happy if he had not pursued an extravagant and personal policy till he made all the rational sentiment of France warmly hostile to him, or coldly indifferent! But what he said is true; it is impossible for the State, in modern France, to go counter to a great current of rational sentiment. It must, in its acts, have its stand upon some ground of reason, and it can afford to treat cheaply only unreason. When a priest demands to rebaptise dissenters admitted to a public school, when a dissenter demands to be exempted from school taxation because it hurts his conscience to help to maintain schools in which may be taught a religion which he dislikes, such pretensions as these the French State treats as phantoms which it may confidently disdain—for they are *irrational.*

I say, then, that by its form and by its contents, by its letter and by its spirit, by its treatment of reason and by its treatment of prejudice, in what it respects and in what it does not respect, the school-legislation of modern France fosters, encourages, and educates the popular intelligence and the popular equity.

This is a great national advantage. But there are some national disadvantages which sometimes flow, or seem to flow, from national education; disadvantages which those who never inquire beyond the school itself are apt to overlook, but which all those to whom schools are interesting mainly as instruments of general civilisation, will certainly desire to find noticed by me. Some alleged disadvantages there are, which, in France as in England, hardly merit discussion. Eminent personages complained to me that already popular education in France was carried so far that society began to be dislocated by it; that the labourer would no longer stay in his field, nor the artisan in his workshop; that every labourer would be an artisan, every artisan a clerk. This is the language which we have all heard so often, from those who think that the development of society can be arrested because a farmer's wife finds it hard to get a cookmaid. It is sufficient to say to those who hold it, that it is vain for them to expect that the lower classes will be kind enough to remain ignorant and unbettered merely for the sake of saving them inconvenience. But there are other disadvantages which are more serious. I say boldly, that an English or a French statesman might well hesitate to establish an elaborate system of national education, if it were proved to him that the necessary result of such a system must be to produce certain effects which have accompanied it elsewhere—to Prussianise his people or to Americanise it.

I speak with respect of an important nation, which has done great things with small means, and with which rests the future of Germany. To what I say of it, I cannot here give due development; I must leave it to the judgment of the best European observers. But I say that the Prussian people, under its elaborate system of education, has become a studious people, a docile people, a well-informed people, if you will—but also a somewhat pedantic, a somewhat sophisticated people. I say that this pedantry, this formalism, takes away something from a people's vital strength. I say that a people loses under them much of the genial natural character, much of the rude primitive vigour, which are the great elementary force of nations.

I speak with more than respect, with warm interest, of a great nation of English blood, and with which rests, in large measure, the future of the world. With a boundless energy of character, with a boundless field for adventure, the American people has unquestionably not been enervated by education; but under a universal system of comparatively advanced education, without certain correctives, the American people has become an energetic people, a powerful people, a highly-taught people, if you will but also an overweening, a self-conceited people. I say that this self-conceit takes away much from a nation's vital worth. The two grand banes of humanity, says Spinoza, are indolence and self-conceit: self-conceit is so noxious because it arrests man in the career of self improvement; because it vulgarises his character and stops the growth of his intellect. The Greek oracle pronounced wisest of men him who was most convinced of his own ignorance: what, then, can be the wisdom of a nation profoundly convinced of its own attainment? After all that has been said, it remains immutably true that "a little knowledge is a dangerous thing," unless he who possesses it knows that it *is* a little; and that he may know this, it is almost indispensable for him to have before his eyes objects which suggest heights of grandeur, or intellect, or feeling, or refinement, which he has never reached. This is the capital misfortune of the American people, that it is a people which has had to grow up without ideals.

The proud day of priesthoods and aristocracies is over, but in their day they have undoubtedly been, as the law was to the Jews, schoolmasters to the nations of Europe, schoolmasters to bring them to modern society; and so dull a learner is man, so rugged and hard to teach, that perhaps those nations which keep their schoolmasters longest are the most enviable. The great ecclesiastical institutions of Europe, with their stately cathedrals, their imposing ceremonial, their affecting services; the great aristocracies of Europe, with their lustre of descent, their splendour of wealth, their reputation for grace and refinement—have undoubtedly for centuries served as ideals to ennoble and elevate the sentiment of the European masses. Assuredly, churches and aristocracies often lacked the sanctity or the refinement ascribed to them; but their effect as distant ideals was still the same: they remained above the individual, a beacon to the imagination of thousands; they stood, vast and grand objects, ever present before the eyes of masses of men in whose daily avocations there was little which was vast, little which was grand; and they preserved these masses from any danger of overrating with vulgar self-satisfaction an inferior culture, however broadly sown, by the exhibition of a standard of dignity and refinement still far above them.

The masses of the great American people have grown up without this salutary standard. Neither in Church nor in State have they had the spectacle of any august institution before their eyes. The face of the land is covered with a swarm of sects, all of them without dignity, some of them without decency. They have no aristocracy. Accustomed to see nothing grander or more venerable than himself and his fellows, but accustomed to see everywhere a certain mediocre culture diffused with indisputable breadth, the common American, who possesses this, and who sees none higher, grows up with a sense of advantage, which is natural, but also with a sense of perfect self-satisfaction, which is deteriorating. The occasional contact with real superiority finds him half incredulous, half resentful. Thus widely cultured, but thus limited in its culture, and thus unconscious of its limitation, the American people offers a spectacle full of interest, indeed, but inspiring the most grave reflections; — the spectacle of a people which threatens to lose its power of intellectual and moral growth.*

Is it to be apprehended (the question involuntarily arises) that diffused and improved education may possibly make the common people of France and England pedantic like the Prussians, or self-conceited like the Americans? England and France have many safeguards against either danger. Against the first they have ample security in the extraordinary fulness with which both retain, amidst all their civilisation, the activity of what the poet calls "the savage virtues of the race." In both, though manifesting itself in very different forms, is stubbornly operant a constitutional preference for the animal over the intellectual life; excessive in one point of view, indeed, requiring greatly to be tempered by education; but, in another point of view, natural and reassuring. In the figured language of which he is a master, M. Michelet said to me of his own people, that it was a *nation de barbares, civilisée par la conscription.* The civilising influence of the conscription may be matter for question; but there can be no question that the masses, both of the French and of the English people, retain a superabundance of the native and barbarous vigour of

* The above was written at the beginning of last year, when the important events now agitating the American States had not yet occurred.

primitive man, which book-learning may wholesomely temper, but will never vanquish.

Against the second danger the preservatives which England possesses must be evident to every one. The most aristocratic people in the world, as one of the most eloquent of its admirers called it, has naturally the aristocratic virtue of not too easily admiring; it has seen so much which is grand and splendid that it is not likely to be unduly enchanted with a mediocre culture, even when that culture is its own. Democratic France, it might at first sight seem, can have no such safeguards. But it must not be forgotten through what an education of hierarchies and grandeurs the French people has passed. The Revolution is of yesterday; the imagination of the French people was fashioned long before. For more than a thousand years France had the most brilliant aristocracy in Europe; her common people were the countrymen of the Montmorencies, the Birons, the Rohans. She is the eldest child of the Roman Catholic Church, a church magnificent even in its decline. At the present hour, when her feudal magnates are gone, when her ecclesiastical magnates are shorn of their splendour, she has an aristocracy to meet the best demands of the modern spirit — an aristocracy the choicest of its class in the world: she has the Institute. The servility which has degraded the scientific and learned societies of some other nations has, in the French Institute, not been allowed to triumph. It is a true aristocracy of the intellect of France; and, in worthily commanding national respect, where great objects to awaken national respect are rare — in rigidly tempering, in the domain of intellect, science, arts, and letters, the natural self-confidence of a democratic society — in making impossible, for the intelligent French common people, a vulgar and provincial self-satisfaction with a low rate of culture, however general — the blessings which it confers on France are incalculable.

I confess that when I contemplate the probable common immunity of England and France from two of the worst dangers which threaten the future progress of other nations, and when I call to mind other points in which the two peoples have at least an important negative resemblance, the interest with which I regard, in France, the constitution and prospects of a great national agent like popular education, becomes unbounded. The two peoples are alike in this, that they are each greater than all others, each unlike to any other. It is in vain that we call the French Celts, and ourselves Teutons: when nations have attained to the greatness of France and England, their peoples can have no profound identity with any people beyond their own borders. Torrents of pedantry have been poured forth on the subject of our Germanic origin; in real truth, we are at the present day no more Germans than we are Frenchmen. By the mixture of our race, by the Latinisation of our language, by the isolation of our country, by the independence of our history, we have long since severed all vital connection with that great German stem which sixteen centuries ago threw out a shoot in this island. France is equally dissociated, by her own eminence, from her once fellow Celtic or Latin races. It is the same with the greatness of the peoples; each is unique, and has no adequate counterpart but in that of the other. From Messina to Archangel, and from Calais to Moscow, there reigns a universal striving after Parisian civilisation; the ideas which move the masses (I do not speak of aristocratic and learned coteries) are, when ideas reach them at all, French ideas. Cross the Straits and you are in another world: in a world where French ideas have not a breath of influence; in a country assuredly not less powerful than France, assuredly of not less weight among the nations than France, but which owes that power and that weight to a different cause — to its incomparable faculty of extending and of establishing *itself*. Each of the two peoples is alike in its immense national feeling; each is alike, too, in its genuine surprise at the shortcomings of the other. An Englishman is astonished that, in an empire boasting of its civilisation, the newspapers should not be allowed to say, on political matters, what they like; that the private citizen should have no remedy by civil action against the public functionary who exceeds his powers; that he should be without the protection which in England the Habeas Corpus Act affords against arbitrary imprisonment. A Frenchman is astonished that, in an empire boasting of its civilisation, out of funds levied upon the Irish people for the maintenance of religion, the church of the small minority should be endowed, the church of the vast majority receive nothing; that, instead of being equal with the rest of the community before the law, a nobleman who commits a crime is not tried by the same judge as another man; that in the English army an officer, in the nineteenth century, buys his office.

To all these resemblances, which I call negative, the two peoples add the important positive resemblance above mentioned: that of all civilised nations they are incomparably the most natural, while of all unsophisticated nations they are incomparably the most civilised.

Well, then, to two nations thus alike in greatness,

and so constituted that education can only augment their power and worth, what system of education do their Governments offer? In France, a national system, which, though very unpretending, is all that a government can prudently attempt to make universal — a system fixing a low level, certainly, of popular instruction, but one which the mounting tide of national wealth and well-being will inevitably push up higher. And this system is so framed as not only not to favour popular unreason or popular intolerance, but positively to encourage and educate popular reason and popular equity. In England, a system not national, which has undoubtedly done much for superior primary instruction, but which for elementary primary instruction has done very little. That it may accomplish something important for the latter, some have conceived the project of making it national. Against this project there are, it seems to me, grave objections. It is a grave objection, that the system is over centralised — that it is too negligent of local machinery — that it is inordinately expensive. It is a graver, that to make it national would be to make national a system not salutary to the national character in the very points where that character most needs a salutary corrective; a system which, to the loud blasts of unreason and intolerance, sends forth no certain counterblast; which submissively accompanies the hatefullest and most barren of all kinds of dispute, religious dispute, into its smallest channels; — stereotypes every crotchet, every prejudice, every division, by recognising it; and suggests to its recipients no higher rationality than it finds in them.

POPULAR EDUCATION OF SWITZERLAND

POPULAR EDUCATION OF SWITZERLAND.

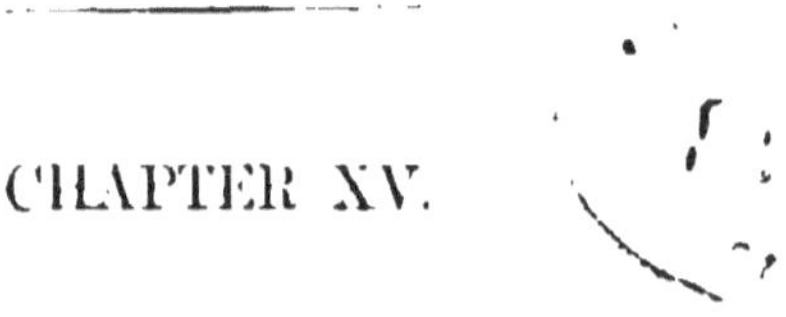

CHAPTER XV.

POPULAR EDUCATION IN FRENCH SWITZERLAND.

I ARRIVED in Switzerland at the end of June, and found the primary schools just closed for the holidays. Holidays are long in Switzerland, and I could not wait there until they should be over. The Normal School at Lausanne—the only normal school in French Switzerland was also closed. To see the Swiss schools in actual operation, therefore, I found impossible.

I regretted this the less because there is no dispute as to the quality of these schools, which in Geneva, Vaud, and Neufchâtel, are confessedly among the best in Europe. Schools exist everywhere; they are well supplied with efficient teachers and most numerously attended.* As to the actual merit of the schools themselves there exist, therefore, no doubts requiring a personal inspection to resolve them. What I wished to learn was, the system under which these schools were established, the degree of completeness with which that

* For a view of the present situation of primary instruction in all the principal Cantons, both German and French, of Switzerland, see the Table (compiled from official documents) at the end of this volume.

system had fulfilled the designs which its authors had in view, and the influence which this system, combined with the other circumstances of their condition, tends to exercise upon the population.

This I could learn even though the schools were in vacation. Both at Geneva and at Lausanne I had the advantage of consulting persons among the best informed and the most intelligent in Europe, to whom private letters of introduction had given me access. Recommended by the kind offices of the British Minister and the British Consul to the Government authorities, I received from them the most courteous attention, and official information which they alone could command. At Lausanne I had the pleasure of conversing with the President of the Council of State, with the Councillor at the head of the Department of Public Instruction, and with the Director of the Normal School, on the state of popular education in the important Canton of Vaud. At Geneva, M. Piguet, the Councillor of State charged with the Department of Public Instruction, not only gave me oral information of the greatest value, but had the kindness to procure for me the whole body of printed documents relating to public education in the French Cantons. These I have carefully studied, and of that study I now proceed to state very briefly the result, controlled by the explanations with which I was furnished on the spot.

I have to speak of five Cantons; Geneva, Vaud, Fribourg, Neufchâtel, and the Valais. Of these, Geneva has a population of 66,000; Vaud, of 206,000; Fribourg, of 100,000; Neufchâtel, of 80,000; the Valais, of from 80,000 to 90,000. In Geneva, popular instruction has long prospered, although in the Catholic communes added by the Treaty of Vienna to the territory of the Canton it is more backward than in the rest of the State, where Protestantism, ever since the Reformation, has fostered it. In Vaud, likewise, it has long been well cared for. The industrious and thriving Canton of Neufchâtel, which has redoubled its activity since its separation from Prussia, has lately bestowed zealous care upon its primary instruction, and is at present, of all the French Cantons, that in which it most flourishes. Of Fribourg I shall speak presently. The poverty and wretchedness of the Valaisans, which every traveller has noticed, make their primary schools much inferior to those of the four richer French Cantons. But the school-system of all five was, until very recently, the same in its main outlines; it was, in each, a consequence of the triumph of the democratic and anti-clerical party; it was, in most, a system designed to put public education in harmony with the new democratic constitutions established after the war of the Sonderbund, in 1847. It was founded by law in Vaud in 1846, in Geneva and Fribourg in 1848, in the Valais in 1849, in Neufchâtel in 1850. I shall first notice the points in which these laws mostly agree; special points in which they differ I shall notice afterwards.

It is the general scope of all of them to base Swiss education upon the "principles of Christianity and democracy."* Religious instruction is to be given, but it is regarded as the proper province of the minister of religion, not of the schoolmaster; and it is the only part of the instruction with which the minister is per-

* See, for instance, the preamble to the school law of the Canton Vaud: — "Vu l'article de la Constitution, portant: L'enseignement dans les écoles publiques sera conforme aux principes du christianisme et à ceux de la démocratie," &c.

mitted to interfere. Into the ordinary school-lessons the teacher is forbidden to introduce anything of religious dogma; the hours for religious instruction are strictly limited, and, if this instruction is given by the teacher at all, it must be at the request and under the responsibility of the minister of religion whose place he thus consents to fill. This Christian and democratic education is generally, also, compulsory and gratuitous. It embraces all young persons from their eighth to their sixteenth year. If children are privately educated, the State must be satisfied that their education is sufficient. They are liable to be called up for examination with the scholars of the public schools, and to be transferred by authority to a public school if their instruction is found inferior. A certificate of emancipation attests that the obligatory course of learning has been duly fulfilled.

The communes provide and maintain the public schools; but the State assists them when their resources fall short. Every place with more than twenty children of school age is, as a general rule, bound to have its school. When the number of scholars exceeds fifty or sixty, a second school must be established, a third when the second school has passed this limit, and so on. Boys and girls attend the same school. Infant schools the communes are not compelled to establish; but the State recommends their establishment, and aids it.

It is needless to say that this public school system is under the control of the State. The supreme executive of each Canton, the Council of State, delegates its controlling functions to a board of public instruction, consisting of two or three members, and presided over by a Councillor of State. But on any grave matter an appeal lies from this body to the Council of State itself.

and it is the Council alone which has the power to dismiss a teacher. Three out of the five Cantons have school-inspectors. Where there are no school-inspectors, their functions are discharged by the members of the board of public instruction, or by a local body, the communal school-committee. This body, consisting generally of from four to seven members, is named by the municipality. The minister of religion is not a member of it, unless the municipality choose to nominate him. The local committee should visit the schools of its commune not less than once a fortnight, besides holding a public general examination of them once a year.

Teachers must be certificated, and their examination for the certificate is conducted by the central board of public instruction. They are afterwards elected to their situations by competition, and have thus a second examination to undergo. This second examination is conducted by the local school-commission. Their salaries are fixed at about 500 francs a year, with a house and garden.

The instruction given in the primary schools has two or even more degrees.* The subjects taught are religion, reading, writing, grammar, arithmetic and book-keeping, geography, Swiss history, and singing. Instruction is of the elementary or superior degree, according as these subjects are taught with more or less extension. Instruction in both degrees may be given in the same school and by the same master.

* Six in the Canton of Geneva. In this Canton the scholars who have most distinguished themselves in the two highest degrees may be admitted, on the inspector's attestation, into a public secondary school; and, if poor, may there receive free schooling for one year.—*Règlement général des Écoles primaires et des Écoles moyennes du Canton de Genève*, Geneva, 1859, art. 13, 22, 23.

In thus regulating popular education the five Cantons generally agree. They do not *exactly* agree, however; and, even where there is agreement in their laws, there is sometimes variety in their practice.

In the Canton of Geneva, instruction is not by law compulsory; in the other four Cantons it is. I was anxious to ascertain exactly in what this compulsoriness of instruction consisted, and how far it was really made effectual. I read in the law that parents not sending their children to school were to be warned, summoned, sentenced to fine or imprisonment, according to their various degrees of negligence; I found due provision made for the recovery, by means of the ordinary tribunals, of such a fine; for the execution, by their means, of such a sentence of imprisonment. I asked myself, as the English reader will ask himself, In the Cantons of Vaud, Fribourg, Neufchâtel, and the Valais, must every child between the ages of seven and fifteen actually be at school all the year round, and, if he is not, are his parents actually punished for it?

In the first place I soon discovered that he need not be at school all the year round. To take one of the poorest of the Cantons, a Canton in which it seemed to me incredible that the compulsory principle should be fully carried out; the Canton Valais. The law of the Canton Valais proclaims that education is compulsory. But it also proclaims that the school year shall not be of less than—what does the reader suppose?—five months.* It is for five months in the year, then, not for ten, that children in the Valais are obliged to go to

* *Loi sur l'Instruction publique*, Sion, 1849, art. 6.—*Règlement du 6 Septembre* 1849 *sur les Écoles primaires du Canton du Valais*, art. 29.

school. Again, I take the Canton of Fribourg, and I find that there, also, education is obligatory up to the age of fifteen. But the law gives power to the inspector to exempt from this obligation of attendance at school children who are sufficiently advanced, and "children whose labour their parents cannot do without." What a safety-valve to the high pressure of a compulsory system is here! In the Canton of Fribourg, again, the school-vacations, says the law, must not exceed three months in the year.* These are long holidays for primary schools. But I take the largest and richest of all the French Cantons, the Canton of Vaud. In the Canton of Vaud the law makes attendance at school compulsory on all young persons between the ages of seven and sixteen. Are there no exceptions? I go on reading the law, and I find presently that the local school-committee may grant dispensations to all children above twelve years of age whose labour is necessary to their parents. It is made a condition, however, that these children continue to attend school a certain number of times in a week. But the master may grant a child leave of absence for two days in the week, the president of the school-committee may grant him leave for a week at a time, the school-committee itself for a month at a time.† Children above twelve years of age, then, may in one way or another get their school-time very much abridged; but, on any children at all, or on any parents, is the obligation written in the law ever actually enforced? At Geneva the best-informed persons did not hesitate to assure me that the obliga-

* *Loi sur l'Instruction publique*, Fribourg, 1848; art. 51, 60, 53.

† *Loi du 12 Novembre 1846 sur l'Instruction publique*, Lausanne, 1851; art. 61, 62, 68, 69.

tion of school-attendance in the Canton of Vaud was perfectly illusory. When I mentioned this at Lausanne, it was indignantly denied; I was told that the schools of Vaud were excellently attended, its population almost universally instructed. But of this I had no doubt: so they are everywhere in the prosperous Swiss Cantons; so they are in Geneva, where education is not compulsory. What I wanted to find out was, whether the legal obligation was actually put in force to constrain the attendance of children who without such constraint would not have attended: whether in Vaud, where education is compulsory, children went to school, who in Geneva, where it is not compulsory, would have been at home or at work. I could not find that they did. I was told that it was necessary to execute the law with the greatest tact, with the greatest forbearance; but in plain truth I could not discover that it was really executed at all. But perhaps this is because, in Vaud, the children so universally attend school that the executive has no cause of complaint against them, and no infringement of the law ever occurs? By the kindness of the President I was furnished with a copy of the last published Annual Report of the Council of State of Vaud on all the branches of the Cantonal administration. In that part of the Report which relates to schools, I find the following:—"The number of children attending school has somewhat diminished; this diminution is probably caused by the introduction into the Canton of different branches of industry, which give employment to the children in their neighbourhood, who are thus drawn off from school. Under these circumstances *the Council of Public Instruction has great difficulty in reconciling the consideration due to the wants of poor families with the demands of the* *law.*" Returns are then given to show that from 1846, the date of the law, to 1858, the date of the Report, the number of children attending school has steadily diminished.* The Report then continues: — "There is a great number of children who attend no school. Were the Council of Public Instruction more zealously seconded by the prefects, the municipalities, and the local school-committees, the attendance in the primary schools would not exhibit this serious falling-off. With respect to the attendance at school of those children whose names are actually on the books, even this leaves much to be desired, in spite of the efforts of the Council of Public Instruction."

These words are not mine; they are those of the Government of the Canton. And this is in presence of a law of compulsory education! What compulsory education is in America and in Germany I cannot tell; in the only place where I have been able to examine it closely, it is what I have described. Not that primary instruction is unprosperous in the Canton of Vaud; on the contrary, it is most flourishing. What I say is, that the making it compulsory by law has not there added one iota to its prosperity. Its prosperity is due to the general comfort and intelligence of the population; where these are equally present, as in Geneva, the prosperity of education is equal though there is no compulsion; where these fail, the compulsion of the

* There were at school in —

1846	34,781 children.		1855	30,930 children.	
1852	32,853	,,	1856	30,717	,,
1853	32,061	,,	1857 .	30,615	,,
1854 .	31,720	,,	1858 .	30,184	,,

See *Compte rendu par le Conseil d'État du Canton de Vaud sur l'Administration pendant l'année* 1858, *seconde partie*, p. 12.

law is powerless to prevent the inevitable check inflicted on education by their absence.

The school-law of French Switzerland generally, prescribes that primary instruction shall be gratuitous; in point of fact it is gratuitous only in Geneva and in the Valais. In Geneva alone are school-books and materials gratuitously supplied to all the scholars. In the other Cantons all but the poor have to purchase these; and in Vaud, Neufchâtel, and Fribourg, the communes are authorised to exact school fees from all who can afford to pay them, the poor alone having free admission. It must be remembered, however, that in a communal school supported by communal taxation, every family, however poor, contributes something to its support. Where nearly all are poor, as in the Valais, the bare maintenance thus obtained for the school and its teacher must be accepted as sufficient. Where there is wealth, there is a desire to raise the condition of the school and teacher somewhat above this bare maintenance-point. This is effected in Vaud, Neufchâtel, and Fribourg, by levying school fees upon those scholars who can afford to pay them; it is effected in Geneva by direct grant from the State. The direct State-expenditure on education in the little Canton of Geneva, is on this account much greater than the direct State expenditure on education in the large Canton of Vaud. In Geneva, in 1859, it was 115,450 francs; in Vaud, in 1858, the last year for which I have any account, it was only 93,002 fr. 50 c.

Perhaps the Canton of Neufchâtel adopts the best course, by leaving those who can afford it to pay their school-fees, while it reserves its own liberality to augment the salaries of the teachers, generally far too low in French Switzerland as in France. In Geneva, indeed, these are much better than in Vaud, Fribourg, or the Valais. In Vaud, where the salaries of teachers have lately been raised, the legal *minimum* of a master's salary is even now fixed at 20*l.* a year, that of a mistress's at 12*l.* a year, the salaries of both rising 2*l.* a year after ten years' service, 4*l.* a year after twenty years' service. In Geneva, a master (or *regent* as he is called in Switzerland) has in the town of Geneva itself a fixed salary of 56*l.* a year, in the other communes of 40*l.* a year; a mistress (or *regentess*) has 36*l.* a year in the town, 28*l.* in the country. Besides this all teachers in the Canton of Geneva have a *casual*, paid by the State, of threepence a month for every child present in school up to the number of 50 children; twopence a month for every child above that number.* But in Neufchâtel the State does much more. Municipalities and their school-committees fix the teachers' salaries †; but these salaries the State, on certain conditions, and in a certain combined proportion with the commune, increases as high as 80*l.* a year. This is the salary of a teacher of the highest class, but all teachers, even those of the *Écoles d'hiver* ‡, have their proportionate augmentation. By this means Neufchâtel, though without a normal school of its own, easily procures as its primary teachers the best of the students trained at Lausanne.

This normal school of Lausanne is the only normal school in French Switzerland. It was attended in 1859

* *Loi générale sur l'Instruction publique*, Geneva, 1848; art. 101, 102.

† But for the *minimum* which they propose they must obtain the sanction of the Council of State.—*Loi sur l'Instruction primaire*, Neufchâtel, 1850; art. 59.

‡ Schools open during the winter months only; an institution common in Switzerland, and particularly successful in the Canton of Neufchâtel.

by 94 students, 57 of them being young men, 37 young women. It is conducted by a director, to whom I had the pleasure of paying a long visit, and by 11 masters. There is a lady superintendent, with an assistant, to take general charge of the young women, and to teach them needlework and domestic economy. The training school is held in a building which furnishes only lecture rooms and an office for the director; the students board in the town, at boarding-houses approved and inspected by the director. The course for young men lasts three years, for young women two years. There are no practising schools. The expense of a young man's training is about 14*l.* a year, that of a young woman's about 12*l.* For the last six years the State has on an average allowed to each student 6*l.* a year towards the expense of his or her training, the rest is paid by the students themselves. From 25 to 30 students go out every year to take charge of schools. The best go to Neufchâtel and Geneva, where the teachers are best paid. Fribourg will probably soon establish a training school of its own: at present it trains its French teachers in private establishments, its German teachers in the training schools of German Switzerland.*

The school law of every Canton requires the teacher to possess a certificate of capacity. But this requirement is not always enforced. In Vaud, for instance, five years' service in a public school legally exempts a teacher from the obligation of the certificate. But this is not all. I have said that teachers are appointed to schools after a competitive examination held by the local school-committee. To this examination no can-

* See *Règlement pour les Écoles Normales du Canton de Vaud.* Lausanne, 1849.

didate can properly be admitted unless entitled by the certificate of capacity, or by the five years' service. But, where no such candidates present themselves, the law allows school-committees to examine and elect other persons, who may be provisionally continued without a certificate from year to year for five years, at the end of which term they are exempt, as I have mentioned, from the obligation of the certificate Nor is the examination held by the school-committee any effectual substitute for the certificate-examination held by the Central Education Department. The inefficiency of the examinations conducted by the local school-committees I found generally complained of; on the other hand, the certificates granted by the Central Education Department are real guarantees of capacity. The examination for them extends, as in France, only to the subjects taught in the primary schools, and to the art of teaching; but it is serious, and it is conducted by duly qualified persons.

In Vaud and in Neufchâtel the local school-committees are left to fulfil also the functions elsewhere discharged by inspectors: but they supply the want of State-inspection as inefficiently as they supply the want of State-examination. Geneva, Fribourg, and the Valais have inspectors. There are not two opinions as to the value of the services which may be rendered by these functionaries; and they will probably soon be employed by the two Cantons which are now without them.

The school-laws of Geneva and of Neufchâtel appear to me to be superior to those of Vaud and of Fribourg in this,—that their framers had a more single regard to the welfare of primary instruction and to that only, than the framers of the others. The framers of the others undoubtedly had zeal for primary instruction;

but zeal for the ascendancy of the democratic party was too strongly present to their minds at the same time. They have, therefore, omitted provisions for the welfare of the schools which were of great importance; they have introduced provisions to bind the individual, which on educational grounds have no necessity, and which sometimes defeat their own object, by making the law which sanctions them intolerable.

This has been the case in Fribourg. Fribourg is a very powerful canton; its population, though fanatical, is exceedingly vigorous. Until the war of 1847, it was in the hands of the clerical party: the issue of the Sonderbund struggle gave full power to the enemies of the clerical party, to the democrats. The new government, knowing its adversaries' strength, procured its own nomination for a period of nine years, and, in order to indoctrinate the population with liberal ideas, instituted, by the law of 1848, a very developed system of primary instruction. But nine years of Radical government, and the law of 1848, were insufficient to convert the stiffnecked people of Fribourg. At the first elections which took place after the struggle of 1847—the elections of 1856—the clerical party regained its ascendancy, the democratic party fell, and the law of 1848 fell with its authors instead of saving them. When the English reader is informed of some of its provisions, he will not, I think, be much surprised at its fate.* It provided—(in the country of the Père Girard!)—that no religious society, under any denomination whatever, should henceforth be allowed to teach.

* *Loi sur l'Instruction publique*, Fribourg, 1848; art. 8, 9, 11, 42, 6, 51, 5, 101.—*Règlement pour les Écoles primaires du Canton de Fribourg*, Fribourg, 1850; art. 180, 176, 177, 178, 179.

It provided that, for the future, persons educated by the Jesuits, or by any of the orders affiliated to the Jesuits, should be incapable of holding any office in Church or State. It proclaimed the object of primary schools to be "the development of man's moral and intellectual faculties in conformity with the principles of Christianity and democracy." It imposed a political oath on the schoolmaster. It made instruction obligatory and gratuitous. Lest the rising generation should still escape it, it directed, first, that no child living in the Canton should, under any circumstances whatever, be educated at home. Next, that if it was proposed to educate a child in a private school, the parent must first submit the name of the private school to the inspector and to the communal school-committee for their approval. If this was obtained, the pupil was still bound to attend the public half-yearly examinations of the communal school. If he failed to attend, or if he attended and passed a bad examination, the private school which educated him was to be closed. Finally, the resources of the religious, charitable, and grammar-school foundations of communes were henceforth to be made available for the support of primary schools.

This I call the very fanaticism of meddling. But, at the same time, the law instituted an undoubtedly good programme of school-instruction. The reaction swept away both the noxious meddling and the sound programme. By an order dated the 12th of January, 1858, the new Council of State restored foundations to their original uses, relaxed the obligation of attendance at the public schools, gave parents liberty to educate their children at home or in private schools, made the clergyman a necessary member of the local school-committee, freed the teacher from the necessity of taking an oath, raised his salary, and reduced the programme of primary school instruction.

Reaction and Obscurantism! cry the Liberals. Alas, that reaction and obscurantism should sometimes speak the language of moderation and liberty, and that they should invariably cease to speak it the moment they have the power to use, like their adversaries, that of exaggeration and tyranny! For the clerical party in Fribourg this moment has happily not yet arrived. But the future, in Switzerland at any rate, belongs to democracy; and one would gladly see Swiss democracy more rational and more equitable. It has undoubtedly striven to develope popular education; but the spirit in which it has striven for this object has not been without an unfavourable influence upon education itself.

It is the spirit in which highly-instructed peoples live and work that makes them interesting, not the high instruction itself. Placed between France and Germany, Switzerland is inevitably exposed to influences which tend to prevent her democracy from exercising, unchecked, the pulverising action which democracy exercises in America. But the dominant tendency of modern Swiss democracy is yet not to be regarded without disquietude. It is socialistic, in the sense in which that word expresses a principle hostile to the interests of true society—*the elimination of superiorities*. The most distinguished, the most capable, the most high-minded persons in French Switzerland, are precisely those most excluded from the present direction of affairs; they are living in retirement. Instruction may spread wide among a people which thus ostracises all its best citizens; but it will with difficulty elevate it.

POPULAR EDUCATION OF HOLLAND

* 0

POPULAR EDUCATION OF HOLLAND.

CHAPTER XVI.

POPULAR EDUCATION IN HOLLAND UNDER THE LAW OF 1806. REPORTS OF M. CUVIER AND M. COUSIN.

M. COUSIN, whose admirable reports on popular instruction in Germany and Holland have made the education of those countries so widely known, was inclined to prefer the school-law of Prussia to the school-law of Holland: but for the Dutch primary schools themselves he expressed the highest admiration. The admiration for them expressed by M. Cuvier, who, in 1811, was deputed by the University of France to visit Holland, and to report on its system of public education, was even warmer. The great naturalist speaks unfavourably of the Grammar-schools and Universities of Holland: these, he said, were in some respects beneath criticism. But of the primary schools he said, that they were above all praise. He has described the emotion of astonishment and delight with which on his first entrance into one of them he was struck*; so unlike was

* "Nous aurions peine," say M. Cuvier and his colleague, M. Noel, "à rendre l'effet qu'a produit sur nous la première école primaire où nous sommes entrés en Hollande.—La premiere vue de cette école nous avait causé une surprise agréable; lorsque nous fûmes entrés dans tous les détails, nous ne pûmes nous défendre d'une véritable émotion."

it to any school for the poor which he had ever seen, or which at that time was anywhere to be seen out of Holland. For it was in 1811.

The popular instruction of other countries has grown up since that time; but I have seen no primary schools worthy to be matched, even now, with those of Holland. Other far more competent observers have come to the same judgment. It is the school-law which in 1811 M. Cuvier found in operation, which has produced these results. That school-law has lately been altered; of the alterations made in it I will speak presently. They are important, but they are not of a character materially to change the popular education of Holland; even if they were, they are too recent to have yet produced that effect. Up to 1857, the school law of Holland, the law of 1806, with the four general regulations which accompanied it, subsisted without change. As M. Cuvier found it in 1811, so M. Cousin found it in 1836; the same fruits which it was bearing in 1836, it had been bearing in 1811. How that school-law arose, M. Cuvier's report makes known. This report, which is a perfect model of its kind, and which well deserves reprinting, very few, probably, of my readers have seen; for it is not printed in the collection of M. Cuvier's works, it is not to be found even in the library of the British Museum, and it is almost impossible to procure it. I shall therefore repeat, as briefly as I can, the account which it gives of the foundation of the excellent primary instruction of Holland.

Towards the end of the last century, the Dutch schools for the poor resembled those of all other countries; that is to say, they were exceedingly bad. It is remarkable that even in Holland, even in a stronghold of Protestantism — that Protestantism which is com monly thought to have done so much for the instruction of the people — primary schools should by explicit testimony be declared to have been, eighty years ago, thus inferior. We should probably hear the same of the schools of Scotland at the same period, had there been any capable person to judge and to tell us of them. Not that the credit which Protestantism has received for its zeal in teaching the people is wholly undeserved; Protestantism had, in truth, the zeal to found schools, but it had not the knowledge to make good schools. In Holland, eighty years ago, there were no schools for the poor, except schools in connection with the different religious communions; children whose parents were not enrolled members of some church could attend no school at all. But, at any rate, for the children of its own communion Protestantism built schools; there were Protestant schools in connection with the Protestant churches. In connection with the Roman Catholic churches there were no schools whatever. But the Protestant schools were under the inspection of the church-deacons, who changed continually, and who had no fixed principles of management; there was no provision for the training of fit teachers: the schoolmasters were ignorant, and the instruction beggarly.

Such was the state of things when, in 1784, John Nieuvenhuysen, a Mennonite minister in North Holland, founded, with the assistance of several friends, the Society for the Public Good. This society proposed, first, to prepare and circulate among the common people useful elementary works, not only on religious and moral subjects, but also on matters of every-day life. This first object it accomplished with such success, that in two or three years an improved calendar published by the society beat the popular calendar, a tissue of absurdities and superstitions, the *Moore's Almanack* of Holland, out of the field. The society's second object was to establish model and temporary schools, with libraries, for the use of workpeople who had left school. It proposed, thirdly, to conduct inquiries into the true principles of the physical and moral education of children, and into school-method.

The society prospered. In 1809 it numbered 7000 members, and had spread its operations as far as to the Cape of Good Hope. It formed departments in all the localities where it had subscribers, and to these departments it entrusted the inspection and the management of its schools. The government gradually adopted its plans; in 1797, the magistrates of Amsterdam built their public schools in accordance with the suggestions of the two departments of the society established in their city.

In 1801, the celebrated Orientalist, M. Van der Palm, the agent for public instruction in the Batavian Republic, drew up an educational law, which he further improved in 1803, and which laid the base of the final legislation on this subject. In 1805, M. Schimmelpenninck became Grand Pensionary, and M. Van der Palm retired from public life; but his law was the foundation of the law of 1806, proposed by M. Van den Ende, "the father of public instruction in Holland," who from 1806 till 1833 directed, as Commissioner acting under the authority of the Minister for the Home Department, the popular education of his country.

The law of 1806 was very short and very simple. It adopted the existing schools; but it did two things, which no other school law had yet done, and which were the foundations of its eminent success;—it established a thorough system of inspection for the schools, a thorough system of examination for the teachers.

To organise inspection: — this is, in fact, the grand object of the law of 1806; with this it begins, and with this it ends. To keep the system of inspection efficient was the central thought, the paramount aim of its author, up to the very last days of his life, when, a venerable old man, he received M. Cousin at Haarlem in 1836, and said to him: — "Take care how you choose your inspectors; they are men whom you ought to look for with a lantern in your hand." * And inspection in Holland was organised with a force and completeness which it has attained nowhere else.

Each province of Holland was formed into a certain number of school-districts, and at the head of each school-district was placed an inspector. The united inspectors of the province formed the provincial commission for primary instruction. This commission met three times a year, and received a report on his district from each inspector who was a member of it. It examined teachers for certificates. It was in communication with the provincial government. Once a year it sent as its deputy one of its members to the Hague, to form with the deputies from other provinces a commission, to discuss and regulate school matters, under the immediate direction of the Minister for the Home Department and his inspector-general. In his own district, by this law, each inspector is supreme; local and municipal school-committees can only be named with his concurrence, and he is the leading member of

* *De l'Instruction publique en Hollande*, par M. Cousin. Paris, 1837; p. 30.

them all; no teacher, public or private, can be appointed without his authorisation; and he inspects every school in his district twice a year. These powerful functionaries were to be named by the State, on the presentation, for the inspectorships of each province, of the assembled commission of inspectors for that province. They were excellently chosen, amongst the laymen and clergymen who had shown an intelligent interest in popular education. Following a practice not rare in Holland, where the public service is esteemed highly honourable, and where the number of persons able and willing to take part in it is greater than in any other country, they gave their services nearly gratuitously. They received allowances for their expenses while engaged in the business of inspection, but no salaries. Either they were men with private means, or men exercising at the same time with their inspectorship some other function, which provided them with an income. Their cost to the State was, therefore, very small. There were at first 56 inspectors, whose travelling allowances together amounted to 1840*l.*; and this sum, with 320*l.* a year for an inspector general's salary, and with a small charge for the office and travelling expenses of this functionary, was the whole cost to the State of the administration of primary instruction.

Four general regulations accompanied and completed the law of 1806. The provincial and communal administrations were charged to occupy themselves with providing proper means of instruction in their localities, with insuring to the teacher a comfortable subsistence, with obtaining a regular attendance of the children in the schools; but there were no provisions exacting from the communes an obligatory establishment of schools, a legal *minimum* of salary for teachers; none exacting from the children a compulsory school-attendance. Neither did the State enter into any positive undertaking as to its own grants. In general terms, it reserved to itself the right to take such measures as it should think fit, to improve the teacher's position, and to promote the good instruction of the young. It left the rest to the stimulating action of its inspectors upon provincial and communal administrations singularly well disposed to receive it.

Its confidence was justified. The provincial governments fixed the teacher's salary for each province at a rate which made the position of the Dutch schoolmaster superior to that of his class in every other country. Free schools for the poor were provided in all the large towns; in the villages, schools which taught the poor gratuitously, but imposed a small admission-fee on those who could afford to pay it. Ministers of religion and lay authorities combined their efforts to draw the children into the schools. The boards which distributed public relief, imposed on its recipients the condition that they should send their children to school. The result was a popular education, which, for extent and solidity combined, has probably never been equalled. Even in 1811, in the reduced Holland of the French Empire, M. Cuvier found 4451 primary schools, with nearly 200,000 scholars, one in ten of the population being at school. In the province of Groningen the prefect reported, as in 1840 the administration reported in the town of Haarlem, that there was not a child who could not read and write. In Amsterdam there were eleven schools for the poor, so well frequented that candidates for admission to them had to put down their names long beforehand, and scholars who passed out of them were eagerly sought after as servants or apprentices. The deacons' schools, or private parish schools in connection with the churches and under the superintendence of the parish deacons, were gradually giving way before the competition of the public schools. The Lutheran deacons' schools of Amsterdam had recently been closed when M. Cuvier wrote. The village schools were, as at this day, even more prosperous than the poor schools of the towns; for, being attended by children of a somewhat richer class, they gave a somewhat more advanced instruction: the commune, however, paid for the schooling of the poor, and the school-fee of the rest was only about a penny a week. In the thriving villages of North Holland, M. Cuvier found large schools of 200 or 300 children, exciting his admiration by the same cleanliness, order, and good instruction which he had witnessed in the towns. School was held for two hours in the morning, two hours in the afternoon, two hours in the evening: the evening school was for old scholars who had gone to work, and was most numerously and diligently attended. Finally, and this M. Cuvier justly thought one of the grand causes of the success of the Dutch schools, the position of the schoolmasters was most advantageous. Municipalities and parents were alike favourable to them, and held them and their profession in an honour which then, probably, fell to their lot nowhere else. Hardly a village schoolmaster was to be found with a salary of less than 10*l.* a year; in the towns many had from 120*l.* to 160*l.*, and even more than that sum; all had, besides, a house and garden. The fruits of this comfort and consideration were to be seen, as they are remarkably to be seen even at the present day, in the good manners, the good address, the self-respect without presumption, of the Dutch teachers. They are never servile, and never offensive.

The teacher in Holland, in order to enter his profession, had to obtain a *general admission*. To exercise it, he needed a *special admission*. The general admission was obtained by successfully passing the certificate examination. There were four grades of certificate: to be appointed either a public or a private schoolmaster in the towns it was necessary to hold a certificate of the first or second grade; the first grade could be attained by no one who was not twenty-five years old. The third grade qualified a teacher to hold a village school. The fourth grade was reserved for under-masters and assistants. The examination for the higher grades was considerably higher than the certificate-examination of France, considerably lower than ours, for which, indeed, with its twelve hours of written exercises in mathematics alone*, it would be difficult to find a parallel. But the Dutch regulation, instructing the examiners to admit to the highest grade those candidates only who gave signs of a *distinguished culture*, assigned to the schoolmaster's training a humanising and educating direction, which is precisely what we, with our exaggerated demand for masses of hard information, have completely missed. School-methods, also, and pedagogic aptitude, occupied more space in the Dutch examination than in the French or in ours.

The teacher had now his general admission. If he wished to become a public teacher, he presented himself as a candidate for some vacant public mastership, and underwent a competitive examination. This second examination I found in Switzerland also; it exists

* Lately reduced, I am happy to say, to nine.

neither in France nor amongst ourselves. If successful, the teacher then received his special admission. Of the judges who examined him for this, the law made the inspector of the district necessarily one; if dissatisfied with the decision of his colleagues, the inspector had the right of appealing against it to the Minister. For special admission as a private teacher no second examination was necessary. But the candidate required the authorisation of the municipality; and this authorisation was not granted except with the inspector's concurrence.

The legislation of 1806 did not institute normal schools. How, then, was an efficient body of schoolmasters formed? It was formed by permitting, in the schools of the Society for the Public Good, the best scholars to stay on at school for two or three years longer than usual, without paying, on condition that they acted as teachers: these became, first, assistants; then, under-masters; finally, head masters. Great eagerness was manifested to be nominated one of these retained scholars. M. Cuvier found this system in operation when he visited Holland, and he speaks warmly of its success. It was the first serious attempt to form a body of regularly trained masters for primary schools. In our eyes it should have a special interest: we owe to it the institution of pupil-teachers.

Finally, under the legislation of 1806 it was not permitted to public schools to be denominational. The law required that the instruction in them should be such as to "train its recipients for the exercise of all social and Christian virtues," but no dogmatic religious instruction was to be given by the teacher, or was to be given in the school. Measures were to be taken, however, said the law, that the scholar should not go without the dogmatic teaching of the communion to which he belonged. Accordingly, the Minister for the Home Department exhorted by circular the ministers of the different communions to co-operate with the government in carrying the new law into execution, by taking upon themselves the religious instruction of the school children belonging to their persuasion. The religious authorities replied favourably to this appeal. They willingly took upon themselves the task required of them; and nowhere, perhaps, has the instruction of the people been more eminently religious than in Holland, while the public schools have remained, by law, unsectarian. M. Cuvier found that the school children, in 1811, were taught the dogmatic part of their religion on Sundays, in church, by their own minister; that on Saturdays, when Jews were absent, they were instructed in school by the schoolmaster in the New Testament and the life of Christ; on other days, in the truths common to all religions. M. Cousin found, in 1836, the same avoidance of dogmatic teaching in the Dutch schools, the same prevalence of sound religious instruction among the Dutch people.

M. Cuvier concludes his report by pointing out the foundation on which the excellent school-system of Holland appeared to him to repose. It reposed, he said, upon three things; the comfort of the schoolmaster, the effectiveness of the inspection, the superiority of the school-methods. To these three advantages the Dutch schools still owe their prosperity.

M. Cousin, in 1836, found two important modifications introduced into the school-system of Holland since the visit of M. Cuvier. M. Cuvier had noticed with approbation the mode of training schoolmasters which I have above described; in truth, this was a more careful mode of training them than any which at that time was pursued elsewhere: but it left something to be desired; it was not yet the training of the Normal School. Normal schools were established in 1816, under the auspices of M. Van den Ende. One was placed at Haarlem, for Holland; another at Lierre, near Antwerp, for the Belgian provinces, at that time united with Holland. These two institutions, however, sufficed but for a select number of students, the most promising subjects among the future schoolmasters of Holland; for the ordinary majority the training which M. Cuvier had praised continued in use. The normal school at Haarlem became justly celebrated for its success, due to the capacity and character of its director, M. Prinsen. M. Prinsen was still at its head when M. Cousin visited Holland. He received M. Cousin at Haarlem; and the vigour of the man, and the personal nature of his influence over his pupils, is sufficiently revealed in his reply to M. Cousin's request for a copy of the regulations of his school: "I am the regulations," was M. Prinsen's answer.*

The other change was in the town schools. In the towns the public schools for the poor, well managed, well taught, regularly inspected, had become very superior to the private schools, the offspring of individual speculation, which received the children of the lower middling classes. The requirement of the certificate of indigence, in the public free schools of the towns, excluded these children from benefits which they could enjoy in the public paying schools of the country; and there was danger that their education would sink below that of the class beneath them. To avert this danger,

* *De l'Instruction publique en Hollande*, p. 35.

intermediate schools (*tusschen-Schoolen*) were instituted in towns; and in these schools, by payment of a small fee, rarely exceeding 4*d.* a week, children of the middling classes could obtain an instruction invested with a public character and fenced with public guarantees. Above the *tusschen-School* was the French school (*Fransche School*), where a still higher education, including the modern languages, but not yet classical, was afforded for a higher fee; above the French school came the classical, the Latin school.

The classical and superior education of Holland M. Cousin judged with not much more favour than M. Cuvier. I have not to deal with this education here; probably it deserved in most respects the strictures passed upon it by its French critics. But it was impossible for me to enter without emotion the halls and lecture-rooms of Leyden and Utrecht, illustrious by the memory of a host of great names, and recalling by their academic costume, their academic language, or their classical predilections, the venerable Universities of our own country. Perhaps the feeling that these, too, long maintained a course which the modern spirit, not altogether without justice, decried as antiquated, but which nevertheless formed generations able to fill, not ignobly, their part in Church and State, inspired me with indulgent tenderness towards their Dutch sisters. Yet this tenderness does not prevent me from acknowledging, with M. Cuvier and M. Cousin, that it is by its primary schools and its popular education that Holland is since 1800 eminently distinguished.

CHAPTER XVII.

PRESENT SCHOOL LEGISLATION OF HOLLAND. LAW OF 1857.

What could have been the inducement to the Dutch Government to alter a legislation which worked so well? Why, when the law of 1806 was there, should the Chambers have been called upon to vote the law of 1857? I proceed to reply very briefly to these questions.

In the first place, in 1848, Holland had the disease from which it seems that, since the French Revolution, no constitutional state on the Continent can escape;—it wrote down its constitution. The Constitution of 1848 proclaimed* liberty of instruction. The legislation of 1806 had fettered this liberty by requiring the private teacher to obtain a special authorisation before he might open school. It was necessary to bring school-legislation on this point into harmony with the new Constitution.

It was asserted, too, that the body of schoolmasters, satisfactory as was their position in general, were yet left too dependent on the will of the local municipality for the amount of their salaries; that there were many cases in which these were quite insufficient; and that it was desirable to establish by law a rate of salary below which local parsimony might not descend.

* Art. 194

It was said, also, that the legislation of 1806 had not determined with sufficient strictness the obligation of communes to provide schools, and that in some quarters popular education was in consequence suffering. Returns were quoted to show that the attendance of children in the Dutch schools, satisfactory as compared with that which many countries could boast, was yet unsatisfactory as compared with that which Holland could boast formerly. In 1835 the proportion of the inhabitants of Holland in school was 1 to 8·3; in 1848, when it reached its highest point, it was 1 to 7·78; but in January 1854 it had fallen to 1 to 9·35, and in July of the same year yet lower, to 1 to 9·83. The number of children attending no school, estimated at but 21,000 for 1852, was estimated at 38,000 for 1855. For Holland, this was a suffering state of popular education. Many desired to try whether legislation could not amend it.

Yet, after all, these were light grievances to allege against a law which had in general worked admirably. The special authorisation required for private teachers had never in Holland been felt as a serious grievance, because in Holland it was almost always accorded or refused with fairness. The Dutch schoolmaster had, in general, reason rather for satisfaction than for complaint. The diffusion of instruction among the Dutch people was such as might inspire their rulers with thankfulness rather than disquietude.

Another, a graver embarrassment, placed the legislation of 1806 in question. It arose out of those very provisions of the law which had been supposed essentially to characterise it, and which observers had the most applauded. It arose out of the imposition on the schools of a non-denominational character.

M. Cousin's convictions led him to disapprove an instruction for the people which was either purely secular or not directly and dogmatically religious; but he had not been able to refuse his testimony to the success of the non-dogmatic instruction of the primary schools of Holland. He had seen, he declared, in the great schools of Amsterdam, of Rotterdam, of the Hague, Jews, Catholics, and Protestants seated side by side on the same benches, troubled by no religious animosity, receiving harmoniously a common instruction. But what struck him most was that this instruction seemed to him "penetrated with the spirit of Christianity, though not with the spirit of sect;" that it formed men "sincerely religious and in general moral."

This was high praise from such a quarter, and it tended to dissipate the objections most formidable to such a school system as the Dutch. If, in fact, religious training did not suffer in neutral or non-denominational schools, these schools were inevitably to be preferred to all others; for the advantages of their neutrality no one disputes, and the one supposed *dis*advantage of their neutrality was shown not to exist. Precisely on this plea, that, while the Dutch schools were unsectarian, they were yet truly Christian, the venerable M. Van den Ende upheld the system which he had founded. "Yes," he said to M. Cousin in 1836*, "primary schools ought to be Christian, but neither Protestant nor Catholic. They ought to belong to no one communion in particular, and to teach no positive dogma.—Yes, you are right, the school ought to be Christian, the school must be Christian. Toleration is not indifference.—I

* *De l'Instruction publique en Hollande*, par M. Cousin, Paris, 1837, pp. 28, 29.

cannot approve that the schoolmaster should give any dogmatic religious instruction; such instruction should be given by the ministers of the different denominations, and out of school. I allow that the schoolmaster may in some cases have the catechism said; but even this is not without its inconveniences.—Remember that you are in Holland, where the Christian spirit is very widely spread among the people."

It escaped, I think, M. Van den Ende, it escaped. I think, M. Cousin, that it would have been more strictly to the purpose to say:—"You are in Holland, where the *Protestant* spirit is very widely spread among the people." I think it escaped them, that the religious teaching of the Dutch public schools, a sincere, a substantial religious teaching no doubt, was at the same time substantially a *Protestant* teaching. I think it escaped them, that this Protestant teaching passed without raising difficulties in the Dutch schools, because the religious spirit of the Dutch people in general was a decidedly Protestant spirit, which the Protestant teaching of the public schools of course did not offend. But, in that case, the triumph of the neutral school in Holland was more apparent than real. The Dutch system had not, in that case, yet solved the difficult problem of uniting in a religious instruction genuine Christian teaching with absolute exclusion of dogma.

Events have singularly proved this. In 1848 all religious denominations in Holland were placed by law on a perfect equality. Protestantism lost its exclusive predominance. What was the first step taken by the Catholics in the assertion of their equal rights? It was to claim an exact and literal observance of the law of 1806. "The word *Christian* in the law of 1806," said the Catholics, "had become in practice merely another word for *Protestant;* if possible, banish the word *Christian* altogether, for of that word in a neutral school partisans are sure to take sectarian advantage: but, even if the word remains, the law clearly proscribes all dogmatic teaching, clearly limits the Christianity to be taught to morality only; execute the law, forbid the teacher to give any dogmatic religious instruction whatever, banish from the school the Bible, which contains dogma as well as moral precepts." The law was clearly on the side of the Catholics, and they succeeded in having it strictly put in force. M. Van den Ende's own words to M. Cousin, which I have quoted above, show that probably the Catholics had ground for complaint, show that probably the teacher sometimes actually broke the law by taking part in teaching dogmatic formularies. But even though formularies be excluded, it is hard not to impress a Protestant or Catholic stamp on the religious instruction of a school, if a school admits any religious instruction at all. We have had this difficulty even in the national schools of Ireland, where religious teaching may be supposed to have been reduced to its *minimum.* In the excellent schools of the British and Foreign School Society religious teaching has a more considerable place; it much resembles* the religious teaching of the Dutch schools under the law of 1806. The British schools are unsectarian; they profess themselves, they honestly believe themselves, unsectarian. But if the Catholics in great numbers had to use them, we should soon, I imagine, hear complaints that they were Protestant.

No sooner was the law of 1806 put strictly in force,

* The exclusion of dogmatic formularies of religion from the British schools is, however, complete.

no sooner did the public schools of Holland become really non-denominational, than the high Protestants began to cry out against them. They discovered that the law of 1806 was vicious in principle. They discovered that the public schools which this law had founded were "godless schools," were "centres of irreligion and immorality."

The dissatisfaction of this formidable party was the real cause which made the revision of the law of 1806 inevitable. Either the government, while introducing into the school-law of Holland the lesser modifications necessitated by the Constitution of 1848 or by other causes, must obtain from the Chambers a fresh sanction for the important principle of the neutral school, or this principle must be publicly renounced by it. The law of 1857 raised the question.

Never, perhaps, has it been better discussed than in the debates which followed the introduction of that law into the Dutch Chambers. It does honour to Holland that she should have for her representatives men capable of debating this grave question of religious education so admirably. I greatly doubt whether any other parliamentary assembly in the world could have displayed, in treating it, so much knowledge, so much intelligence, so much moderation. These debates prove the truth of what I have before said, that in the upper classes of no country is the education for public affairs so serious or so universal as in Holland; they prove, too, that nowhere does the best thought and information of these classes so well succeed in finding its way into the legislature. A most interesting account* of the discussion has been published in the French lan-

* *Débats sur l'Enseignement primaire dans les Chambres Hollandaises*, par Émile de Laveleye; Gand, 1858.

guage by M. de Laveleye, a Belgian, and a warm partisan of the cause of neutral schools; I strongly recommend the study of his book to all who desire to see the question of religious education fully debated. My space permits me here only to indicate, with the utmost brevity, the parties on each side in this discussion in the Dutch Chambers, and its issue.

Against the neutral school the high Protestant party stood alone; but its strength, though unaided, was great. This party is at the same time the great conservative party of Holland; it was strong by its wealth, by its respectability, by its long preponderance, by the avowed favour of the King. It was strongest of all, perhaps, by the character of its leader, M. Groen van Prinsterer, a man of deep religious convictions, of fervent eloquence, and of pure and noble character. As a pamphleteer and as an orator, M. Groen van Prinsterer attacked the neutral school with equal power. "No education without religion!" he exclaimed, "and no religion except in connection with some actual religious communion! else you fall into a vague deism which is but the first step towards atheism and immorality."

If the opponents of the non-denominational school were one, its supporters were many. First of all stood the Roman Catholics; insisting, as in states where they are not in power they always insist, that the State which cannot be of their own religion shall be of no religion at all; that it shall be perfectly neutral between the various sects; that no other sect, at any rate, shall have the benefit of that State-connection which here it cannot itself obtain, but which, when it can obtain it, it has never refused. Next came the Jews and dissenters; accustomed to use the public schools, desiring to make them even more neutral rather than less neutral, apprehensive that of public schools, allotted separately to denominations, their own share might be small. Next came an important section of the Protestant party, the Protestants of the New School, as they are called, who have of late years made much progress, and whose stronghold is in the University of Groningen: who take their theology from the German rationalists, and, while they declare themselves sincerely Christian, incline, in their own words, "to consider Christianity rather by its moral side and its civilising effect, than by its dogmatic side and its regenerating effect." For these persons, the general character of the religious teaching of the Dutch schools under the law of 1806, the "Christianity common to all sects" taught in them, was precisely what they desired. Finally, the neutral schools were upheld by the whole liberal party, bent in Holland, as elsewhere, to apply on every possible occasion their favourite principle of the radical separation of Church and State; bent to exclude religion altogether from schools which belong to the State, because with religion, they said, the State ought to have no concern whatever.

The party which really triumphed was that of the Protestants of the New School. They owed this triumph less to their own numbers and ability than to the conformity of their views with the language of the legislation of 1806. That legislation was dear, and justly dear, to the people of Holland; a school-system had grown up under it of which they might well be proud; they had not generally experienced any serious inconvenience from it. The new law, therefore, while it forbade, more distinctly than the old law, the schoolmaster to take part in dogmatic religious teaching, while it expressly abandoned religious instruction to the ministers of the different religious communions, while it abstained from proclaiming, like the old law, a desire that the dogmatic religious teaching of the young, though not given in the public school, might yet not be neglected,—nevertheless still used, like the old law, the word *Christian*. It still declared that the object of primary education was "to develope the reason of the young, and to train them to the exercise of all *Christian* and social virtues."* This retention of the word *Christian* gave great offence to many members of the majority. It gave offence to the Liberals, because, they said, this word was "in evident opposition with the purely lay character of the State; for the State, as such, has no religion." Yet the Liberals accepted the new law as a compromise, and because, after all, it still repelled the introduction of the denominational school. But the Catholics were less pliant. To the last they insisted on excluding the word *Christian*, because in practice, they said, this word signified *Protestant;* and most of them voted against the law, because this word was retained. The law passed, however, and by a large majority.

Popular instruction in Holland is, therefore, still Christian. But it is Christian in a sense so large, so wide, from which everything distinctive and dogmatic is so rigorously excluded, that it might as well, perhaps, have rested satisfied with calling itself moral. Those who gave it the name of Christian were careful to announce that by Christianity they meant "all those ideas which purify the soul by elevating it, and which prepare the union of citizens in a common sentiment of

* "Christelijke en maatschappelijke deugden."

mutual good will;" not "those theological subtleties which stifle the natural affections, and perpetuate divisions among members of one commonwealth." They announced that the Christianity of the law and of the State was "a social or lay Christianity, gradually transforming society after the model of ideal justice;" not "a dogmatic Christianity, the affair of the individual and the Church." They announced that this Christianity did not even exclude the Jew; for "the Jew himself will admit that the virtues enjoined by the Old Testament are not in opposition with the word of Christ considered as a sage and a philosopher."* The Jews, on their part, announced that this Christianity they accepted. "In a moral point of view," said M. Godefroi, a Jew deputy from Amsterdam, "I believe and hope that there is no member of this Chamber, be he who he may, who is not a Christian. The word Christian, in this sense, I can accept with a safe conscience."†

The Jews might be satisfied, but the orthodox Protestants were not. In a speech of remarkable energy, and which produced a deep impression upon the country, M. Groen van Prinsterer made a final effort against the new law. "If this law passes," he cried, "Christianity itself is henceforth only a sect, and in the sphere of government its name must never more be pronounced. We shall have not only the *ne plus ultra* of the separation of Church and State, but we shall have the separation of State and religion." "But the Constitution," retorted M. Groen's adversaries, "but the Constitution

* See the speech of M. Schimmelpenninck, in M. de Laveleye's *Débats sur l'Enseignement primaire*, &c. p. 23.

† *Débats sur l'Enseignement primaire*, &c. p. 53.

is on our side!" "If the Constitution," replied M. Groen, "makes the irreligious school a necessity, revise the Constitution!" When the law passed, he resigned his seat in the Chamber and retired into private life.

It is too soon yet to pronounce on the working of the law of 1857, for it has been in operation but two years. There seems at first sight no reason why the religious instruction of the Dutch schools should not follow the same course under the law of 1857 as under the law of 1806, for both laws regulate this instruction in nearly the same words. But the question of distinctive religious teaching has been raised; the strict execution of the letter of the law has been enforced; the orthodox Protestants have been made to see that, under that law, a religious instruction such as they wished could be given only whilst their adversaries slumbered — could be withheld the moment their adversaries awoke. The able and experienced inspector who conducted me round the schools of Utrecht, M. van Hoijtema, in pointing out to me a private elementary school, remarked that such schools had a much greater importance in Holland now than a few years ago. I asked him the reason of this; he replied that in the large towns, at any rate, there was an increasing dissatisfaction with the inadequate religious instruction of the public schools, an increasing demand for schools where a real definite religious instruction was given. He added that this was a grave state of things; that in his opinion it was very undesirable that the schools of the State, with their superior means of efficiency, should not retain the education of the people *: that Government would probably be

* In Belgium, where the number of children attending some school or other is pretty nearly the same as in Holland, but where,

driven to do something in order to try to remove the present objections to them. I was greatly struck by these words of M. van Hoijtema; his testimony is above suspicion; he is a Government official, and a man of great intelligence, experience, and weight. At the same time that he is school-inspector of Utrecht, he is also first judge of the Military Court of the province. But I do not regard his testimony as decisively establishing the failure of the recent school-law of Holland; on the contrary, the hour has not yet come for judging this law decisively. But it is evident, at the same time, that the example of Holland cannot at this moment be appealed to as exhibiting the complete success of the non-denominational principle.

In fact, it may perhaps be doubted, whether any body of public schools anywhere exists, satisfying at the same time the demands of parents for their children's genuine moral and religious training, and the demands of the partisans of a strict religious neutrality. Secular schools exist, but these do not satisfy the great majority of parents. Schools professing neutral religious teaching exist, but these do not satisfy rigid neutrals. They may profess to give "an instruction penetrated with Christianity, yet without any mixture of Christian dogma," * but they have not yet succeeded in giving it. In America the prevalent religious tone of the country is the religious tone of Protestant Dissent, and this, secular as the American school-system

of that number, the proportion attending private, not public schools, is much greater, the instruction is incredibly inferior to that of Holland. See *Débats sur l'Enseignement primaire*, (the author of which is himself a Belgian), p. 7.

* See the Speech of the Minister of Justice, M. Van der Bruggen, *Débats sur l'Enseignement primaire*, &c. p. 17.

may profess itself, becomes the religious tone of the public education of the country, without violence, without opposition. In England, the religious tone of the schools of the British and Foreign School Society is undoubtedly also the religious tone of Protestant Dissent; but in England Protestant Dissent is not all-pervading and supreme. The British schools, therefore, have to try to neutralise their religious tone, so far as they can do this without impairing its religious sincerity; and, precisely because they have to try to do this, precisely because they have to attempt this impossible feat, these excellent schools are not thoroughly succeeding. While they are too biblical for the secularist, they are yet far too latitudinarian for the orthodox. And not the orthodox only, but the great majority of mankind — the undevout, the indifferent, the sceptical — have a deep-seated feeling that religion ought to be blended with the instruction of their children, even though it is never blended with their own lives. They have a feeling equally deep-seated, that no religion has ever yet been impressively and effectively conveyed to ordinary minds, except under the conditions of a dogmatic shape and positive formularies.

The State must not forget this in legislating for public education; if it does, it must expect its legislation to be a failure. The power which has to govern men, must not omit to take account of one of the most powerful motors of men's nature, their religious feeling. It is vain to tell the State that it is of no religion; it is more true to say that the State is of the religion of all its citizens, without the fanaticism of any. It is most of the religion of the majority, in the sense that it justly establishes this the most widely. It deals with all, indeed, as an authority, not as a partisan; it deals with all lesser bodies contained in itself as possessing a higher reason than any one of them, (for if it has not this, what right has it to govern?); it allows no one religious body to persecute another; it allows none to be irrational at the public expense; it even reserves to itself the right of judging what religious differences are vital and important, and demand a separate establishment*; — but it does not attempt to exclude religion from a sphere which naturally belongs to it; it does not command religion to forego, before it may enter this sphere, the modes of operation which are essential to it; it does not attempt to impose on the masses an eclecticism which may be possible for a few superior minds. It avails itself, to supply a regular known demand of common human nature, of a regular known machinery.

It is not, therefore, unreasonable to ask of those "Religions of the Future" which the present day so prodigally announces, that they will equip themselves with a substantial shape, with a worship, a ministry, and a flock, before we legislate for popular education in accordance with their exigencies. But, when they have done this, their neutralism will be at an end,

* It is worthy of remark that in France a separate establishment, in virtue of Art. 2 of the law of 1833, was conceded only to schools connecting themselves with one or other of the three *cultes reconnus par l'État*, the Catholic, Protestant, and Jewish. It was not thought expedient to recognise minor divisions as constituting sufficient grounds for separating school-children. The difference between the religious tenets of a Baptist and a Roman Catholic, for instance, would in France be held sufficient to make their claim for separate schools reasonable; not so the difference between a Baptist and a Wesleyan. See an interesting decision of the Council Royal on this subject in M. Kilian's *Manuel* already quoted, p. 72.

denominationalism will have made them prisoners; the denominationalism of Groningen or Tübingen, instead of that of Utrecht or Geneva.

The principal change made by the law of 1857 is the establishment of greater liberty of instruction. The certificates of morality and capacity are still demanded of every teacher, public or private; but the special authorisation of the municipality, formerly necessary for every private teacher before he could open school, and not granted except with the district-inspector's sanction, is demanded no longer.* This relaxation makes the establishment of private schools more easy. The programme of primary instruction, and that of the certificate-examination of teachers, remain much the same as they were under the law of 1806. Primary instruction, strictly so called, is pronounced by the law of 1857 to comprehend reading, writing, arithmetic, the elements of geometry, of Dutch grammar, of geography, of history, of the natural sciences, and singing. This is a much fuller programme than the corresponding programme of France or Belgium. The certificate-examination is proportionately fuller also.

The new law expressly prescribes † that primary schools, in each commune, shall be at the commune's charge. The law of 1806 had contained no positive

* A certificate from the municipality, to the effect that they have seen the private teacher's certificates of morality and capacity, and found them in regular form, is still required. But if the municipality refuse or delay the issue of such certificate, the teacher may appeal to the States' deputies and to the King. See Law of August 13th, 1857; Art. 37, 38. A translation of the whole of this important law (for which I am indebted to the kindness of Mr. Ward, the British Secretary of Legation in Holland), will be found at the end of the volume.

† Art. 31.

prescription on this point. The schools are to be in sufficient number, and the States' deputies and the supreme government have the right of judging whether in any commune they are in sufficient number or not.* School-fees are to be exacted of those who can afford to pay them, but not of "children whose families are receiving public relief, or, though not receiving public relief, are unable to pay for their schooling."† If the charge of its schools is too heavy for a commune, the province and the State aid it by a grant, of which each contributes half.‡ The exact amount of charge to be supported by a commune before it can receive aid, is not fixed by the Dutch law; neither is a machinery established for compelling the commune and the province to raise the school-funds required of them. In both these respects the French law is superior. But in the weakest point of the French law, in the establishment of a *minimum* for the teachers' salaries, the Dutch law is commendably liberal. The *minimum* of a schoolmaster's fixed salary, placed at 8*l.* a year by the Belgian and by the French law, the Dutch law places at nearly 34*l.*§ I need not remind the reader that the sum actually received by a schoolmaster in Holland is much greater. An undermaster's salary is fixed at a minimum of 200 florins; one-half of the salary fixed for head-masters.

Under the law of 1857 the public schoolmaster is still appointed by competitive examination. The district-inspector retains his influence over this examination. After it has taken place, he and a select body of the municipality draw up a list of from three to six names, those of the candidates who have acquitted

* Art. 17.

† Art. 33.

‡ Art. 35.

§ 400 florins.

themselves best. From this list the entire body of the communal council makes its selection. The communal council may also dismiss the teacher, but it must first obtain the concurrence of the inspector. If the communal council refuse to pronounce a dismissal which the inspector thinks advisable, the States' deputies of the province may pronounce it upon the representation of this functionary.*

The law fixes the legal staff of teachers to be allowed to public schools. When the number of scholars exceeds 70, the master is to have the aid of a pupil-teacher (*kweekeling*, from *kweeken*, to foster); when it exceeds 100, of an undermaster; when it exceeds 150, of an undermaster and pupil-teacher; for every 50 scholars above this last number he is allowed another pupil teacher, for every 100 scholars another undermaster.† The head master receives two guineas a year for each pupil teacher.

The law of 1857, like that of 1806, has abstained from making education compulsory. But it gives legal sanction to a practice already long followed by many municipalities, and which I have noticed above; it enjoins the municipal council to "provide as far as possible for the attendance at school of all children whose parents are in the receipt of public relief." Great efforts had been made, in the debates on the clauses of the law, to procure a more decided recognition by the State of the principle of compulsory education. It was proposed at least to make the payment of the school-fee obligatory for each child of school age, if the Chamber would not go so far as to make his actual attendance at school obligatory. This obligation of

* Art. 22. † Art. 18.

payment (*schoolgeld-pligtigheid*) had already, it was said, been enforced by the governments of three provinces, Groningen, Drenthe, and Overyssel, with excellent effect.* The usual arguments for compulsory education were adduced—that other countries had successfully established it—that ignorance was making rapid strides for want of it—that in China, where it reigns, all the children can read and write. It was replied that compulsory education was altogether against the habits of the Dutch people. Even in the mitigated form of the *schoolgeld-pligtigheid*, a large majority of the Chamber refused to sanction it.

The new legislation organised inspection somewhat differently from the law of 1806. It retained the local school-commissions, and the district-inspectors; but at the head of the inspection of each district it placed a salaried provincial inspector.† It directed that these provincial inspectors should be assembled, once a year, under the presidency of the Minister for the Home Department, to deliberate on the general interests of primary instruction. The Minister for the Home Department, assisted by a Referendary, is the supreme authority for the government of education. Between the provincial inspectors and the Minister, the law of 1857 has omitted to place inspectors-general. M. de Laveleye, in general the warm admirer of the Dutch school-legislation, considers this omission most unfortunate.

* In Groningen the number of children attending school had risen from 20,000 to 30,000, in consequence of the adoption in 1839, by the provincial government, of a regulation requiring the payment of the school-fee for every child of from 5 to 12 years of age, whether he attended school or not. See *Débats sur l'Enseignement primaire*, p. 57.

† Art. 58.

The 16th article of the law declares that children are to be admitted into the communal school without distinction of creed. For the much-debated 23rd article the wording finally adopted was as follows: —

"Primary instruction, while it imparts the information necessary, is to tend to develope the reason of the young, and to train them to the exercise of all Christian and social virtues.

"The teacher shall abstain from teaching, doing, or permitting anything contrary to the respect due to the convictions of dissenters.

"Religious instruction is left to the different religious communions. The school-room may be put at their disposal for that purpose, for the benefit of children attending the school, out of school-hours."

CHAPTER XVIII.

PRESENT CONDITION OF POPULAR EDUCATION IN HOLLAND.

IN Lord Napier's absence, Mr. Ward, the British Chargé d'Affaires at the Hague, to whose kindness I am much indebted, presented me to M. Vollenhoven, the Referendary charged with the department of primary instruction under the authority of the Minister for the Home Department, M. van Tets. M. Vollenhoven not only furnished me with all the official documents which I wished to consult on the subject of primary instruction in Holland, but obligingly placed me in communication with the school-inspectors of the localities which I proposed to visit. My guide at the Hague was M. van Citters, a member of one of the best families in Holland, of good fortune, and a man of letters, but, with the public spirit of which I have before spoken as distinguishing his countrymen, giving his services gratuitously as a school-inspector. Under his guidance I visited one of the public schools of the Hague. It was a mixed school, containing 320 boys and 330 girls; the teaching staff consisted of a head-master, four under-masters, and five pupil-teachers. The head-master has 1000 florins a-year, with a house, fire, and lights; the under-masters have from 350 to 600 florins a-year; the pupil-teachers from 50 to 100, and their instruction. This instruction is organised somewhat differently from that of our pupil-teachers; in each town of Holland the whole body of public schoolmasters forms one community, jointly giving instruction to the whole body of pupil teachers, each master taking his own subject. In Holland, as in our own country, there are at the present moment many complaints that pupil teachers are exceedingly hard to obtain. Those whom I saw appeared to me in general admirably trained; but yet more remarkable was the training of the principal masters. Many of the pupil teachers spoke a little French, one or two of them a little English; but among the head-masters it is not rare to find men speaking English or French well, and having a considerable acquaintance with the literature of both languages.

The external appearance of the children, in this school at the Hague, and their discipline, were excellent; yet this was one of the four free schools of the capital; there is also one intermediate or paying school. My imperfect knowledge of the Dutch language prevented me from orally examining the scholars; but I saw enough of their work on their slates and in their copy-books, to convince me of the solidity of their instruction. The school opens daily with general prayer, general enough (it is supposed) for all to join in it; and the head master teaches scripture history as part of the school-course. Out of school hours, between 12 and 1 o'clock, special instructors attend, to give, in the school-room, religious instruction to the Protestant scholars; neither Roman Catholics nor the Jews use the school-room for this purpose, though at liberty to do so. I asked if any inconvenience was experienced from the mixture of boys and girls in one school; I was told, none whatever; the practice is universal in Holland. The three large school-rooms were well lighted and airy; though the weather was hot, and the rooms were somewhat overcrowded, the ventilation was perfectly good. In Holland, as in France, it is common, when a school is wanted, to adapt existing buildings to the purpose, instead of erecting new; the adaptations which I saw were generally successful, and much expense is thus saved.

I visited Haarlem; but M. Prinsen, the celebrated director of the normal school, is no longer there. The present director is M. Geerligs, who is at the same time the school-inspector of the district. M. Geerligs obligingly conducted me through the primary schools of the town. Here, as at the Hague, the public schools for the poor are four in number. Of two of these which I visited, one had 500 scholars, under a head-master with a yearly salary of 1200 florins, five under-masters, and one pupil-teacher. The other, with a somewhat lower instruction, had a head-master with a salary of 1000 florins, six under-masters, and three pupil-teachers, with an attendance of 600 scholars. Both schools were overcrowded. Of the two other public schools in Haarlem, one has 700 scholars, the other 500. The pupil-teachers here have from 12 to 25 florins a-year; the rate of their payment differs in different places. The order and cleanliness in both the large poor-schools which I visited were quite exemplary.

The law of 1857 is to be completed by regulations reorganising the normal schools of Holland; but these regulations have not yet appeared. Meanwhile the normal school of Haarlem is provisionally continued. It contained, when I visited it, 25 students. They are not boarded in the institution, but lodge in the town; this arrangement is undoubtedly faulty, and the new regulations will change it. The institution is entirely at the charge of the State, which allows 200 florins a-year for the maintenance of each student in it. Admission is eagerly sought for. The course lasts four years. The students attend lectures from 8 to 9 in the morning, and from $5\frac{1}{2}$ to $7\frac{1}{2}$ in the evening; the first-year students attend lectures in the afternoon also. But the mornings of all the students, the mornings and afternoons of students of the second, third, and fourth year, are spent in teaching in the different schools of Haarlem. They are practised in schools of all kinds; schools for the poor, schools for the middle class; schools (without Greek and Latin) for the rich. The children of the latter, at an age when in England they would probably be still at home, almost universally attend school in Holland. A school for the richer class of children is attached to the normal school, and belongs to the present director, M. Geerlings. The students commence in the poor schools, and go gradually upwards, finishing their practice in schools for the richer class, where the attainment required in the teacher is, of course, more considerable than in the others. In Holland this mode of training the future teacher so as to fit him for any kind of primary school, is found convenient; the superior address and acquirement of the best Dutch teachers is probably to be attributed to it. It is possible that in other countries it might be found to have disadvantages. But, at any rate, the large part assigned in the Dutch system of training to the actual practice of teaching, is excellent. Our normal school authorities would do well to meditate on this great feature of the Haarlem course. The reader will perceive that when I said that, in Holland, the training of the future schoolmaster was much more strictly practical and professional than with us, it was not a vain form of words which I was using.

Holland has at present a population of 3,298,137 inhabitants. For her eleven provinces, she has 11 provincial inspectors and 92 district inspectors. In 1857, her public primary schools were 2,478 in number, with a staff of 2,409 principal masters, 1,587 under-masters, 642 pupil-teachers, 134 schoolmistresses and assistants. In the day and evening schools there were, on the 15th of January, 322,767 scholars. Of these schools 197 were, in 1857, inspected three times; 618, twice; 1,053, once. In 817 of them the instruction is reported as very good; in 1,236 as good; as middling in 367; in 55 as bad. There were, besides, 944 private schools, giving instruction to 83,562 scholars. There were 784 infant schools, receiving 49,873 young children. Boarding-schools, Sunday-schools, and work-schools, with the pupils attending them, are not included in the totals above given.*

The proportion of scholars to the population, not yet so satisfactory as in 1848, was nevertheless in 1857 more satisfactory than in 1854; in January of the latter year, but 1 in every 9·35 inhabitants was in school; in the same month of 1857, 1 in every 8·11 inhabitants. But, in truth, the suffering state of popular education in Holland would be a flourishing state in most other countries. In the debates of 1857 one of the speakers, who complained that popular education in Holland was going back, cited, in proof of the justice of his complaint, returns showing the state of in-

* See Tables I. and II. (compiled from official sources) at the end of this volume.

struction of the conscripts of South Holland in 1856. In this least favoured province, out of 6086 young men drawn for the army, 669 could not read or write. Fortunate country, where such an extent of ignorance is matter of complaint! In the neighbouring country of Belgium in the same year, out of 6617 conscripts in the province of Brabant, 2,254 could not read or write; out of 5910 conscripts in the province of West Flanders, 2088 were in the same condition; out of 7192 in East Flanders, 3153. And, while in East Flanders but 1820 conscripts out of 7192 could read, write, and cipher correctly, in South Holland, in the worst educated of the Dutch provinces, no less than 5268 out of 6086 possessed this degree of acquirement.*

Such, in Holland, is the present excellent situation of primary instruction. In Prussia it may be even somewhat more widely diffused; but nowhere, probably, has it such thorough soundness and solidity. It is impossible to regard it without admiration. Yet I will freely confess that I do not feel in regarding it that lively interest which I should feel if it were produced under conditions more resembling those which exist, or which are likely to exist, in our own country. The circumstances of Holland, though in some external respects singularly like our own, are yet profoundly and essentially different. They are different both in their defects and in their advantages. Holland differs from us in that which most materially influences the course of a nation's life,—in the present temper and genius of her people.

C'est une nation éteinte, a clever Frenchman said to

* [illegible] p. 53.

me of the Dutch people. This is too strong; yet this people, undoubtedly, is no longer in the heyday and flush of its national life; it has no longer the enthusiasm and the aspirations of confident youth or powerful maturity. Although very far, assuredly, from the weakness of decrepitude, its genius moves with the mechanic and unelastic march of a spirit whose prime is over. The Dutch people has now, as a people, two strong aspirations only — for the maintenance of its separate nationality, and for the retention of its colonial dominion. These are respectable aspirations certainly; but such aspirations are not the whole enthusiastic life of great peoples. They were not the sole aspirations of the great Holland of the sixteenth century — of the Holland of William the Silent. They are not the sole aspirations of the England, the France, the Russia, the America, of the present day, looking inquisitively and ardently towards an unbounded future. They are not the sole aspirations of a mighty and growing people, full of life, full of movement, full of energy.

But the sober and limited spirit of the Dutch people regulates all the positive affairs of life with exemplary precision. It regulates them with a precision difficult of attainment for more impulsive and mobile nations. Above all, it regulates them with a precision which its comparatively small numbers render comparatively easy for it. It is easier to have a model village than a model city; it is easier minutely to provide, watch, and keep in order a mechanism for three millions of men, than for thirty millions. What will it be when the three millions are at the same time individually far more still and tractable than the thirty? I do not think we can hope, in England, for municipalities which, like the Dutch municipalities, can in the main safely be trusted to provide and watch over schools; for a population which, like the Dutch population, can in the main safely be trusted to come to school regularly; for a government which has only to give good advice and good suggestions in order to be promptly obeyed.

Even the Government of Holland, however, has regulated popular education by law; even the school-loving people of Holland, so well taught, so sober-minded, so reasonable, is not abandoned in the matter of its education to its own caprices. The State in Holland, where education is prized by the masses, no more leaves education to itself, than the State in France, where it is little valued by them. It is the same in the other country of which I have described the school-system—in Switzerland. Here and there we may have found, indeed, school-rules in some respects injudicious, in some respects extravagant; but everywhere we have found law, everywhere State-regulation. English readers will judge for themselves, whether there is anything which makes the State, in England, unfit to be trusted with such regulation; whether there is anything which makes the people in England unfit to be subjected to it. They will judge, whether there is any danger in intrusting to a State-authority, the least meddlesome, the least grasping, the least prone to over-government in the world—to a State-authority which, even if it wished to change its nature in these respects, would be powerless against the resistance which would confront it—the superintendence of an important concern which the State superintends in all other countries, and which Burke, no friend to petty governmental meddling, would indisputably have classed with religion among the proper objects of State establishment*, had this question of popular education come to the surface in his day. They will judge, whether there is any inherent quality in the English people, fitting it to regulate well by itself a concern which no other people has by itself well regulated.

For a certain part of its education, undoubtedly, the English people is sufficient to itself. In the air of England, in the commerce of his countrymen, in the long tradition and practice of liberty, there is for every Englishman an education which is without a parallel in the world, and which I am the last to undervalue. If I do not extol it, it is because every one in England appreciates it duly. This education of a people governments neither give nor take away. This it receives, not by the disposition of legislators, but by the essential conditions of its own being. But there are some things which neither in England nor in any other country can the mass of a people have by nature, and these things governments can give it. They can give it those simple, but invaluable and humanising, acquirements, without which the finest race in the world is but a race of splendid barbarians. Above all, governments, in giving these, may at the same time educate a people's reason, a people's equity. These are not the qualities which the masses develope for themselves. Obstinate resistance to oppression, omnipotent industry, heroic valour, all these may come from below upwards; but unprejudiced intelligence, but equitable moderation — never. If, then, the State

* See the remarkable passage in *Thoughts and Details on Scarcity*, Burke's *Works*, London, 1852, vol. v. p. 210.

disbelieves in reason, when will reason reach the mob?

In England the State is perhaps inclined to admit too readily its powerlessness as inevitable. It too easily resigns itself to believe that there exists in the country no such thing as a party of reason, capable of upholding a government which should boldly throw itself upon it for support. Perhaps such a party exists; perhaps it is stronger than governments think. No doubt the State has in this country to confront, when it attempts to act, great suspicion, great jealousy. But in other countries, also, it has had its adversaries to contend with; and it has sometimes, even when most despotic, relied for success not on superior brute force, but on an arm which the most constitutional State might blamelessly wield—on superior reason. The Consular legislation of 1802, which I have already mentioned, supplies a notable instance. In his great work of reorganising French society, Napoleon determined to revive, by the institution of the justest system of public recompenses ever founded—the Legion of Honour—those distinctions of rank which are salutary and necessary to society, but which feudalism had abused and anarchy had abolished. Distinctions are in nature; but there are the essential distinctions of Nature herself, and there are the arbitrary distinctions of accident or favour. The decorations of governments usually follow the latter. The Legion of Honour was instituted to do homage to the former. The fanatics of an impossible equality declaimed violently against the First Consul's project. He persevered and succeeded; but both in the Tribunate and in the Legislative Body his measure encountered strenuous resistance. "We have gone a little too fast," said Napoleon to those about him, when he heard of this opposition: "we have gone a little too fast, that must be allowed. *But we had reason on our side; and, when one has reason on one's side, one should have the courage to run some risks.*" Noble words of a profound and truly creative genius, which employed, in administration, something solider than makeshifts!

APPENDIX

FRANCE.

Décret sur l'Organisation de l'Instruction primaire.—3 Brumaire, An 4 (25 Octobre 1795).

Titre 1.—Écoles primaires.

Art. 1. Il sera établi dans chaque canton de la République une ou plusieurs écoles primaires, dont les arrondissemens seront déterminés par les administrations de département.

2. Il sera établi dans chaque département plusieurs jurys d'instruction: le nombre de ces jurys sera de six au plus, et chacun sera composé de trois membres nommés par l'administration départementale.

3. Les instituteurs primaires seront examinés par l'un des jurys d'instruction, et sur la présentation des administrations municipales; ils seront nommés par les administrations de département.

4. Ils ne pourront être destitués que par le concours des mêmes administrations, de l'avis d'un jury d'instruction, et après avoir été entendus.

5. Dans chaque école primaire on enseignera à lire, à écrire, à calculer, et les élémens de la morale républicaine.

6. Il sera fourni par la République, à chaque instituteur primaire, un local tant pour lui servir de logement, que pour recevoir les élèves pendant la durée des leçons.

Il sera également fourni à chaque instituteur le jardin qui se trouverait attenant à ce local. Lorsque les administrations de département le jugeront plus convenable, il sera alloué à l'instituteur une somme annuelle, pour lui tenir lieu du logement et du jardin susdits.

7. Ils pourront, ainsi que les professeurs des écoles centrales et spéciales, cumuler traitement et pensions.

8. Les instituteurs primaires recevront de chacun de leurs élèves une rétribution annuelle, qui sera fixée par l'administration de département.

9. L'administration municipale pourra exempter de cette rétribution un quart des élèves de chaque école primaire pour cause d'indigence.

10. Les règlements relatifs au régime des écoles primaires seront arrêtés par les administrations de département, et soumis à l'approbation du directoire exécutif.

11. Les administrations municipales surveilleront immédiatement les écoles primaires, et y maintiendront l'exécution des lois et des arrêtés des administrations supérieures.

Loi sur l'Instruction primaire. 28 Juin 1833.

Titre I.—*De l'Instruction primaire et de son objet.*

Art. 1.

L'instruction primaire est élémentaire ou supérieure.

L'instruction primaire élémentaire comprend nécessairement l'instruction morale et religieuse, la lecture, l'écriture, les éléments de la langue française et du calcul, le système légal des poids et mesures.

L'instruction primaire supérieure comprend nécessairement, en outre, les éléments de la géométrie et ses applications usuelles, spécialement le dessin linéaire et l'arpentage, des notions des sciences physiques et de l'histoire naturelle applicables aux usages de la vie, le chant, les éléments de l'histoire et de la géographie, et surtout de l'histoire et de la géographie de la France.

Selon les besoins et les ressources des localités, l'instruction primaire pourra recevoir les développements qui seront jugés convenables.

Art. 2.

Le vœu des pères de famille sera toujours consulté et suivi en ce qui concerne la participation de leurs enfants à l'instruction religieuse.

Art. 3.

L'instruction primaire est privée ou publique.

Titre 2. — Des Écoles primaires privées.

Art. 4.

Tout individu âgé de dix-huit ans accomplis pourra exercer la profession d'instituteur primaire et diriger tout établissement quelconque d'instruction primaire, sans autres conditions que de présenter préalablement au maire de la commune où il voudra tenir école,

1. Un brevet de capacité obtenu, après examen, selon le dégré de l'école qu'il veut établir.

2. Un certificat constatant que l'impétrant est digne, par sa moralité, de se livrer à l'enseignement. Ce certificat sera délivré, sur l'attestation de trois conseillers municipaux, par le maire de la commune ou de chacune des communes où il aura résidé depuis trois ans.

Art. 5.

Sont incapables de tenir école,

1. Les condamnés à des peines afflictives ou infamantes.

2. Les condamnés pour vol, escroquerie, banqueroute, abus de confiance ou attentat aux mœurs, et les individus qui auront été privés par jugement de tout ou partie des droits de famille mentionnés aux paragraphes 5 et 6 de l'article 12 du Code pénal.

3. Les individus interdits en exécution de l'article 7 de la présente loi.

Art. 6.

Quiconque aura ouvert une école primaire en contravention à l'article 5, ou sans avoir satisfait aux conditions prescrites par l'article 4 de la présente loi, sera poursuivi devant le tribunal correctionnel du lieu du délit, et condamné à une amende de cinquante à deux cents francs ; l'école sera fermée. En cas de récidive, le délinquant sera condamné à un emprisonnement de quinze à trente jours et à une amende de cent à quatre cents francs.

Art. 7.

Tout instituteur privé, sur la demande du comité mentionné dans l'article 19 de la présente loi, ou sur la poursuite d'office du ministère public, pourra être traduit, pour cause d'inconduite ou d'immoralité, devant le tribunal civil de l'arrondissement, et être interdit de l'exercice de sa profession à temps ou à toujours.

Le tribunal entendra les parties, et statuera sommairement en chambre du conseil. Il en sera de même sur l'appel, qui devra être interjeté dans le délai de dix jours, à compter du jour de la notification du jugement, et qui en aucun cas ne sera suspensif.

Le tout sans préjudice des poursuites qui pourraient avoir lieu pour crimes, délits ou contraventions prévus par les lois.

Titre 3.—Des Écoles primaires publiques.

Art. 8.

Les écoles primaires publiques sont celles qu'entretiennent, en tout ou en partie, les communes, les départements, ou l'État.

Art. 9.

Toute commune est tenue, soit par elle-même, soit en se réunissant à une ou plusieurs communes voisines, d'entretenir au moins une école primaire élémentaire.

Dans le cas où les circonstances locales le permettraient, le Ministre de l'Instruction publique pourra, après avoir entendu le conseil municipal, autoriser, à titres d'écoles communales, des écoles plus particulièrement affectées à l'un des cultes reconnus par l'État.

Art. 10.

Les communes chefs-lieux de département, et celles dont la population excède six mille âmes, devront avoir en outre une école primaire supérieure.

Art. 11.

Tout département sera tenu d'entretenir une école normale primaire, soit par lui-même, soit en se réunissant à un ou plusieurs départements voisins.

Les conseils généraux délibéreront sur les moyens d'assurer l'entretien des écoles normales primaires. Ils délibéreront également sur la réunion de plusieurs départements pour l'entretien d'une seule école normale. Cette réunion devra être autorisée par ordonnance royale.

Art. 12.

Il sera fourni à tout instituteur communal,—

1. Un local convenablement disposé, tant pour lui servir d'habitation que pour recevoir les élèves.

2. Un traitement fixe qui ne pourra être moindre de deux cents francs pour une école primaire élémentaire, et de quatre cents francs pour une école primaire supérieure.

Art. 13.

A défaut de fondations, donations, ou legs, qui assurent un local et un traitement, conformément à l'article précédent, le conseil municipal délibérera sur les moyens d'y pourvoir.

En cas d'insuffisance des revenus ordinaires pour l'établissement des écoles primaires élémentaires et supérieures, il y sera pourvu au moyen d'une imposition spéciale, votée par le conseil municipal, ou, à défaut du vote de ce conseil, établie par ordonnance royale. Cette imposition, qui devra être autorisée chaque année par la loi de finances, ne pourra excéder trois centimes additionnels au principal des contributions foncière, personnelle et mobilière.

Lorsque des communes n'auront pu, soit isolément, soit par la réunion de plusieurs d'entre elles, procurer un local et assurer le traitement au moyen de cette contribution de trois centimes, il sera pourvu aux dépenses reconnues nécessaires à l'instruction primaire, et, en cas d'insuffisance des fonds départementaux, par une imposition spéciale, votée par le conseil général du département, ou, à défaut du vote de ce conseil, établie par ordonnance royale. Cette imposition, qui devra être autorisée chaque année par la loi de finances, ne pourra excéder deux centimes additionnels au principal des contributions foncière, personnelle et mobilière.

Si les centimes ainsi imposés aux communes et aux départements ne suffisent pas aux besoins de l'instruction primaire, le Ministre de l'Instruction publique y pourvoira au moyen d'une subvention prélevée sur le crédit qui sera porté annuellement pour l'instruction primaire au budget de l'État.

Chaque année il sera annexé à la proposition du budget un rapport détaillé sur l'emploi des fonds alloués pour l'année précédente.

Art. 14.

En sus du traitement fixe, l'instituteur communal recevra une rétribution mensuelle, dont le taux sera réglé par le conseil municipal et qui sera perçue dans la même forme et selon les mêmes règles que les contributions publiques directes. Le rôle en sera recouvrable, mois par mois, sur un état des élèves, certifié par l'instituteur, visé par le maire, et rendu exécutoire par le sous-préfet.

Le recouvrement de la rétribution ne donnera lieu qu'au remboursement des frais par la commune, sans aucune remise au profit des agents de la perception.

Seront admis gratuitement dans l'école communale élémentaire ceux des élèves de la commune ou des communes réunies, que les conseils municipaux auront désignés comme ne pouvant payer aucune rétribution.

Dans les écoles primaires supérieures un nombre de places gratuites, déterminé par le conseil municipal, pourra être réservé pour les enfants qui, après concours, auront été designés par le comité d'instruction primaire, dans les familles qui seront hors d'état de payer la rétribution.

Art. 15.

Il sera établi dans chaque département une caisse d'épargne et de prévoyance en faveur des instituteurs primaires communaux.

Les statuts de ces caisses d'épargne seront déterminés par des ordonnances royales.

Cette caisse sera formée par une retenue annuelle d'un vingtième sur le traitement fixe de chaque instituteur communal. Le montant de la retenue sera placé au compte ouvert au trésor royal pour les caisses d'épargne et de prévoyance; les intérêts de ces fonds seront capitalisés tous les six mois. Le produit total de la retenue exercée sur chaque instituteur lui sera rendu à l'époque où il se retirera, et, en cas de décès dans l'exercice de ses fonctions, à sa veuve, ou à ses héritiers.

Dans aucun cas, il ne pourra être ajouté aucune subvention, sur les fonds de l'État, à cette caisse d'épargne et de prévoyance; mais elle pourra, dans les formes et selon les règles prescrites pour les établissements d'utilité publique, recevoir des dons et legs dont l'emploi, à défaut de dispositions des donateurs ou des testateurs, sera réglé par le conseil général.

Art. 16.

Nul ne pourra être nommé instituteur communal, s'il ne remplit les conditions de capacité et de moralité prescrites par l'article 4 de la présente loi, ou s'il se trouve dans un des cas prévus par l'article 5.

Titre 4.—Des Autorités préposées à l'Instruction primaire.

Art. 17.

Il y aura près de chaque école communale un comité local de surveillance composé du maire ou adjoint, président, du curé ou pasteur, et d'un ou plusieurs habitants notables désignés par le comité d'arrondissement.

Dans les communes dont la population est répartie entre différents cultes reconnus par l'État, le curé ou le plus ancien des curés, et un des ministres de chacun des autres cultes, désigné par son consistoire, feront partie du comité communal de surveillance.

Plusieurs écoles de la même commune pourront être réunies sous la surveillance du même comité.

Lorsqu'en vertu de l'article 9 plusieurs communes se seront réunies pour entretenir une école, le comité d'arrondissement désignera, dans chaque commune un ou plusieurs habitants notables pour faire partie du comité. Le maire de chacune des communes fera en outre partie du comité.

Sur le rapport du comité d'arrondissement, le Ministre de l'Instruction publique pourra dissoudre un comité local de surveillance et le remplacer par un comité spécial, dans lequel personne ne sera compris de droit.

Art. 18.

Il sera formé dans chaque arrondissement de sous-préfecture un comité spécialement chargé de surveiller et d'encourager l'instruction primaire.

Le Ministre de l'Instruction publique pourra, suivant la population et les besoins des localités, établir dans le même arrondissement plusieurs comités, dont il déterminera la circonscription par cantons isolés ou agglomérés.

Art. 19.

Sont membres des comités d'arrondissement :—

Le maire du chef-lieu ou le plus ancien des maires du chef-lieu de la circonscription.

Le juge de paix ou le plus ancien des juges de paix de la circonscription.

Le curé ou le plus ancien des curés de la circonscription.

Un ministre de chacun des autres cultes reconnus par la loi, qui exercera dans la circonscription, et qui aura été désigné comme il est dit au second paragraphe de l'article 17.

Un proviseur, principal de collège, professeur, régent, chef d'institution, ou maître de pension, désigné par le Ministre de l'Instruction publique, lorsqu'il existera des collèges, institutions, ou pensions dans la circonscription du comité.

Un instituteur primaire, résidant dans la circonscription du comité, et désigné par le Ministre de l'Instruction publique.

Trois membres du conseil d'arrondissement, ou habitants notables désignés par le dit conseil :

Les membres du conseil général du département, qui auront leur domicile réel dans la circonscription du comité.

Le préfet préside de droit tous les comités du département, et le sous-préfet tous ceux de l'arrondissement ; le procureur du roi est membre de droit de tous les comités de l'arrondissement.

Le comité choisit tous les ans son vice-président et son secrétaire ; il peut prendre celui-ci hors de son sein. Le secrétaire, lorsqu'il est choisi hors du comité, en devient membre par sa nomination.

Art. 20.

Les comités s'assembleront au moins une fois par mois. Ils pourront être convoqués extraordinairement sur la demande d'un délégué du Ministre : ce délégué assistera à la délibération.

Les comités ne pourront délibérer s'il n'y a au moins cinq membres présents pour les comités d'arrondissement, et trois pour les comités communaux ; en cas de partage, le président aura voix prépondérante.

Les fonctions de notables qui font partie des comités dureront trois ans ; ils seront indéfiniment rééligibles.

Art. 21.

Le comité communal a inspection sur les écoles publiques ou privées de la commune. Il veille à la salubrité des écoles et au maintien de la discipline, sans préjudice des attributions du maire en matière de police municipale.

Il s'assure qu'il a été pourvu à l'enseignement gratuit des enfants pauvres.

Il arrête un état des enfants qui ne reçoivent l'instruction primaire ni à domicile, ni dans les écoles publiques ou privées.

Il fait connaître au comité d'arrondissement les divers besoins de la commune sous le rapport de l'instruction primaire.

En cas d'urgence, et sur la plainte du comité communal, le maire peut ordonner provisoirement que l'instituteur sera suspendu de ses fonctions, à la charge de rendre compte dans les vingt-quatre heures, au comité d'arrondissement, de cette suspension et des motifs qui l'ont déterminée.

Le conseil municipal présente au comité d'arrondissement les candidats pour les écoles publiques après avoir préalablement pris l'avis du comité communal.

Art. 22.

Le comité d'arrondissement inspecte, et, au besoin, fait inspecter par des délégués pris parmi ses membres ou hors de son sein, toutes les écoles primaires de son ressort. Lorsque les délégués ont été choisis par lui, hors de son sein, ils ont droit d'assister à ses séances avec voix délibérative.

Lorsqu'il le juge nécessaire, il réunit plusieurs écoles de la même commune sous la surveillance du même comité, ainsi qu'il a été prescrit à l'article 17.

Il envoie chaque année au préfet et au Ministre de l'Instruction publique l'état de situation de toutes les écoles primaires du ressort.

Il donne son avis sur les secours et les encouragements à accorder à l'instruction primaire.

Il provoque les réformes et les améliorations nécessaires.

Il nomme les instituteurs communaux sur la présentation du conseil municipal, procède à leur installation, et reçoit leur serment.

Les instituteurs communaux doivent être institués par le Ministre de l'Instruction publique.

Art. 23.

En cas de négligence habituelle, ou de faute grave de l'instituteur communal, le comité d'arrondissement, ou d'office, ou sur la plainte adressée par le comité communal, mande l'instituteur inculpé; après l'avoir entendu, ou dûment appelé, il le réprimande ou le suspend pour un mois avec ou sans privation de traitement, ou même le révoque de ses fonctions.

L'instituteur frappé d'une révocation pourra se pourvoir devant le Ministre de l'Instruction publique, en Conseil royal. Ce pourvoi devra être formé dans le délai d'un mois, à partir de la notification de la décision du comité, de laquelle notification il sera dressé procès verbal par le maire de la commune. Toutefois, la décision du comité est exécutoire par provision.

Pendant la suspension de l'instituteur, son traitement, s'il en est privé, sera laissé à la disposition du conseil municipal, pour être alloué, s'il y a lieu, à un instituteur remplaçant.

Art. 24.

Les dispositions de l'article 7 de la présente loi, relatives aux instituteurs privés, sont applicables aux instituteurs communaux.

Art. 25.

Il y aura dans chaque département une ou plusieurs commissions d'instruction primaire, chargées d'examiner tous les aspirants aux brevets de capacité, soit pour l'instruction primaire élémentaire, soit pour l'instruction primaire supérieure, et qui délivreront les dits brevets sous l'autorité du Ministre. Ces commissions seront également chargées de faire les examens d'entrée et de sortie des élèves de l'école normale primaire.

Les membres de ces commissions seront nommés par le Ministre de l'Instruction publique.

Les examens auront lieu publiquement, et à des époques déterminées par le Ministre de l'Instruction publique.

I.—GENERAL

Showing the Progress of STATE-EXPENDITURE

	[illegible]	[illegible]	[illegible]	[illegible]
	Fr. c.	Fr. c.	Fr. c.	Fr. c.
Faculties of Law	[illegible]	[illegible]	2[illegible]	28[illegible]
Faculties of Medicine	264,611 71†	25[illegible]	17[illegible]	—
Secondary Instruction	1,710,768 [illegible]	1,200,[illegible]	1,016,[illegible]	1,7[illegible]
Primary Instruction		[illegible]		[illegible]
Institute	287,165 [illegible]	[illegible]	[illegible]	[illegible]
College of France	124,711 [illegible]	[illegible]	11[illegible]	[illegible]
Museum of Natural History	[illegible]	[illegible]	[illegible]	[illegible]
Bureau of Longitudes	120,[illegible]	[illegible]	[illegible]	[illegible]
Imperial Library	171,[illegible] 00	200,000 00	[illegible] 71	207,000 00
Mazarine Library	21,905 00	28,[illegible] 00	21,1[illegible]	[illegible]
Arsenal Library	82,001 [illegible]	[illegible]	[illegible]	[illegible]
Ste. Geneviève Library	[illegible]	[illegible]	[illegible]	[illegible]
Academy of Medicine				
School of Oriental Languages and School of Charters	17,[illegible]	[illegible]	[illegible]	[illegible]
Encouragement to Societies and the Arts	111,[illegible]	[illegible]	97,671 [illegible]	71,[illegible]
Subscriptions to Scientific Literary and Scientific Works	151,[illegible] 00	140,[illegible] 00	[illegible]	164,[illegible]73 15
Donations to Artists	[illegible]	37,[illegible]	[illegible]	13,170 00
Total	[illegible] 71	[illegible]	[illegible] 95	[illegible] 977 47

* The [illegible] Tables following [illegible] extracted from *[illegible]* [illegible] Ministère de l'Instruction publique [illegible] Paris, 1867.

† Divided between the faculties of Law and Medicine.

TABLE.*

on PUBLIC INSTRUCTION from 1809 to 1834.

1821.		1824.		1827.		1829.		1832.		1834.	
Fr.	c.	Fr.	c.	Fr.	c.	Fr.	c.	Fr.	c.	Fr.	c.
—		—		—		—		—		—	
—		—		—		—		—		—	
1,794,924	86	1,768,107	31	1,741,117	25	1,725,000	00	1,587,942	91	1,689,856	19
58,630	37	49,387	45	44,473	85	99,677	00	984,979	29	1,501,296	91
459,994	62	421,991	48	424,994	81	425,439	43	420,543	09	496,785	20
112,357	29	111,756	62	116,939	05	119,047	85	134,044	20	126,079	97
334,008	00	325,000	01	335,246	33	338,041	30	337,471	59	369,255	18
121,405	54	114,900	54	113,999	55	113,699	36	114,932	51	105,999	60
205,710	00	201,160	34	202,930	00	205,000	00	204,333	22	267,681	65
	‡	34,999	68	34,999	68	34,999	68	33,999	01	35,000	00
32,999	56	32,999	56	32,710	87	32,833	30	33,000	00	35,000	80
37,000	00	37,000	00	37,000	00	36,999	36	37,999	88	39,499	83
		22,183	93	40,739	27	39,945	22	39,999	93	41,999	85
37,790	02	43,751	97	44,989	58	47,896	47	51,856	89	55,276	01
94,655	31	132,368	00	61,209	97	72,693	00	77,832	67	171,345	21
169,615	67	116,679	66	98,866	50	132,490	70	135,595	70	96,628	55
49,800	00	49,250	00	48,750	00	50,050	00	49,250	00	48,908	32
3,508,991	24	3,491,536	55	3,379,166	71	3,473,812	67	4,213,770	99	5,033,013	27

‡ In 1821 the expense of the *Bibliothèque Mazarine* is included in that of the Institute.

§ The expense of the central administration is not shown in the above table. This was for 1835, 471,278 fr. 22c.; for 1845, 521,037 fr. 54c.; for 1855, 638,312 fr. 66c.

II.

Table of State-Expenditure on Primary Instruction, from 1835 to 1855.

Years	Ordinary and Obligatory Expenditure	Extraordinary Expenditure	Special Expenditure	Total
	Fr. c.	Fr. c.	Fr. c.	Fr. c.
1835	511,104 25	1,040,660 14		[illegible]
1836	610,182 72	982,590 02		[illegible] 772 94
1837				[illegible]
1838				[illegible]
1839	[illegible] 612 97	[illegible] 274 80		[illegible] 217 77
1840	[illegible]	[illegible] 737 40		[illegible]
1841	[illegible] 815 1[illegible]	[illegible]		[illegible]
1842	[illegible] 112 97	1,855,570 06		[illegible]
1843	[illegible] 117 71	[illegible] 814 17		[illegible]
1844	728,[illegible] 66	[illegible] 418 6[illegible]		[illegible]
1845	77[illegible]	[illegible] 25 77		[illegible]
1846	700,821 10	[illegible]		[illegible]
1847	[illegible] 66	[illegible]		[illegible]
1848	[illegible] 20	[illegible] 721 15	[illegible] 20	[illegible] 401 [illegible] 87
1849	[illegible] 96	[illegible]		[illegible] 05
1850	[illegible] 901 00	[illegible] 421 187 92	[illegible] 17	[illegible] 05
1851	[illegible] 745 8[illegible]	1,842,190 29	[illegible] 87	[illegible] 71 92
1852	[illegible] 112 [illegible]	[illegible] 77	17,710 [illegible]	[illegible] 12
1853	[illegible] 967 0[illegible]	1,71[illegible]	[illegible]	[illegible]
1854	[illegible] 597,[illegible] 97	1,71[illegible]	51,617 6[illegible]	[illegible] 22
1855	[illegible] 811 81	[illegible] 02	38,611 71	[illegible] 071 87

III.

TABLE of DEPARTMENTAL EXPENDITURE on PRIMARY INSTRUCTION from 1835 to 1855.

Years.	Ordinary Expenditure.		Extraordinary Expenditure.		Arrears of Expenditure.		Total.	
	Fr.	c.	Fr.	c.	Fr.	c.	Fr.	c.
1835							2,888,912	59
1836							3,231,162	63
1837							3,859,541	82
1838							3,873,412	46
1839	2,684,249	85	1,309,832	04	21,696	42	4,015,778	05
1840	2,694,661	72	1,387,039	71	18,704	37	4,100,405	80
1841	2,749,371	66	1,328,014	73	22,262	08	4,099,648	47
1842	2,753,521	73	1,326.638	70	26,230	75	4,106,391	18
1843	2,760,351	57	1,231,747	50	18,381	14	4,040,480	61
1844	2,787,351	79	1,477,541	90	135,016	86	4,399,432	52
1845	2,809,240	77	1,570,118	87	24,531	11	4,404,313	75
1846	2,852,387	61	1,477,063	87	49,022	39	4,378,528	50
1847	2,913,810	89	1,504,891	11	98,920	66	4,517,622	66
1848	2,898,545	39	1,440,029	97	86,960	02	4,425,535	58
1849	2,945,891	32	1,496,387	71	105,118	41	4,547,697	47
1850	2,877,361	14	1,541,864	01	117,299	92	4,536,528	10
1851	4,015,381	47	720,131	75	116,151	01	4,851,667	26
1852	4,188,100	72	1,177,145	29	165,803	14	5,531,049	15
1853	4,241,405	79	1,201,318	13	91,646	89	5,537,370	81
1854	4,232,409	47	1,227,288	90	75,484	59	5,535,182	96
1855	4,134,418	18	1,088,828	77	189,619	71	5,412,866	66

IV.

TABLE showing SUMMARY of STATE, DEPARTMENTAL, and COMMUNAL* EXPENDITURE on PRIMARY INSTRUCTION for the Years 1837, 1846, 1850, 1852 and 1855.

Nature of Receipts and Expenses	1837	1846	1850	1852	1855
	Fr. c.	Fr. c.	Fr. c.	Fr. c.	Fr. c.
Received by [illegible]	8,619,153 00	9,027,704 00	8,745,408 40	8,770,626 27	8,951,817 [illegible]
Expenses charged on the Communes	7,217,861 85	8,511,865 00	9,876,7[illegible]8 89	10,71[illegible] 9[illegible]	1[illegible] 7[illegible]
Expenses charged on the Departments	2,853,511 82	4,378,5[illegible]8 50	4,58[illegible] 1	[illegible],[illegible]71 [illegible]19 15	[illegible],112,866 0[illegible]
Expenses charged on the State	1,845,567 15	2,808,914 21	[illegible] 19	6,211,1[illegible]2 6[illegible]	5,7[illegible]7,957 0[illegible]
Expenses charged on the resources of the Primary Normal Schools†	255,8[illegible]8 01	556,290 77	182,851 3[illegible]	140,[illegible]39 0[illegible]	215,71[illegible] 1[illegible]
Totals	21,78[illegible] [illegible]01 91	25,[illegible]8,2[illegible]2 48	29,[illegible]87,[illegible] 2[illegible]	[illegible]1,[illegible]98,022 10	32,210,819 3[illegible]

* This Table is incomplete as regards the Communes. Their extraordinary expenditure [illegible] not being included in it. The expenditure averages six times the amount [illegible] of the State for the same object. [illegible] the figures given in the last [illegible] represent the whole expenditure [illegible] upon French primary instruction [illegible] printed forms.

† The [illegible] of the property of the State Primary Normal Schools [illegible] by legacies or [illegible] are received by the State, which afterwards pays them back as a separate [illegible] to the expenses of primary instruction.

V.

TABLE* showing the **NUMBER** of **CRIMINALS** accused, acquitted, and condemned, in **FRANCE**, from 1826 to 1850.

Years.	Population according to the Census of each Period.	Accused.	Acquitted.	Condemned.
1826		6,988	2,640	4,348
1827	31,857,961	6,929	2,693	4,236
1828		7,396	2,845	4,551
1829		7,373	2,898	4,475
1830		6,962	2,832	4,130
				21,740
1831		7,606	3,508	4,098
1832	32,561,463	8,237	3,592	4,645
1833		7,315	3,118	4,197
1834		6,952	2,791	4,161
1835		7,223	2,825	4,398
				21,499
1836	33,540,910	7,232	2,609	4,623
1837		8,094	2,977	5,117
1838		8,014	2,853	5,161
1839		7,858	2,795	5,063
1840		8,226	2,750	5,476
				25,440
1841		7,462	2,446	5,016
1842	34,230,178	6,953	2,251	4,702
1843		7,226	2,342	4,884
1844		7,195	2,295	4,900
1845		6,685	2,234	4,451
				23,953
1846		6,908	2,275	4,633
1847	35,401,761	8,704	2,873	5,831
1848		7,352	3,048	4,304
1849		6,983	2,774	4,209
1850		7,202	2,696	4,506
		185,075	68,960	23,483
				116,115

* Extracted from the *Rapport présenté au Prince Président de la République, par le Garde des Sceaux, sur l'Administration de la Justice Criminelle en France, pendant les années* 1826 *à* 1850; Paris, September 1852.

RÈGLEMENT pour les ÉCOLES COMMUNALES LAÏQUES de GARÇONS de la VILLE de PARIS.

[illegible] 25 [illegible] 1852.

I. – TABLEAU DE L'EMPLOI DU TEMPS.

Heures	1re CLASSE	Heures	2me CLASSE
8 1/2	OUVERTURE DE L'ÉCOLE, ARRIVÉE DES MAÎTRES. [illegible]		
9	Prière : *[illegible]* Dei.	9	Prière : *[illegible]* Dei.
	INSTRUCTION MORALE ET RELIGIEUSE. Tous les jours.		INSTRUCTION MORALE ET RELIGIEUSE. [illegible]
10	LANGUE FRANÇAISE. Tous les jours.	10	LECTURE. [illegible]
11	ÉCRITURE: Lundi, Mercredi, Vendredi. — HISTOIRE ET GÉOGRAPHIE: Mardi, Jeudi, Samedi.	11	ÉCRITURE.
12	Prière : *[illegible]*	12	Prière : *[illegible]*
	Déjeuner et Récréation [illegible] préaux.		Déjeuner et Récréation [illegible] préaux.
	GYMNASTIQUE [illegible]		
1	Prière : *[illegible]* Sancte.	1	Prière : *[illegible]* Sancte.
	ARITHMÉTIQUE ET SYSTÈME MÉTRIQUE. [illegible]		CALCUL.
2	DESSIN LINÉAIRE: Lundi, Mercredi, Vendredi. — EXPLICATIONS ET INTERROGATIONS [illegible] Mardi, Samedi.	2	ÉCRITURE. — DESSIN LINÉAIRE [illegible]
3	LECTURE: Mardi, Samedi. — CHANT: Lundi, Mercredi, Vendredi.		LECTURE.
4	Prière : *[illegible]*	4	Prière : *[illegible]*
	CHANT DU *DOMINE*		CHANT DU *DOMINE*

DÉPART DES ÉLÈVES.

[illegible]

Indication du Temps consacré, en somme, à chaque enseignement, par semaine.

—	1re Classe.	2me Classe.	—
	Heures.	Heures.	
Instruction morale et religieuse	6	6	
Lecture . .	4	11	
Écriture . .	3	11	
Langue française . .	6	„	ORTHOGRAPHE, 6 heures pour les élèves les plus avancés.
Arithmétique et Système métrique . . .	5	5	
Dessin linéaire . . .	3	„	6 heures pour les élèves les plus avancés.
Chant . .	3	„	
Histoire et Géographie .	3	„	
	33 heures	33 heures	

Nota.—La gymnastique a lieu pendant les récréations.

II.—Mode d'Enseignement.

Première Classe.

La première classe, celle des élèves avancés, sera dirigée selon le mode simultané ; l'enseignement y sera donné directement par l'instituteur.

Cependant, pour plusieurs facultés, dans lesquelles les élèves sont ordinairement de forces inégales, et doivent faire des devoirs différents, telles que l'arithmétique et l'orthographe, on formera plusieurs divisions qui recevront successivement leçon du maitre.

Avant son arrivée dans une division, ou après qu'il y aura donné leçon, le maître sera remplacé par un moniteur.

Seconde Classe.

Pour la partie la plus élémentaire de l'enseignement donné dans la seconde classe, ou classe des commençants, des moniteurs seront employés. On prendra, pour en remplir les fonctions, et à tour de rôle, les élèves de la classe avancée.

Cependant des élèves non encore admis dans cette dernière classe seront utilisés comme moniteurs, s'ils sont capables de l'être, et s'ils reçoivent tous les jours, sur ce qu'ils enseignent, une leçon directe du maître.

L'autre partie de l'enseignement, dans la seconde classe, sera donnée par le maître lui-même, comme il va être dit dans les articles suivants.

III.—Procédés d'Enseignement à suivre dans la Seconde Classe.

1° Instruction morale et religieuse.

Prières.

Un moniteur placé à l'estrade récitera à haute voix, lentement, et plusieurs fois, la prière qui lui sera indiquée par l'instituteur.

Les élèves qui ne savent pas lire, placés dans les bancs devant le moniteur, l'écouteront (première demi-heure), et plusieurs d'entre eux devront, à la fin de cet exercice, réciter successivement la prière assignée (seconde demi-heure).

Catéchisme et Histoire-Sainte.

Quant aux élèves qui savent lire, ils étudieront individuellement, aux bancs, le catéchisme et l'histoire-sainte (première demi-heure).

Ils réciteront ensuite au maître (seconde demi-heure).

2° Lecture.

Aux groupes, devant les tableaux, pour les commençants.

Epellation avec l'aide du moniteur (première demi-heure).

Commencement de lecture courante dans la partie du tableau qui aura été épelée (seconde demi-heure).

Pour les élèves plus avancés dans la lecture des tableaux, l'épellation n'aura plus lieu, on emploiera le procédé de lecture courante seulement.

Aux tables, dans les livres.

Les élèves arrivés à la lecture courante dans les livres, seront réunis aux tables, en divisions plus ou moins nombreuses, pour y être exercés par le maître, suivant le mode simultané, à la lecture à haute voix.

3° Ecriture.

L'enseignement de l'écriture aura lieu sur modèles, sans dictées, dans toutes les divisions de la classe.

La correction sera continue; elle sera faite par le maître, secondé de quelques moniteurs.

4° Orthographe.

Il y aura pour les élèves les plus avancés de la seconde classe enseignement de l'orthographe au moyen de dictées graduées, d'explications données par le maître, de corrections par l'épellation et de copies de ces dictées.

5° Calcul.

Enseignement de la Numération.

L'enseignement de la numération sera donné au tableau noir avec le secours de tableaux gradués contenant d'abord les cent premiers nombres dans l'ordre naturel; les suivants, des nombres de trois chiffres; d'autres, des nombres de quatre chiffres; enfin, les derniers, des nombres de un, deux, trois, et quatre chiffres, alternativement; et l'on fera usage avec ces tableaux des deux procédés suivants:

Énonciation par les élèves, avec l'aide du moniteur, des nombres qui leur seront indiqués (première demi-heure).

Écriture sur le tableau noir, par les élèves, des nombres qu'ils entendront énoncer par le moniteur (seconde demi-heure).

Les élèves passeront à l'addition quand ils sauront énoncer et écrire des nombres de quatre chiffres. Ensuite, l'enseignement de la numération aura lieu conjointement avec celui des quatre règles.

Enseignement des quatre Règles.

Le moniteur ayant énoncé les nombres sur lesquels il s'agit d'opérer, et un élève les ayant écrits sur le tableau noir, chaque élève du groupe, à son tour, avec l'aide du moniteur, fera une partie différente de l'opération.

On opérera ensuite de même sur d'autres nombres (première demi-heure).

Des nombres étant encore énoncés et écrits, les élèves opéreront successivement, mais sans être aidés (seconde demi-heure).

Indépendamment des groupes autour de la salle, on formera aux bancs, pour les élèves les plus avancés, des divisions plus ou moins nombreuses, où le travail, en calcul, se fera sous la direction du maître, suivant les procédés du mode simultané.

6° Dessin linéaire.

Aux groupes, sur les tableaux noirs.

Le maître ou le moniteur commencera par dessiner lui-même, à main levée, la figure à copier, et il la nommera.

Chaque élève du groupe la tracera à son tour.

On opérera ensuite de même pour d'autres figures (première demi-heure).

La figure à dessiner sera seulement nommée par le moniteur, et montrée par lui sur le tableau modèle.

L'élève désigné la dessinera.

Ensuite, même opération sur d'autres figures (seconde demi-heure).

La correction sera effectuée par le maître ou par le moniteur à l'aide des instruments.

7° Sont maintenues toutes les autres prescriptions actuellement observées dans les écoles communales laïques de garçons à Paris, et contenues dans les anciens réglements, concernant l'admission des élèves, l'ordre, la discipline, la propreté, le service de santé, les récompenses, les congés, les examens, les registres, et tous les devoirs des instituteurs.

Pour extrait conforme :

Le Recteur de l'Académie de la Seine,

Signé CAŸX.

TABLE, showing Comparative Situation of PRIMARY INSTRUC-

CANTONS.	Population in 18[illegible].	Schools and Teachers.	Maximum of Scholars per School.
ZURICH -	260,000	[illegible]80 schools, 474 teachers. 1 school to every 684 inhabitants, 1 teacher to every 548.	120 scholars. Above that number an under-master.
BERNE - -	470,000	About 1300 schools. 1 school to every 362 inhabitants.	80, 90, and 100.
FRIBOURG -	100,000	288 schools. 1 school to every 347 inhabitants.	70. Above that a second school.
BASLE-TOWN -	31,000. Numbers in school, 1802. 1 school for 64 children.	28 schools. 1 school to every 1107 inhabitants.	60 to 70.
ST GALL -	175,000	384 schools (Cath. 230, Protestant 154). Average 1 school to every 456 inhabitants.	70 to 90 in Catholic schools, 90 in Protestant schools.
ARGOVIA -	201,000	197 schools. 1 school to every 410 inhabitants.	120 scholars.
NEUCHÂTEL -	80,000	2[illegible]1 schools. 1 school to every 315 inhabitants.	50 to 60. Above that a second school.
GENEVA - -	66,000. Numbers in school, 5110. 1 school to every 68 children, 1 teacher to every 45 children.	75 schools, and 113 masters, mistresses, and [illegible]. 1 school to every 880 inhabitants.	20 to 100 scholars and above.
VAUD	200,000. Numbers in school, 32,000. 1 school to every 44 children.	731 schools, or masters and mistresses. 1 school to every 273 inhabitants.	60. Above that a second school.

* The teacher receives in addition, half [illegible] francs, amounting to from 1 f. 50 c. to 3 f. a year per scholar.

† The salary is paid by the State. There is a school-fee of from 10 cents to 1 f. per month for each child.

ION in the following CANTONS of SWITZERLAND, in 1859.

Minimum of Salaries.	Contribution of State to Salaries.	Contribution of Communes to Salaries.	CANTONS.
525 f.; 584 f.; 700 f.; 800 f., and above.*	207,057 f. for primary instruction, of which 145,000 f. for pensions.	?	ZURICH.
500 f. There are higher salaries.	270,696 f.	360,000 f.	BERNE.
600 f.	25,000 f.	Communes pay, as a rule.	FRIBOURG.
Town.—from 2028 f. to 2564 f. Country. — from 1000 f. to 1074 f.	40,011 f. †	?	BASLE-TOWN.
420 f.; 500 f.; up to 1000 f., and above.	25,000 f.	Communes pay the salaries.	ST. GALL.
Town.—1857 f. Country.—528 f. and 682 f.	100,000 f.	270,000 f.	ARGOVIA.
600 f. 2000 f.	251,329 f. for primary instruction, of which 64,690 f. for pensions.	Communes, . 67,595 f. School-fees, 56,567 f. Other sources, 19,750 f.	NEUFCHÂTEL.
1000 f., 1400 f., and a good *casual* paid by the State.	97,000 f. for primary instruction, of which 71,685 f. for pensions.	Communes contribute a quarter or half.	GENEVA.
522 f., but half the salaries are under this amount. 600 f.; 700 f.; 800 f.; 1000 f. in the towns.	46,666 f.	298,377 f. ‡	VAUD.

‡ 176 Communes are authorised to receive school-contributions.

N.B.—In all these Cantons the teacher has, in addition, a house, and a small piece of ground, or an equivalent.

HOLLAND.

Law of the 13th August 1857, on Primary Instruction.

We William III, by the Grace of God, King of the Netherlands, Prince of Orange-Nassau, Grand Duke of Luxemburg, &c. &c.

To all who shall see or hear these, greeting!

Whereas We have taken into consideration that Art. 194 of the Fundamental Law provides that the establishment of public instruction, with due respect to every man's religious principles, shall be regulated by law; that throughout the kingdom sufficient public primary instruction shall be given on the part of the authorities, and that education shall be free, subject always to the superintendence of the authorities, and, as far as concerns middle and primary instruction, subject also to examination into the capacity and morality of the master; all of this to be established by law;

That, in the meanwhile, and until provison shall be made for the regulation of middle and higher instruction, it is necessary to give effect to these provisions as far as primary instruction is concerned;

Therefore We, having heard the Council of State, and by and with the advice of the States General, have thought good and determined as We think good, and determine by these presents:

Title I.—General Provisions.

Art. 1.

Primary instruction is distinguished into ordinary and more extended instruction.

Ordinary instruction includes:—

a. Reading.
b. Writing.
c. Arithmetic.
d. The principles of Grammar.
e. of the Dutch language.
f. of Geography.
g. of History.
h. of Physics.
i. Singing.

The more extended instruction is considered to include:—

k. The principles of the knowledge of the Modern Languages.
l. of Mathematics.
m. of Agriculture.
n. Gymnastics.
o. Drawing.
p. Needlework.

Art. 2.

Primary instruction may be given either in schools, or in the houses of the parents or guardians of the children.

The former is school education, the latter private education.

Instruction given to the children collectively of not more than three families shall still be considered as private education.

Art. 3.

Primary schools shall be distinguished as public and private schools.

Public schools are those established and maintained by the communes, the provinces, and the government, severally or in common; all others are private schools.

Assistance may be granted to private schools on the part either of the commune or of the province under such conditions as the communal or provincial authority may deem necessary. Schools thus assisted shall be open to any children, without distinction of religious creed. The 1st and 2nd clauses of Art. 23 are applicable to these schools.

Art. 4.

No school instruction shall be given in such buildings as shall be pronounced detrimental to health by the district school inspector, or insufficient in point of room for the number of children attending the school. In the event of the decision of this officer not being acquiesced in, the matter shall be decided by the States Deputies, after a fresh and independent inquiry.

Further appeal,* from the decision of the school inspector as well as from that of the States Deputies, must be made within fourteen days, counted from the day when notice of the decision has been received by the parties interested.

All those are qualified thus to appeal to whose prejudice the decision may operate; that is to say, the parents or guardians of the children attending the school, if the school inspector shall have acquiesced in the decision of the States Deputies. Pending the final decision, instruction may continue to be given in the building objected to.

Art. 5.

School education shall be given by head masters and assistant teachers, head mistresses and female assistant-teachers, and both male and female apprentice teachers.

Apprentice-teachers are those who, not having yet attained the age at which they can be admitted for examination as assistant-teachers, assist in giving school instruction.

* This final appeal is to the Minister for the Home Department. See Art. 13 of this Law.

Having attained that age, they may continue as apprentice-teachers during the time that is yet to elapse before they can be admitted for examination. Apprentice-teachers failing to pass the examination mentioned in the 2nd and 3rd clauses, or having been unable, for reasons satisfactory to the provincial inspector, to present themselves for examination, may notwithstanding continue as apprentice-teachers until the next examination.

Art. 6.

Nobody is allowed to give primary instruction, who shall not possess the proofs of capacity and morality required by this law.

Foreigners require, besides, Our permission.

Art. 7.

The provisions of the preceding Article are not applicable to—

a. The apprentice-teachers, as far as instruction is concerned in the school where they are employed;

b. Those who give primary instruction to the children of one family exclusively;

c. Those who, not making a profession of primary instruction, but being willing to be employed without any pecuniary remuneration, may have obtained Our permission to give such instruction.

d. Candidates and Doctors in Arts and Sciences in so far as by reason of their academical degrees they are qualified to give instruction in one or other of the branches mentioned in Art. 1.

Art. 8.

Any person giving primary instruction without being qualified, or in violation of the 1st clause of Art. 4, shall for the first offence be punished with a fine of twenty-five and not exceeding fifty florins; for the second offence with a fine of fifty and not exceeding a hundred florins, and imprisonment for eight and not exceeding fourteen days, cumulatively or separately; and for each subsequent offence with imprisonment for one month and not exceeding one year.

Any person giving primary instruction beyond the limits of his qualification, shall be liable to half the amount and duration of the above-mentioned punishments. Assistant-teachers, temporarily placed at the head of a school, provided the temporary occupation does not last longer than six months, are excepted from these provisions— Art. 463 of the Penal Code, and Art. 20 of the Law of the 29th of June, 1854 (Staatsblad No. 102), are applicable to these provisions.

Art. 9.

On every judgment of fine it shall be declared by the judge that, on failure of payment of the fine and costs by the offender within two months after having been summoned to pay, the penalty inflicted shall be changed into imprisonment for not more than fourteen days if the fine exceed fifty florins, and for not more than seven days if a fine not exceeding fifty florins has been imposed.

Art. 10.

Except in the cases mentioned hereafter, the qualification to give primary instruction ceases for any person condemned by final sentence, —

a. for crimes.

b. for theft, swindling, perjury, breach of trust, or immoral conduct.

Art. 11.

Any person having lost his qualification for giving primary instruction, cannot recover it.

In the cases mentioned in the 7th clause of Art. 22, and in Art. 39, it can be granted again by Us.

Art. 12.

For the education of teachers there shall be at least two

Government training schools; and normal lessons shall be established in connection with some of the best primary schools by the authority of the Government.

The education of male and female teachers in the primary schools shall be promoted by State authority as much as possible.

Art. 13.

From every decision taken by the States Deputies in virtue of this law, an appeal lies to Us.

Art. 14.

The provisions of this law concerning male teachers are likewise applicable to female teachers, as far as it does not contain any exceptions for the latter.

Art. 15.

This law is not applicable: —

a. To those who give instruction exclusively in one of the branches mentioned in the *classes* marked *i*, *n*, *o*, and *p*, of Art. 1, and to the schools destined for those purposes.

b. To military instructors and the instruction given by them to military men.

Title II. — Of Public Instruction. — § 1. Of the Schools.

Art. 16.

In every commune, primary instruction shall be given in a certain number of schools, sufficient for the number and requirements of the population, and open to any children, without distinction of religious creed.

The instruction shall include at least the branches classed from *a* to *i* in Art. 1. Wherever any want exists of extension, such being practicable, all the branches classed from *k* to *p* in Art. 1, or one or more of them, shall be included in the instruction.

Two or more adjoining communes may, in conformity

with Art. 121 of the Law of June 29, 1851 (Staatsblad No. 85), join in the establishment and maintenance of united schools.

Art. 17.

The council of the commune shall fix the number of schools. Its resolution shall be communicated to the States Deputies.

If the States Deputies think the number insufficient, they shall order an augmentation.

If it shall appear insufficient to Us, an augmentation may be ordered by Us.

The extension of instruction mentioned in the 2nd clause of the last Article shall be established in the same way.

§ 2. — *Of the Teachers.*

Art. 18.

If the number of pupils in one school shall exceed seventy, the head-master shall be assisted by one apprentice-teacher; in schools not exceeding one hundred, by one assistant-teacher; exceeding one hundred and fifty, by one assistant and one apprentice. Beyond the latter number, he shall be assisted by one apprentice for fifty, and by one assistant for one hundred pupils respectively.

Art. 19.

A yearly salary shall be assigned to every head-master, besides a house rent free, with a garden, if possible.

In case no house rent free can be provided for him, he shall receive an equitable compensation for house-rent.

In case of disagreement between the council of the commune and the teacher with respect to the amount of such compensation, the question shall be decided by the States Deputies.

For every apprentice mentioned in the last article, an additional sum shall be granted to the head-master.

To every assistant-teacher a yearly salary shall be assigned.

The yearly salaries and additions shall be fixed by the council of the commune, subject to the approbation of the States Deputies.

The amount of the yearly salary for a head-master shall be at least 400 florins; for an assistant-teacher at least 200 florins. The amount of the additional sum shall be at least 25 florins.

Art. 20.

In those communes where, on account of their large and scattered population, a greater number of schools shall be required than otherwise would be necessary, a head-master or assistant-teacher, whose yearly salary shall be at least 200 florins, may be placed at the head of those schools respectively, subject to the approbation of the States Deputies.

Art. 21.

In order to be qualified for the appointment of head-master or assistant-teacher, the candidate is required to possess —

a. A certificate of capacity to give school instruction.

b. Testimonials of good moral conduct delivered by the council of administration of the commune or communes where the candidate has been living during the last two years.

Art. 22.

The head-masters shall be appointed by the council of the commune from a list containing not less than three nor more than six names prepared by the burgomasters and councillors, in concert with the district school-inspector, after a competitive examination conducted by the latter, or under his inspection, in presence of the burgomaster and councillors, or of a deputation from their body, and of the local committee for school affairs, or of a deputation from that committee. The members of the council of the commune shall be invited to be present at the examination.

The assistant-teachers shall be appointed by the council of

the commune from a list containing three names prepared by the burgomaster and councillors, in concert with the head-master and the district school-inspector.

The head-masters and assistant-teachers may be suspended by the burgomaster and councillors, after consultation with the school-inspector. The burgomaster and councillors shall give as soon as possible an account of their decision to the council of the commune.

The head-masters and assistant-teachers may be dismissed by the council of the commune on the requisition of the burgomaster and the councillors, and the district school-inspector. Resignations must be made to the council of the commune directly.

If suspension or dismissal should be necessary, either according to the opinion of the local committee for school affairs, or of the district school-inspector, and the communal council delay or refuse to proceed thereto, such suspension or dismissal may be effected by the States Deputies.

Suspension shall never exceed a term of three months, and the salary may continue to be paid, or be partially or entirely withheld during suspension.

Those who are dismissed on account of scandalous conduct, or of propagation of doctrines inconsistent with morality, or tending to excite disobedience to the laws of the country, may be declared by the States Deputies to have lost their qualification to give instruction.

The appointment and dismissal of apprentice-teachers is made by the head-master, subject to the approbation of the district school-inspector.

In cases of suspension, of dismissal, or of a vacancy in the place of head-master or assistant-teacher, the burgomaster and councillors shall provide for the temporary occupation of the vacant place; in the case of a head-master, in concert with the district school-inspector, and with the head-master in the case of an assistant-teacher. The place of head-master shall be filled up within six months at least after becoming vacant.

Art. 23.

The system of education in the schools, while imparting suitable and useful information, shall be made conducive to the development of the intellectual capacities of the children, and to their training in all Christian and social virtues.

The teacher shall abstain from teaching or permitting to be taught anything inconsistent with the respect due to the religious opinions of dissenters. Religious instruction is left to the ecclesiastical communities. The school-rooms shall be at their disposal for that purpose out of school hours, for the benefit of children attending the school.

Art. 24.

The head-master and assistant-teachers are not allowed to hold any office or employment otherwise than with the approbation of the States Deputies, after consultation with the burgomaster and councillors, and in communes of 3000 inhabitants and upwards with the local committee for school affairs, and in other communes with the district school-inspector. They are not allowed to carry on any business, to work at any trade, or to exercise any profession: this prohibition is applicable also to the members of the families of the head-masters and assistant-teachers, as far as relates to carrying on the prohibited occupation in their houses.

Art. 25.

The head-master and assistant-teachers shall be entitled to a pension from Government in the following cases and under the conditions thereto annexed.

Art. 26.

A right to a pension is acquired after receiving an honourable discharge on acquiring the age of sixty-five years, and completing the period of forty years' service.

A pension may likewise be granted to those who after ten years' service have become incapable of performing the duties of their calling on account either of mental or bodily infirmities, and have received an honourable discharge on such grounds.

The incapacity shall be established by the declaration of the district school-inspector and of the State's Deputies. In calculating the amount of the pension, such services only shall be taken into consideration as they have been performed as head-master or as assistant-master under this law, or, previously to this law coming into operation, as teacher of a public school, being engaged in primary instruction.

Those who have not received an honourable discharge, forfeit their right to a pension.

Art. 27.

The pension shall amount for each year's service to one-sixtieth part of the yearly salary which during the last twelve months previous to an honourable discharge may have served as a basis for the payment of the contributions mentioned in Art. 28; it shall not however in any case exceed two-third of such yearly salary.

Art. 28.

As a contribution to the pension fund, the head-master and assistant-teachers shall pay from the day on which the law comes into operation, two per cent. per annum of the yearly salary annexed to their appointment. The contributions shall be collected on behalf of the State, at the charge of the officers of the commune, and accounted for to the public treasury.

Art. 29.

Those communes in which any head-masters or assistant-teachers shall be pensioned by virtue of this law, shall make good to the Government a third part of the amount of such pensions.

Art. 30.

The provisions of Arts. 22, 23, 24, 26, 27, 28, 29, 30, 31, 32, 37, 40 and 41 of the Law of 9th May, 1846 (Staatsblad No. 24), with the alterations enacted by the Law of 3rd May, 1851 (Staatsblad No. 49), are applicable to pensions of head-masters and assistant-teachers.

§ 3. — *Of the Cost of Instruction.*

Art. 31.

Each commune shall provide for the charges of its primary instruction, as far as these charges are not imposed upon others, or shall not be provided for in any other manner.

Art. 32.

These charges are: —

a. The yearly salary of the head-masters and assistant-teachers.

b. The additional remuneration on account of apprentice-teachers.

c. The charges for the erection and maintenance, or for hire of school-buildings.

d. For providing and keeping in order the school furniture and school-books, and for other school necessaries for the pupils.

e. For light and fire required for the school-rooms.

f. For the erection and maintenance, or for hire of dwelling-houses for the teachers.

g. Compensation to the head-masters in lieu of a house rent-free.

h. The contribution of the commune to the pension of the teachers.

i. The expenses of the local school committee.

Art. 33.

To meet these charges a payment may be required from each child attending the school. Children supported by public charity, and such as, though not receiving relief, are unable to pay for their schooling, shall not be called upon for this payment.

The council of the commune shall provide as far as possible for the school attendance of children of parents receiving relief or in indigent circumstances.

Art. 34.

The fixing of the amount of the school-money, as well as any alteration of such amount, or the entire remission of it, shall be effected in conformity with Arts. 232–236 of the Law of 29th of June, 1851. (*Staatsblad* No. 85.)

The collection shall be regulated by a local order, in conformity with the provisions of Arts. 258–262 of the same Law.

Art. 35.

The school-money shall be the same for all children of the same class in any school.

For two or more children of the same family, attending school at the same time, the rate of payment may be reduced.

Art. 36.

If, after inquiry by the States Deputies, and after the report thereon of the States of the province, We shall judge any commune to be too heavily charged by the expenditure requisite for suitable establishments of primary instruction, such portion thereof as shall continue to be charged upon the commune shall be fixed by Us, and the deficiency shall be provided for by the province, and by the Government, in the proportion of one moiety by each.

Title III. — Of Private Education.

Art. 37.

For conducting education in private schools, or in private houses, the following qualifications are required:

a. A Certificate of Capacity.

b. Testimonials of the same description as those mentioned in Art. 21, Letter *c*.

c. A Certificate that both these documents have been seen and found in due order by the burgomaster and councillors of the commune where the instruction is to be given.

Art. 38.

The burgomaster and councillors shall give their decision respecting the issue of the certificate, mentioned under Letter *c* in Article 37, within four weeks, to be counted from the date of the claim of such certificate. An appeal may be made from such decision to the States Deputies, or an appeal be made if no decision shall have been communicated to the parties interested within the above-mentioned period. After rejection of appeal by the States Deputies, or in default of notice of their decision within six weeks to the parties interested, an appeal may be made to Us.

Art. 39.

Teachers who, in conducting education in private schools, or in private houses, shall propagate doctrines inconsistent with morality, or tending to excite disobedience to the laws of the country, may, on presentment by the burgomaster and councillors, by the local school committee, or by the district school-inspector, be declared by the States Deputies to have lost their qualification to give instruction.

This provision is also applicable to such teachers as make themselves obnoxious to the charge of scandalous conduct.

Title IV.—Of the Certificate of Capacity to give Instruction.

Art. 40.

Certificates of capacity for conducting education in private schools and private houses are to be obtained by passing examinations.

Art. 41.

An opportunity for such examination shall be afforded twice a year in each province by a committee, composed of the superintendent and four school-inspectors.

The board shall hold its sittings in the principal town of the province. It shall be competent to attach to itself assessors, having special acquirements.

The appointment of the school-inspectors and the fixing of the time of meeting of the boards, shall be settled by Our Minister of the Interior.

The examinations shall be held in public, except those of the female teachers.

Art. 12.

The time when the examinations are to take place, shall be made known to the public by advertisement.

Any person desiring to present himself for examination, shall apply in due time to the school-inspector of the district where he resides, or where, if a stranger, he intends to establish himself, with notice of the description of certificate which he requires.

He must further produce one or more testimonials of his good moral conduct, and his certificate of birth.

The time and the place of the examination will be communicated to him by the school-inspector.

He shall present himself for examination in the province where he resides, or, if a stranger, in that where he intends to establish himself.

Art. 13.

In order to be admitted for examination the candidate must have attained the proper age; this is fixed at eighteen years for private and assistant-teachers of either sex, at twenty-three years for head-masters and head-mistresses.

Art. 14.

Candidates for examination for the purpose of obtaining a certificate of capacity as assistant-teacher of either sex, are required:

To read and write well.

To have an adequate knowledge of analysis, of the rules of spelling, and of the elements of the Dutch language.

To be able to express themselves with correctness and ease, as well orally as in writing.

To know the principles of grammar.

To know arithmetic, in whole numbers as well as in vulgar and decimal fractions, applied to money, weights, and measures; in addition to this, the male candidates are required to know the system of logarithms.

To be acquainted with geography and history.

To know the principles of natural philosophy.

To know the theory of singing.

To know the principles of teaching and education.

Art. 45.

Candidates for examination for the purpose of obtaining certificates of capacity as head-mistresses are required to possess attainments of the same description as those required of assistant-teachers, but more advanced, and with application to their profession as head-mistresses.

Art. 46.

Candidates for examination for the purpose of obtaining certificates of capacity as head-masters are required to possess attainments of the same description as those required from assistant-teachers, but more advanced, comprehensive, and developed.

Art. 47.

Candidates desiring to obtain, or having already obtained, one of the certificates mentioned in the last three articles, may, at their request, be further examined in one or more of the subjects marked from *k* to *p* in Art. 1.

Art. 48.

The examination for obtaining a certificate of capacity as private teacher, of either sex, embraces one or more of the subjects mentioned in Art. 1.

For that purpose, equal attainments at least are required as from assistant-teachers.

Art. 49.

When the examination has been passed to the satisfaction of the board, they shall deliver the certificate required to the candidate.

The subject or subjects of more comprehensive primary instruction, in which the candidate may have passed his examination successfully, shall be recorded in the certificate of capacity to give school instruction.

In like manner a record shall be made, in certificates of capacity to give private lessons, of any other subjects of primary instruction in which the examination has been successfully passed.

Art. 50.

Certificates of capacity shall be delivered on payment of ten florins for those of head-masters or head-mistresses; five florins for those of assistant-teachers of either sex; five florins for those of private-teachers, either male or female, in more than one subject; three florins for those of a private-teacher, either male or female, in one subject only.

For the first record (as mentioned in clauses 2 and 3 of the preceding Art.), in the certificate of school-instruction, three florins shall be paid, and in that for private tuition in one subject, only two florins. The first record in the certificate for private tuition in more than one subject, and any further records in general, shall be made gratuitously.

The above-mentioned sums are to provide for the expenses of the meetings of the boards, including the remuneration to the assessors. The surplus shall be paid over to the public treasury.

Art. 51.

Certificates of capacity shall be valid for the whole kingdom.

Certificates for school-instruction shall be also valid for private tuition.

Certificates for private tuition also qualify the holders to give instruction in a school, in one or more of the subjects marked *b*, *c*, and from *i* to *p*, inclusive, in Art. 1.

Certificates of capacity as head-master or head-mistress qualify them equally to hold the place of assistant-teachers.

In addition to the cases provided for in Art. 20, the certificate of assistant-teachers may, under the conditions to be prescribed by Us, qualify the holder to be at the head of a public school.

Title V. — Of the Superintendence of Education.

Art. 52.

The superintendence of education, subject to the supervision of Our Minister of the Interior, is conferred upon—

a. Local committees for school affairs.
b. District school-inspectors.
c. Provincial superintendents.

Art. 53.

There shall be in every commune a committee for school affairs.

In communes united by virtue of the 3rd clause of Art. 16, for the purposes of the erection and maintenance of joint schools, there shall be a joint committee.

Art. 54.

In communes of less than 3000 inhabitants, the duties of the local committee for school affairs are transferred to the burgomaster and councillors.

In other communes the committees shall be appointed by the council of the commune.

The office of member of the committee may be held with that of member of the council of the commune.

Art. 55.

Every province shall be divided by Us into school-districts.

Every district shall be placed under the charge of a school-inspector.

In case of decease, sickness, or absence of the school-inspector, provision may be made for the performance of his duties by Our Minister of the Interior.

Art. 56.

The school-inspector shall be appointed by Us for the period of six years.

On the expiration of their period of service, they may be reappointed.

They may be dismissed at any time by Us.

Art. 57.

The school-inspectors shall receive a certain sum from the public treasury, as compensation for their travelling expenses and maintenance.

Art. 58.

In each province there shall be one superintendent (provincial-inspector).

The superintendents shall be appointed by Us. They may be dismissed at any time by Us.

They shall receive from the public treasury a yearly salary, and compensation for their travelling expenses and maintenance.

Art. 59.

The superintendents shall be summoned to meet together once a year, by Our Minister of the Interior, for the purpose of deliberating upon and promoting, under his authority, the general interests of primary instruction.

Art. 60.

The superintendents shall hold no office or employment without Our permission.

Art. 61.

The members of the local committees for school affairs,

the school-inspectors, and the superintendents, before entering upon their duties, shall take an oath, or promise upon their honour, to discharge them duly and faithfully.

The oath shall be administered, or the promise accepted, in the case of members of the local committees, in communes of 3000 inhabitants and upwards, by the burgomaster; in other communes by the judge of the canton where they are living; in the case of school-inspectors, by Our Commissary in the province, and in the case of superintendents, by Our Minister of the Interior.

Art. 62.

The members of the local committees, the school-inspectors, and the superintendents are empowered to report on any transgressions against this law, or against the further prescriptions concerning primary instruction.

Art. 63.

All schools where primary instruction is given, whether public or private, shall be open at all times to the members of the local committee for school affairs, to the district school-inspector, and to the superintendent of the province.

The teachers are bound to give them any information that may be required concerning the school and the instruction.

Default in this respect shall be punished with a fine of twenty-five florins, or imprisonment for three days, and for every fresh offence with both penalties united. Article 463 of the Penal Code, and Article 20 of the Law of 29th June, 1854 (Staatsblad No. 102), are applicable to these cases.

Art. 64.

The local committees for school affairs shall keep a careful watch over all schools in the commune where primary instruction is given. They shall visit them at least twice a year, either collectively or by a deputation from their body. They shall take care that the regulations concerning primary instruction be strictly observed. They shall keep a record of the person engaged in teaching, of the number of pupils, and of the state of education. They shall deliver to the council of the commune, before the 1st of March in every year, a report, with their remarks thereon, of the state of education in the commune, and they shall send a copy of this report to the district school-inspector. They shall give notice to him of any considerable changes that may have taken place in the state of the schools; they shall furnish him and the provincial superintendent with all the information which they may each require; they shall afford assistance to such teachers as may ask for their advice, aid, or co-operation, and they shall make it their business to promote heartily the prosperity of education.

Art. 65.

The school-inspectors shall take care to be constantly and fully acquainted with the state of school affairs in their district. They shall visit at least twice a year all schools within it where primary instruction is given, and keep an accurate record of such visits. They shall take care that the regulations concerning primary instruction be strictly observed. They shall communicate with the local committees for school affairs, and with the councils of the communes; they shall lay before them, as well as the provincial superintendent, such proposals as they may think conducive to the interests of education. They shall give notice to the said superintendent of anything which in visiting the schools has appeared to them of any importance, and provide him with all such information as he may require. They shall deliver to the superintendent, before the 1st of May in every year, a report on the state of education in their district, with their remarks thereon, and send a copy thereof to the States Deputies. They shall heartily support the interests of the teachers, promote their meetings, and be present at them, as far as possible.

Art. 66.

The school-inspectors shall have admittance to the meetings of all local committees for school affairs in their district, and they shall have consultative voice in such meetings.

Art. 67.

The superintendents shall endeavour, both by visiting the schools and by oral and written communications with the local committees for school affairs, and with the councils of the communes, to promote the improvement and prosperity of the schools. They shall advise Our Minister of the Interior on any questions respecting which their opinions may be asked. They shall prepare from the annual reports of the school-inspectors a report, accompanied with their remarks, concerning the state of education in their province, and send this report, before the 1st of July in each year, to Our above-mentioned Minister.

Title VI.—Transitory Provisions.

Art. 68.

Teachers of either sex, both public and private, and tutors and governesses who at the time of this law coming into operation shall be lawfully engaged in such callings, require no reappointment nor acknowledgment to continue therein.

After that time, any certificates of general admission of the 1st and 2nd rank obtained previously, shall be considered as giving the same rights as certificates of capacity as head-master: certificates of the 3rd rank as giving the same rights as certificates of capacity as assistant-teacher: those of school-mistresses as giving the same rights as certificates of capacity as head-mistress: but only within the province or commune where such certificates have been delivered. Tutors and governesses who after that time desire to settle as such in another commune, are obliged to submit previously to the examination mentioned in Art. 18.

Head-masters of private schools of the 2nd class in existence at the time of this law coming into operation, who hold at least the 2nd rank, may in case of transfer of such schools by the council of the commune, in concert with the district school-inspector, as public primary schools, be appointed as head-masters of such institutions.

The provisions of Art. 22, concerning the proposal of names and the competitive examination, are not applicable to these cases.

Art. 69.

The yearly salaries of all public head-masters and head-mistresses in actual service at the time of this law coming into operation shall, as long as they continue to hold their places, in no case be fixed at an amount less than the income which they have been receiving yearly, at an average, during the five years next preceding the above date; or, for those who have been in service for a shorter time, during such shorter period.

Art. 70.

To carry into effect the provisions respecting the fixing of the number of schools in proportion to the population and their wants, and the extension of the instruction (Arts. 16 and 17), the assistance in teaching to be afforded to the head-master (Art. 18), the yearly salaries and other emoluments of the head-masters and assistant-teachers, and the additional remuneration on account of the apprentice-teachers (Arts. 19 and 20), and the expenses of education (Arts. 31 35), - a term of three years at most is allowed, reckoning from the date of this law coming into operation.

During such term the yearly salaries and contributions of the provinces and of the Government shall be paid to the head-masters and head-mistresses and to the communes at the rate of their receipts for the time being, at the date of this law coming into operation.

Art. 71.

Private schools in receipt of assistance, at the date of this law coming into operation, from the commune or from the province, and not fulfilling the condition of the 4th clause of Art. 3, cannot continue to receive such assistance for a period exceeding one year from the date first abovementioned.

Art. 72.

Pending a settlement by law of the system of secondary instruction, the provisions of this law are equally applicable to all that concerns the more advanced instruction in modern languages, and in mathematical and physical science.

In order to be admitted for examination for the purpose of obtaining a certificate of capacity in one or more of these subjects, the attainment of 18 years at least is required. A single payment of five florins shall be made for the certificate.

Art. 73.

This law shall come into operation on the 1st of January, 1858.

Saving the provisions of Art. 70, all existing general provincial and local regulations concerning primary instruction will then be abolished; the provincial committees of education, local committees for school affairs, and committees for local superintendence of schools, dissolved; the district school-inspectors dismissed; and the system of superintendence of schools, according to the present law, substituted for them.

I. TABLE* showing TOTAL NUMBER of PRIMARY [illegible] of HOLLAND.

Provinces.	Population on 1st January 1851.	Population on 1st January 1857.	School Districts.	Local School Committees.	Number of Schools.
North Brabant	397,133	409,678	9	4	425
Gelderland	373,252	396,421	10	11	442
South Holland	477,567	612,051	9	11	481
North Holland	479,564	512,231	11	6	510
Zealand	161,495	165,791	5	4	160
Utrecht	150,441	159,582	5	2	159
Friesland	249,769	268,119	9	6	370
Overyssel	218,551	233,723	6	3	245
Groningen	189,178	204,481	6	1	255
Drenthe	83,675	92,785	4	2	116
Limburg	208,111	213,489	8	4	226
Total	2,986,869	3,298,137	82	54	3422

* This and the following Tables are extracted from an official Report on [illegible] *Lagere Scholen* [illegible] *Koningrijk der Nederlanden* over 1857 – 1858.

SCHOOLS, TEACHERS, and SCHOLARS in each PROVINCE in 1857.

Teachers.			Scholars.					
			15th January.			15th July.		
Male.	Female.	Total.	Boys.	Girls.	Total.	Boys.	Girls.	Total.
664	263	927	27,360	22,100	49,460	19,723	17,996	37.719
760	134	894	32,065	22,029	54,094	21,072	16,931	38,003
1,225	131	1.356	37.743	29,797	67,540	34,485	28,600	63,085
1,084	188	1.272	31,726	25,849	57,575	31.944	26,927	58,871
323	15	338	11,613	7,640	19,253	7,834	6,486	14.320
347	56	403	9,700	7,619	17,319	8,855	7,567	16,422
622	21	643	21,938	17.040	38,978	18,412	15,581	33,993
467	34	501	17,334	14.691	32,025	13,619	12.387	26,006
439	3	442	16,049	14,260	31,209	14,691	13,666	28,357
200	5	205	7,106	6,202	14.008	4,900	4.659	9.559
349	61	410	14,119	10,749	24,868	10.186	8,097	18,283
6,480	911	7,391	228,353	177,976	106,329	185.721	158,897	344.618

Public Education in Holland, *Verslag nopens den Staat der Hooge, Middle-* The Hague, 1859.

II.

TABLE showing the PROPORTION, in HOLLAND, of PUPILS attending SCHOOL to the POPULATION.

Provinces	Population on 1st January [illegible] to the total number of Scholars as [illegible] to . . .	Population on 1st January 1857 to the total number of Scholars as [illegible] to . .	Population on 1st January [illegible] to the total number of Scholars as [illegible] to . .	Population on 1st January 1867 to the total number of Scholars as [illegible] to
	On the 15th January 1857.		On the 15th July [illegible]	
North Brabant .	122·0	120·7	95·0	92·1
Gelderland .	145·2	136·5	101·8	95·9
South Holland .	141·5	110·4	132·2	105·8
North Holland	120·0	106·2	122·8	108·1
Zeeland .	119·2	116·1	88·7	80·4
Utrecht .	115·1	108·7	100·2	105·0
Friesland .	156·1	115·4	136·1	126·8
Overyssel .	146·5	137·0	119·5	111·3
Groningen .	165·0	152·6	119·9	128·7
Drenthe	167·4	151·0	114·2	10[illegible]
Limburg	120·5	116·5	88·6	85·6
Mean number	136·1	12[illegible]·2	115·4	104·5

THE END.

LONDON
PRINTED BY SPOTTISWOODE AND CO.
NEW-STREET SQUARE

www.ingramcontent.com/pod-product-compliance
Lightning Source LLC
Chambersburg PA
CBHW031854220426
43663CB00006B/618

* 9 7 8 3 3 3 7 1 9 7 9 3 3 *